Rambling on the Road to Rome

Peter Francis Browne

SUMMERSDALE

First published by Hamish Hamilton Ltd in 1990.

This edition published in 2001 by Summersdale Publishers Ltd.

Summersdale Publishers Ltd
46 West Street
Chichester
West Sussex
PO19 1RP

www.summersdale.com

Printed and bound by Creative Print & Design, Wales.

ISBN 1 84024 167 5

Cover image: Simon J. Griffiths

To Mary, Angela and Michael

LECTOR: Why on earth did you write this book?
AUCTOR: For my amusement.
LECTOR: And why do you suppose I got it?
AUCTOR: I cannot conceive . . .

Hilaire Belloc
The Path to Rome

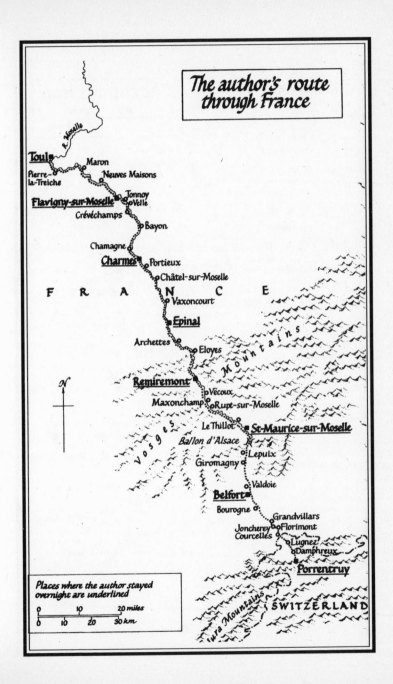

The author's route through France

R. Moselle

Toul
Maron
Pierre-la-Treiche
Neuves Maisons
Flavigny-sur-Moselle
Tonnoy
Velle
Crévéchamps
Bayon
Chamagne
Charmes
Portieux
Châtel-sur-Moselle
Vaxoncourt

F R A N C E

Epinal
Archettes
Eloyes

Mountains

Remiremont
Vécoux
Maxonchamp
Rupt-sur-Moselle
Le Thillot
St-Maurice-sur-Moselle
Ballon d'Alsace
Lepuix
Giromagny
Valdoie
Belfort
Bourogne
Grandvillars
Joncherey
Florimont
Courcelles
Lugnez
Damphreux
Porrentruy

Vosges

N

SWITZERLAND

Jura Mountains

Places where the author stayed
overnight are underlined

0   10   20 miles
0   10   20   30 km

The author's route

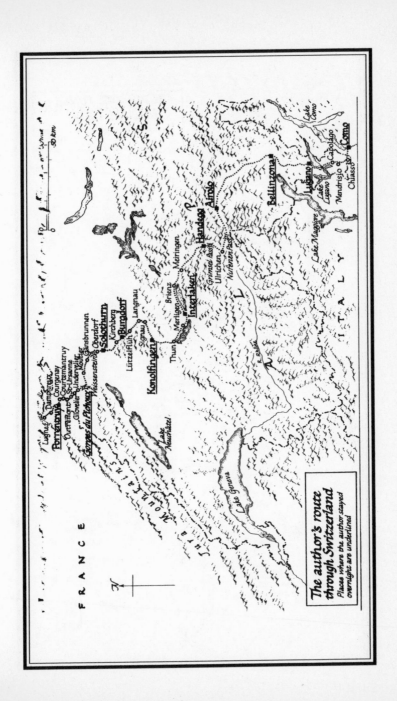

The author's route through Switzerland

Places where the author stayed overnight are underlined

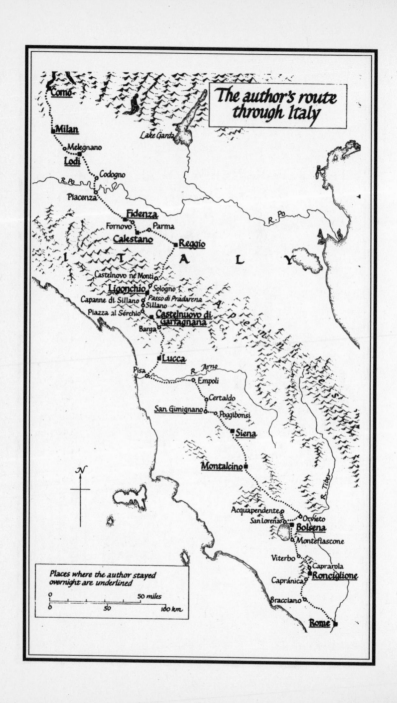

The author's route through Italy

Places where the author stayed overnight are underlined

0   50 miles

0   50   100 km

Contents

Preamble

Near a dark dark wood, in a dark dark house, in a dark dark cupboard there was a graveyard of books whose crumbling headstones were engraved with the names of obscure English martyrs and Machiavellian continental popes.

Such biographies did little to satisfy the burgeoning inquisitiveness of a child whose upbringing had entrapped him in religious orthodoxy. But amongst these decomposing tomes, where a host of booklice thrived, there was a volume, which, like certain saints, had remained incorrupt despite having been written by a far from saintly man.

I assume that *The Path to Rome* was included in our meagre library because Hilaire Belloc was a Catholic writer, and I suspect that his improbable name on the spine prompted me to select it.

The book describes how, in 1901, Belloc made a pilgrimage from Toul, in Lorraine – where he had been a conscript ten years previously – to Rome, mostly on foot.

It is a discursive work and apart from passages describing the landscape I understood little of what he wrote, although the idea of drawing a straight line on a map between two cities, and attempting to follow it, appealed enormously; for when one is ten years old a line seems the most logical means of getting from A to B.

The Path to Rome was the first travel book I read and it opened my mind to a world far beyond the claustrophobic square mile of Surrey – bounded by school, church and home – where I was being raised in order to 'Love God, serve Him in this world, and be happy with Him in the next.'

Was it really possible that an adult could simply take to the road and wander through Europe for no other reason than that it took his fancy? Surely all men – my father included – had to work in London in some dreary business and content themselves with an annual fortnight's holiday in Swanage or Worthing?

One day, I vowed, I would trace Belloc's journey.

Thirty years later I did.

Amble

Toul is an unremarkable city in that north-eastern bulge of France which few visit, apart from those in search of Joan of Arc's birthplace at Domrémy twenty kilometres to the south.

It was closed when I arrived and an icy wind blowing from the Moselle was gusting along narrow and deserted streets whose houses were already – by five o'clock on a late September evening – shuttered against the world.

In the south where the sun glares for most of the year shutters make perfect sense; but here, on the same latitude as Stuttgart, I interpreted their blank stares as a personal affront.

Before marriage and children I had travelled widely, but apart from a brief spell in Spain directing a tits-in-wet-T-shirts promotional film for a holiday company I had been trapped in Britain throughout the Thatcher years. At last, after a decade's exile within my own country, I was abroad. And where had I chosen? Toul! Even Moose Jaw had been more appealing.

Had Belloc really spent a memorable year in this grey garrison town far from the fleshpots of Paris? Apparently; but he had only just flown the nest and had enjoyed the camaraderie of fellow conscripts, whereas I, apprehensive and alone, did not know a soul.

In a square reverberating with the high-pitched whine of under-powered motorbikes ridden by sullen youths I found a bar.

The barman did not look at me but at my rucksack and walking boots which, in this out of the way corner devoid of mountains and passes, must have seemed an eccentricity. His surly black eyes remained downcast, and when I asked for a beer he grunted.

I had forgotten how dreary provincial French bars could be: the Formica-topped tables at which morose customers sat, their skin drained of blood by fluorescent lights; the flickering pinball machine; the bare walls; the torn cloth on the pool table; the complete – almost self-conscious eschewance of homeliness. And I had forgotten how parsimonious the French can be with their measures of beer; always the same diminutive glass half full of froth and tasting of Budweiser or worse.

'Are there any hotels around here?' I asked.

Something fascinating must have been occurring on the floor for he refused to look up. 'Why do you want one?'

How many reasons were there? 'I plan to sleep here.'

'Why?'

This was becoming absurd. 'Because I'm tired.'

My explanation seemed to satisfy him and he gave me the name of the only hotel that was still open, although when I eventually found it I found it closed. A scribbled note pinned to the door promised a welcome at seven and so I sat on a nearby bench with only my paunchy and absurdly heavy rucksack beside me for company.

The cathedral bell chimed seven and still no lights shone from the hotel. I was becoming irritable, but knew that if my journey was to succeed then I would have to learn to curb my impatience. After all, I was in France with the prospect of an unforgettable trip ahead of me. Why worry? I would simply watch the world go by. But nothing went by, and I watched dusk become night while a shallow river of mist began to flood the street.

I was on the point of giving up and going in search of somewhere to pitch my tent when I noticed an elderly woman scurrying up and down outside the hotel muttering to herself.

She saw me and came over.

'Do you speak English?' she asked without the trace of an accent.

'Perfectly.'

'Then perhaps you would explain why the hotel is closed? It plainly says open at seven.'

'I've absolutely no idea. I'm waiting too.'

'Oh, so you're English. How splendid. Isn't it a dreadful place? Everything's shut and my poor husband's driven all the way from Austria today. Through Switzerland. I've left him in the car.'

I assumed he was in a state of terminal exhaustion. How dare they drive so far in one day. If everything went according to plan it would take me a week to walk to the Swiss frontier and a further ten days to cross into Italy.

I was feeling horribly smug. After all, what else would a real traveller like me expect from mere tourists like them?

'You wait here,' she commanded. 'I'll find a phone and call their number.'

Such an obvious solution had not occurred to me and I felt mildly humiliated. I took a swig of duty-free Scotch and awaited developments.

I had left my home in Devon less than twenty-four hours previously, but I had forgotten how travel stretches time. Days can contract when one is enmeshed in routine, but in my estimation one must multiply time at least threefold when one is travelling. It seemed as though I had already been gone for days.

Apart from chatting to a chain-smoking South Korean surgeon who had been learning English in Aberystwyth, my journey via Portsmouth, Le Havre and Paris had been uneventful, although my perceptions, heightened by unfamiliar sights had, I suspect, already begun to overload my unconscious.

On the train from Paris I had fallen asleep and had dreamed of home: my young sons crawling into the double bed and curling up like bolsters between my wife and me; walking on Dartmoor with my dog; cajoling the children to brush their teeth – ordinary everyday occurrences. And when I had opened my eyes and seen the silhouettes of men with shotguns advancing in line across a muddy field towards the train it was as if waking and sleeping had been transposed. Domesticity pervaded my life, and such banal recollections could not be the stuff of which dreams are made. And so I had reacted logically. My dreams were real; the hunters a figment. So much for Descartes. And although I have no intention of turning this account of my journey into a dream diary I will mention just one more.

During that first night my dreams were more conventional. I was torn to pieces by dogs.

Before going to bed I had wandered through the empty, ill-lit streets and had found myself outside the cathedral. The moon was full and had bathed the building in an eerie blue glow which highlighted a pack of grotesque canine gargoyles, their jaws open, their teeth bared.

Such images alone might have been enough to induce a nightmare, but they were linked to a neurotic fear of being bitten during my walk.

Before leaving England I had flicked through a couple of books about backpacking in Europe, one of which was Rob Hunter's *Walking in France*. In a section dealing with potential hazards, I had read that it would be sensible to carry an anti-snakebite serum (hypodermics for self-injection available from most French pharmacies) but I dismissed this advice as being alarmist. However, a paragraph about rabies – *la rage* – held my attention, for I would be tramping, off the beaten track, through a region where this most terrifying of diseases is now endemic. Were I to be bitten by a wild animal or a farm dog I should – I read with increasing disquiet – take the creature, alive or dead, to the nearest doctor, who would be able to test the beast for infection.

What, I wondered, was I supposed to do if a psychotic Alsatian, whose peasant master had failed to train it the Woodhouse way, leapt at me and clamped its foaming fangs around my shins? Club it to death and drag it by its tail along forest paths to the nearest general practitioner? Or should I ignore the wounds? Take my chances, and spend several anxious weeks waiting for phobic symptoms? Would I awake in some Tuscan inn to the intolerable sound of a dripping tap?

In dogs' collective unconscious there is an unshakeable belief that all lone pedestrians with rucksacks are hunchbacks incapable of self-defence. This I know to my cost, and have a certificate of tetanus prevention to prove it.

I could have bought a spray-can of anti-rapist nerve gas for protection – possession of which is legal in France – but chose instead to rely on my grandfather's blackthorn walking stick, a slender cane carved from a single branch whose shaft is studded with vicious barbs. Outside an English football ground on a Saturday afternoon it would doubtless be confiscated as an offensive weapon, and throughout my journey I was careful to affect a limp – when I wasn't limping – whenever I spotted a policeman eyeing me with suspicion; for I reasoned that even a gun-toting gendarme would not rob a cripple of his stick.

However, my blackthorn proved to be a two-edged sword. True, it was useful in several encounters with dogs whose eyes varied in size from teacups to millwheels, but in lonely places ordinary citizens frequently crossed the road at my approach, thereby depriving me of such conversations as,

'Excuse me, but could you tell me the way to X?'

'Certainly. Take the next lane on the left.'

'Thank you.'

'Not at all.'

which would not only have prevented my getting lost, but would have gone some way towards cementing Anglo-French/Swiss/Italian relations.

Toul to Flavigny-sur-Moselle

At six o'clock on Monday morning, having watched my watch for two hours, I rose and took a shower, noting dispassionately how the wiry commas of pubic hairs on the cracked tiles did not match mine.

I ate the ubiquitous bread roll and child's portions of butter and jam washed down with sludgy coffee into which I ladled enough sugar to set any dentist's teeth on edge. As a rule I loathe sweet things, but I was feeling lethargic and hoped that the sucrose would supply me with sufficient fire to burn each bridge I crossed.

Although I did not plan to follow Belloc's route religiously, I thought it appropriate to visit the cathedral before setting off.

I assumed that an early mass would be in progress, but the sepulchral interior was cold and sombre and peopled solely by spectral statues staring at me in the half-light.

Suddenly I felt afraid.

Until now the journey had been an abstraction inextricably woven into the text of Belloc's book, but now I was faced with the reality of actually having to do it. The whole idea seemed improbable. All that way. The Moselle Valley, the Vosges, the Jura, the Alps, the Lombardy Plain, the Apennines, Tuscany. How many kilometres? A thousand? I did not know. Doubts assailed me. Would I even be able to complete the first day's walk? I was over 40, my rucksack weighed twenty kilos, and although I was fitter than most men my age I had never attempted such a ludicrous venture. I had caught jogging disease in America, and for ten years had been running regularly in a vain attempt to stave off middle age. I had even completed my first and only marathon; but that was a mere four hours isolated in a more or less sedentary life, and although my legs were strong I had one Achilles heel – my back.

By rights someone of my height should have more vertebrae than a dwarf, but evolution is indiscriminate. In my mind's eye I see my back as a stack of children's bricks ready to topple at the slightest provocation. Any everyday act, performed carelessly, can upset their verticality: felling a tree, carrying a piano, sex in a non-missionary position. Even lifting a rucksack containing a Dictaphone and a pack of *Learn Italian in a Week* cassettes might set the bones slipping. And when it happens I cannot move – not at all. Days must be spent immobile on the floor with my poor wife impersonating Florence Nightingale.

What if, on some desolate mountain footpath far from civilisation, my back simply said, 'I've had enough of this. You'll have to go on without me'? Would I be forced to crawl metre by metre, day after day, quenching my thirst on dew licked from continental grasses, and eating truffles? And if I survived, would I be able to sell my story to *Reader's Digest*?

Like all true hypochondriacs, I had come prepared, and my side pocket was bulging with painkillers and muscle relaxants. But prevention is better than cure, and so I decided to take care – bend my knees when lacing my boots, remove my pack before squatting behind a bush, and remain celibate.

My other worry concerned my ability to cope with solitude. Like all scribblers, I can delight in my own company, but only for limited periods. I do not believe in astrology, but if it were true then I would conform perfectly to the Gemini stereotype. I oscillate between extremes: one moment plodding moodily from tor to tor across the bogs of Dartmoor; the next scurrying off to the nearest pub, where I am prepared to chat to anyone about anything other than astrology.

When you go on holiday to a resort you inevitably meet people. Faces glimpsed on arrival in lobby or restaurant become Joan and Ralph by the second day. By the third you have unwisely exchanged addresses. Even if, by the fifth, you are taking early breakfasts and moving further down the beach to avoid Joan's infuriating giggle there are always others to take her place. It is not the same when you are constantly on the move.

In the sixties, when, like most self-indulgent students brought up on a half baked diet of Jack Kerouac, I spent my summers hitchhiking through Europe, such ephemerality had its advantages. Then, when I did not know myself, I was content with my own company because my personality was constantly shifting. And in the pre-AIDS era, when to be English was an aphrodisiac, there were the added attractions of countless encounters with pill-popping sophomores who added retrospective sparkle to the crummiest of towns. Zagreb, Sofia, Bonn; none remembered for their architecture.

But Toul would be remembered merely for its shutters and the twin towers of its cathedral. Encounters en route would necessarily be superficial. And now that I knew myself – or so I supposed – I would have to be content with internal dialogues, both parts spoken by the same immutable character who had nothing new to

21

teach me. But I was being presumptive. My journey had not yet begun.

★ ★ ★

I left the cathedral and immediately took the wrong road.

Like all motorists, conditioned to following signposts blindly, I chose directions specifically designed to keep Toul free of traffic, and instead of going south I headed towards Helsinki.

Half an hour later I passed the cathedral, its elegant bulk rising behind hideous concrete ramparts that testified to Toul's history as a frontier town.

Belloc left the city along the Moselle's west bank, but juggernauts had not been invented then, and his road now looked lethal.

I consulted my map and saw that by crossing the river on the Nancy road and following a lane on the east bank I could recross the Moselle at the village of Pierre-la-Treiche a few kilometres upstream.

I stopped in the middle of the bridge and peered down at the Moselle. It was not wildly attractive: a wide canalised stretch reminiscent of the Thames at Putney, its surface whipped into whitecaps by a keen gale. The sky above was uniformly grey, while on the horizon, crossing the German border, there was an armada of piratical black clouds.

In photographic terms the entire vista was $f1.4$, and even with my pupils fully dilated the picture was underexposed. A gaggle of schoolgirls wearing bright anoraks enlivened the otherwise monochromatic scene, but when they passed me and burst into laughter I felt the first twinges of paranoia. Perhaps my red nylon gaiters – bought with the Alps in mind – did look a little incongruous, but I hoped that they would prevent rabid Jack Russells or other below-the-knee dogs from actually drawing blood. Or was the baguette protruding from my plastic Tesco bag the cause of their mirth?

Once over the bridge I turned south, already aware that each step was taking me closer to the Eternal City.

The road passed between nondescript houses, then headed out into a barren floodplain where the skeletal shapes of rusting cranes and dredgers reared above windswept clumps of purple willowherb bordering disused gravel pits.

A woman, her hair horizontal in the gale, was pushing a pram whose wheels squealed like a baby. I smiled and said hello, but she appraised me with dead eyes and passed by without returning my greeting.

A lorry, its engine noise muffled by the wind, shot past, its wing mirror almost hitting my head. I swore at the driver, but should have thanked him for reminding me to walk facing the oncoming traffic.

The lorry turned off into a cement works from which a mongrel guard dog, its legs and sex hidden by matted black hair, scuttled like an oversized wolf spider. It did not bark or rush straight at me, but chose to trot nonchalantly in the direction from which I had come. Then, well practised, it turned, crossed the road, and came at me from behind.

It seemed statistically unfair that I should be forced to confront my deepest anxiety so soon, and I searched for someone who could call the beast to heel. After all it must have been obvious to anyone that a person already weighed down with tent pegs and neuroses had no intention of stealing a bag of cement. But the lorry had evaporated and the works resembled a ghost town with dust devils twirling in the yard and the corrugated iron cladding of a shed clanging like primary school percussion.

I turned to face the dog and said, 'Who's a good boy then?', confident in the knowledge that it was tone rather than vocabulary that mattered.

Disconcerted momentarily, it faltered, but it must have smelt my fear for it began to advance menacingly in a semi-crouching position.

I walked backwards, brandishing my blackthorn, having made up my mind to boot it mercilessly should it attack.

It shadowed me, weaving from side to side like a fish, but after fifty metres I must have passed the olfactory boundary marking its territory for it sniffed the base of a telegraph pole, cocked a leg, and sauntered back, its duty done.

A little further on I stopped to pick up stones, and with my pockets rasping with ammunition I headed towards Rome.

I soon left the squalor behind and knew I was in the country when, on the outskirts of Chaudeney, I saw two deerskins, flanked by underwear, pegged to a clothesline.

Chaudeney is a pretty village whose gardens were heavy with fruit.

An old man with ear tufts like an owl's was perching precariously at the apex of a tapering ladder, which was swaying against branches buffeted by the wind. He was putting apples into bags slung bandolier-fashion over his shoulders, and when he saw me he plucked one and flung it for me to catch. This simple act of kindness made my spirits rise for the first time since leaving England. I thanked him, and with my mouth full of France I continued along a lane now bordered by woods.

To the south-east, beyond the Moselle, I could see the escarpment of the Bois l'Evêque where Belloc, having left Toul in the evening, had halted in a heathery clearing to eat a midnight feast of bread, ham and chocolate. And, of course, wine, which four wandering soldiers he encountered declined to share, 'to my great joy'.

These forested hills, no higher than the Sussex Downs, reminded me that I had chosen to begin my journey late in the year. It was past the equinox, and the foliage was already autumnal, the oaks and beeches prematurely browned by the river valley's microclimate. And amongst the crowns were unfamiliar flames; some species of maple presumably, their tops as red as Christmas candles.

Belloc had travelled in June when the nights were brief and warm, but I would be subject to more moon than sun and would have to confine my observations to the comparatively short daylight hours; for to move at night would, I had decided, deprive me of everything but mileage. And although I knew it was a race against time to reach the Alps before the first snow fell, it was a race in which I was not prepared to participate. I could not control the weather, and if winter arrived early that year then I would simply have to improvise.

A narrow bridge crosses the Moselle at Pierre-la-Treiche, and as it is a habit of mine to stop in the middle of all bridges I did so there and watched a gleaming white cabin cruiser, prodded by a fierce tailwind, slopping through true waves; for the river flows directly east to west here, and the wind was from the east. The boat seemed a fugitive from the Mediterranean with its owner standing resolutely at the wheel, his obese body unsuccessfully disguised by a Hawaiian shirt and orange shorts, while his pale wife, partially covered by a billowing bathrobe, lay cruciform on the foredeck. They must have been dying of cold, and I can only surmise that they were determined to cut a dash when entering their home port.

On the far side of the bridge I met soldiers; not four, like Belloc, but four hundred. Shivering conscripts, amongst whom dapper officers with neat moustaches flitted to and fro, were disconsolately loading spinach-green lorries with camping gear from a site littered with a thousand soft-drink cans.

As I approached they all stopped their tasks as though ordered telepathically, and stared. I waved, but not an eyelid flickered beneath combat caps that seemed maliciously designed to make all wearers appear moronic. Local farm-boys, I assumed, doing their reluctant bit for NATO, and I can only suppose that their bewilderment was induced by the sight of a man carrying a heavy pack voluntarily.

I marched on, thanking fate for releasing my generation from two years of square-bashing and communal living in Nissen huts smelling of stale sweat and semen. And again I wondered how a forceful individual like Belloc could have looked on his barrack life in Toul with such affection, albeit in retrospect. But perhaps I was being too harsh, for at twenty-one every novel experience is an adventure.

Now, like a raw recruit on his first day of manoeuvres, my legs and shoulders were already aching and my stomach was gurgling a request for rations. And so I wandered into Pierre-la-Treiche in search of cheese and fruit, for my mouth was dry and I had neither the spit nor the inclination to cope with plain bread.

As I entered the village the wind drew aside a curtain of cloud to reveal a blue window, and the scene was illuminated by my favourite light: a foreground of houses and flowery gardens reflecting the sun with a stark backdrop of sky whose solid chunks of greys and purples resembled the smooth facets of a slate cliff.

A ginger cat, caught unawares by the heat, flopped down in the middle of the wide empty street, and white smoke gushing from chimney pots suddenly seemed unseasonable.

The shop was closed, and when I entered a bar and asked why this should be so, the barman looked at me as though I were an idiot, shrugged, and said, 'Because it's Monday of course.'

I made do with beer, sat at a table outside, and watched a pair of buzzards wheeling high above the cat, the deserted street, and me.

With a bottle of mineral water adding considerably to the weight of my dangling plastic bag I left the quiet village and made my first map-reading error.

The Moselle bends like a bow through a wooded gorge, and my intended route, the bowstring, passed through a forest. But I was used to working with Ordnance Survey maps, and had not yet come to grips with the scale of my French one. Besides, this map, bought in England, must have been old stock, for the road I took along the riverbank was not even marked.

I trudged two kilometres before realising my mistake, but I was too tired to retreat and reasoned that this road must go somewhere.

The sandy prow of a scraggy island came into view and from my map I saw that from the far end, at a ferry crossing, a lane led off at a right angle, curling up into the forest where I could rejoin Belloc's path; for at this stage, and for many days to come, I was foolishly obsessed with following his exact route.

When I reached the end of the island there was no ferry and no lane; only a monstrous lock with a control tower, all concrete and smoked glass, surveying the empty river. A new bridge crossed to the far bank but would take me miles out of my way.

I sat on a bollard, drank mineral water and wondered what the hell to do.

Perhaps I could scramble up the escarpment and use my compass to find the road? But after inspecting the steep slope I realised that the brambles and saplings were impenetrable.

I had reluctantly decided to retrace my steps when I noticed a sign which read, *Moselle Bicycle Track. Maron 1 Hour*. And there, stretching away in a thin black ribbon beside the river, was an asphalt pavement, doubtless laid by the Lorraine Rural District Council to encourage healthy outdoor activities.

I was already becoming obsessed with time and distance – something I had vowed not to do – and I asked myself a question worthy of an 11+ examination.

Q. If a cyclist averaging 16 kilometres per hour could reach Maron in 60 minutes then how long would I, averaging three miles per hour, take to reach Maron?

A. Three hours, 20 minutes.

There were no villages marked before Maron, but I had bread to eat and water to drink and so I set off, glad to be on a path where vehicles could not follow.

The river was swollen, and at several points opaque grey water lapped the black track, while to my right slopes thick with underbrush precluded any deviation. When the river is in spate the path must be impassable.

I remembered how Belloc had described the Moselle changing into a mountain torrent not far to the south, and I found it hard to believe that this broad expanse would ever, in my timescale, alter its sluggish lowland characteristics.

The lonely path and the proximity of the desolate river fed my fears.

Many things frighten me; seldom because of actual threats to my safety, but because my imagination, fuelled by past experiences and deep-seated anxieties, provides vivid cinematic sequences in which I am the victim of circumstances. No doubt if I paid a psychoanalyst to unravel the old bandages wrapping this underlying streak of pessimism they would reveal that a terror of hellfire, inculcated since I was five, was the cause. And she would probably be right.

Here I was reminded of the Mississippi where it broadens into Lake Pepin between the shores of Wisconsin and Minnesota. There, on a similarly dark and windy day, I had spent an hour of blue funk in a tiny tin boat whose helmsman, deaf to my pleas, had headed at full throttle into the choppy centre where the outboard's propeller screwed its way into a shoal. Finding myself marooned in the middle of a river-lake was almost too much to take; for its very shallowness – its quality of being not-quite-land – made the surrounding deep seem doubly ominous. The owner – one of those devil-may-care twentieth-century urban American backwoodsmen prone to wearing red check shirts and bowie knives – managed to reverse out of danger, but a distrust of wide water had already been filed.

There I stood on the bank of the Moselle watching my wraith clinging to an upturned boat. There was nothing I could do to help, and so I drank the last of my whisky and lobbed the bottle into the river where it bobbed for a few seconds before capsizing and sinking with a final exhalation of bubbles.

An oxbow lake a mile long has been formed where the Moselle bends towards the north, and my route followed a narrow causeway between the flowing and still water. The lake, partly protected by willows, was calm and the colour of jade. Coots and dabchicks cruised jerkily amongst reeds and half submerged trees, while in the distance I saw the silhouettes of seven anorexic herons stooping on the edge of a sandbank. At my approach they rose vertically and flapped away gracelessly into the wind.

A huge barge loaded with gravel, its gunnels almost awash, thudded downstream displacing enough water to cause a semi-cylindrical wave which followed at a constant speed and distance behind the boat like a tidal bore. The skipper waved and shouted something I could not catch, and then he was gone. Another stranger; another extra flitting across the screen to be kept, uncredited and unedited, in those endless corridors of stored rushes deep inside my skull.

I wondered if my journey was destined to be nothing more than a perpetual tracking shot, the camera motor constantly whirring, all random images faithfully catalogued. Or would I be able to impose my own order on events?

I walked on, recalling the arguments for and against free will which had plagued my youth, when philosophical discussion had been more than just a pastime. Since my early twenties such questions had been swept aside or at best brought out after dinner like a game of Scrabble. 'More coffee? No? Then let's play Determinism.' And with thought processes blurred by wine and pragmatism the questions and answers had no longer seemed relevant.

Now, alone by the Moselle, without recourse to a cosy and diverting routine, I was terrified by the prospect of having time to think. My entire body began to tremble, and I wondered if this physical manifestation was the precursor of some sudden mental malfunction, which, like a frustrated understudy, had been waiting in the wings for just such an opportunity to emerge.

Looked at objectively my disquietude seems absurd, but at the time I genuinely believed that I might be on the brink of a breakdown (whatever that is). I was becoming obsessed with functioning as a mere recording machine. Pan left and what did I see? A steep bluff of ochre-coloured rock on which a man, unroped, was climbing solo. Pan right: a soldier with a gun in a watchtower guarding the barbed wire perimeter of a military camp or prison in a forest clearing; a tricolour on a pole. Tilt up: a sky as pallid as a dead man's skin stretched under the sun. Tilt down: boots with red laces moving of their own volition.

How much further to Maron? Five kilometres? I continued quickly, almost jogging, the lake on my right having been replaced by a swamp of black ponds and ditches where bulbous brown fungi grew on dead trees, and where strange ferns, like etiolated palms, sprouted from mud banks draped with rotting slime that filled the air with its stench. A buzzard glided low across the black water, although a pterodactyl would have been more in keeping. But swamp gradually gave way to meadows and although I was drained of energy I was aware that my crisis was subsiding into normal neurosis.

In my haste I had ignored the warning pains in heels and toes, for I was hungry for houses and people and had vowed to keep going until I reached them.

For the third time that day I crossed the Moselle and found myself in Maron, where I bought lemonade, cheese and fruit from a woman whose corneas were like quartered apples with pips for pupils.

The red-roofed village was empty, and I sat on the church steps as the clock struck one. The sun suddenly shone, and I lay back with my pack for a pillow. This is more like it, I thought, as I closed my eyes and allowed the yellow heat to weigh heavy on my eyelids. But the peace was short-lived. Music intruded – not bucolic songs in concert with my preconceived ideas of Bellocian simplicity, but the inimitable sound of B. B. King's blues guitar splitting the air, its source a high-powered hi-fi in a shuttered room across the street.

Still, I like B. B. King and was content to eat my lunch to the strains of his incomparable riffs, even though such plangent playing provided a bizarre soundtrack for the film I was watching.

I pierced an orange with a thumbnail, but found the task of peeling beyond my capabilities. I put the orange down and studied my right hand with growing alarm.

My fingers were moving about uncontrollably as though something was interfering with the wires conducting messages from my brain.

A heart attack? No. That was the left side, wasn't it? And as though on cue, the fingers on my left hand began to twitch independently, stiff and straight like the spines of a sea anemone.

My thoughts raced. Would there be a doctor in such an insignificant village? And where was the nearest hospital? Nancy?

I should have known. It was my own fault for not having had a thorough medical checkup before leaving England. Why the hell did people think it healthy to trek around the countryside with twenty kilos on one's back? After all my heart couldn't differentiate between a rucksack and a sudden weight increase. Any doctor worth his salt would have put me on a crash diet. Please, God, let me survive and I promise to chuck my rucksack in the river and take the first plane home. My wife! My children! And on the first day too.

And then I noticed the pink weals between fingers and palms. All was explained. I was suffering from Tesco's Disease. My heavy plastic bag, carried alternately in right and left hands, had cut off the supply of blood to my fingers, which were now being infused with a fresh will to live.

With this new lease of life came a couldn't-care-less attitude, and without hesitation I decided to break the law; not the French, but Merrill's.

John Merrill has written a book called *Walking My Way*, and on the flyleaf the blurb describes him as the world's leading professional walker. Naturally, having spotted this book on the shelves of Exeter Public

Library, I had read it with scholarly concentration before setting out. And what an education it was. It not only informed me that the foot has two main functions, namely to support the body while standing and to propel it forward when walking, but also convinced me that marathon walking is a *serious business*.

To assist aspiring walkers Mr Merrill has drawn up a list of Laws, one of which is to disregard blisters. Walking barefoot is recommended if the pain becomes unbearable, although I was more inclined to take the advice of my local chemist, who had issued me with a copious supply of moleskins to apply to raw parts of my anatomy as the need arose.

This I proceeded to do on the church steps, watched by an octogenarian who stared at me censoriously throughout my scissoring as though I were committing sacrilege. Only when my naked feet were re-encased in socks did he retreat.

My orange was attracting wasps, and so I decided to leave – although not before breaking another of Merrill's Laws. I drank lemonade.

Not only does Mr Merrill advise walkers to carry no water but to refrain from drinking throughout the day. And by stopping I had contravened yet another Law for I had unburdened myself and rested. Even at lunchtime I should have kept my rucksack on and leaned against a wall. But at least I had not talked to anyone for longer than half an hour; a heinous crime, which could not only have induced a desire to stop walking but could keep me behind schedule.

Well behind schedule, having concocted a shandy in my stomach by the addition of Alsace beer, I set out along the road to Neuves Maisons.

The sun was now beaming from a cloudless sky and the feeling of claustrophobia brought on by following the enclosed bed of the valley was dissipated, not only by the heat but by my first overall view of the region's topography.

Although no higher than thirty metres above the river I could trace its course clearly for its meandering surface was scaled with silver like a slow-worm's back.

Forested plateaus, masquerading as hills, were separated by lateral coombes where hamlets and farmhouses had taken advantage of the rich alluvial soil. All the crops apart from corn had been harvested, and for the next few days the rattle of brittle cornleaves was frequently the sole accompaniment to my footfalls.

I smelt Neuves Maisons before I saw it for it lay due east and the wind carried its sulphurous stink straight towards me.

In Chaligny, a suburb, I passed large residences belonging, no doubt, to the local plant managers, and I wondered how these people could tolerate living within sniffing distance of this persistent industrial fart. But they were obviously proud of their homes, which were not hidden behind high walls but flaunted within hideous enclosures of wire mesh of the kind that surround municipal tennis courts.

On the outskirts of Neuves Maisons I passed through *Zône Industrielle Louis Pasteur*.

Almost everything in France, it seems, is linked to her famous sons and daughters. What provincial town does not boast a Rue Victor Hugo or Avenue Alexandre Dumas? But I am not complaining, for at least such wayside memorials promulgate their achievements.

Perhaps Britain should take a leaf out of the French book. A Laurie Lee Shopping Mall in Slad? The Dylan Thomas Marina at Laugharne? The Gerard Manley Hopkins Wood and Furniture Centre at Binsey?

In Neuves Maisons factory chimneys spewed out columns of brown gas that coalesced to form a dingy canopy behind which the sun, resembling an old leather football, was just visible. The streets were thick with fumes belched from the exhausts of enormous trucks whose gears grated and brakes hissed between grime-encrusted shop fronts and dilapidated dwellings. And for the first time I saw evidence of poverty in France.

Single storey hovels, like run-down Welsh slate-quarrymen's cottages, bordered the street, their walls blackened by a century of industrial filth.

The top half of a stable-style door was ajar, and inside I saw an old woman lying on a bed in what must have been the only habitable room.

Her long tangled white hair was spread on a pillow blotched with stains and her bony fingers lay motionless on a torn blanket. A sallow bulb filled this awful room with shadows, and for a while I thought I was staring at a corpse. But then she turned to stare at me with sad eyes that must once have been blue.

I hurried away feeling like a voyeur caught in the act, for I had invaded the poor woman's privacy with my thoughts as surely as if I had entered her room demanding to take photographs.

The heat was intense and I was saturated with sweat where my rucksack clung like an obese monkey to my back.

I needed a beer, but when I opened the door of a bar I hesitated, dispirited by an impression of dust and squalor. The barman was having trouble with the only customer, a squat muscle-bound drunk who screwed up his Neanderthal features at the unwelcome intrusion of sunlight.

The drunk, his eyes focused on infinity, slid off his stool and beckoned me with hairy fingers.

The barman – who I would have thought needed all the trade he could get – demanded to know what I wanted in a tone that betrayed serious domestic difficulties; either that or he was crazy.

I retreated. If John Merrill could survive for an entire day without liquid then I could go without beer for an hour. I would get a drink a little further on.

I recalled how Belloc had found unfriendliness here when looking for a room, and how he had cursed this miserable place.

And so I, too, cursed Neuves Maisons, and plodded out through its drab suburbs.

I was relieved to reach the countryside again, but there was no shade and, like John Mills struggling across the Sahara to Alexandria, I was seeing visions of ice-cold lager floating in front of me. Each incline had become sand.

The road seemed to go on for ever, undulating through scrubby fields and thickets, its edges armour-plated with crash barriers that provided me with the alternatives of being run down by lorries or taking to steep embankments that put a tremendous strain on my feeble ankle joints.

Rome seemed a long, long way away.

At last, after some kilometres, I saw a roadside bar. *Fermé*. Two more kilometres. A truck-stop. *Fermé*.

I left the main road and took to a lane, but had to endure the proximity of three sources of undrinkable water: a leat carpeted with green pondweed, a khaki canal, and the blue Moselle.

The sun had turned the lane to shimmering liquid, and an approaching angler appeared to be wading through it, his legs invisible below his knees. It was as though he were fishing for trout in mid-road.

My state of dehydration had become so acute, and my legs so wobbly, that I seemed to be gently springing along a surface made from stretched elastic. Then, around a bend, I saw houses, towards which I bounced.

An elderly couple sat soaking up the sun outside their cottage. I tried to speak but my lips were gummed together. 'Are you all right?' the man asked.

'No,' I croaked. 'I need water.'

But instead of disappearing into his cottage to emerge moments later with a glass of crystal-clear water, he pointed to a stone trough in the street.

'Is it drinkable?' I asked, almost past caring.

He laughed, patted his chest, and told me that he had been drinking it for sixty-five years.

No doubt the entire local population was immune to the myriad diphtherial bacteria lurking there.

'Isn't there a bar or a shop in the village?'

'Nothing,' he assured me.

So I flung off my rucksack and, deprived of its weight, toppled several involuntary paces forward.

The bed of the trough was a mosaic of rotting leaves but, as I cupped my hands, the man shouted, 'No, no! Pull the lever!'

And there, set into the wall above the trough, was a pump handle. Translucent spring water gushed from a spout I had not noticed and I drank my fill, allowing the icy liquid to dribble down deliciously inside my shirt.

Beyond this hamlet my quiet tributary of a lane joined the flow of heavy traffic, and I had no option but to follow this busy highway the final few kilometres into Flavigny-sur-Moselle.

The walking was dangerous here, and when, at a complicated junction, I saw the flashing blue lights on police cars parked by the roadside I expected to be harangued or fined for jaywalking. But the police were occupied with the aftermath of a car smash.

A woman was sitting on a grass verge, her face as white as blotting paper with ovoid bloodstains where her fingertips, having explored the gash near an ear, had touched her cheeks.

An ashen man was giving details to a gendarme, who, on seeing my fruitless efforts to cross the road, halted the traffic and ushered me safely across.

Belloc praised Flavigny for its linear structure, which he likened to the Roman method of building towns. For him it was a mark of civilisation but for me it was sheer cruelty. After thirty-five kilometres I was closer to exhaustion than I had ever been – marathon included – and all I craved was a place to sleep.

The sun was setting as I stumbled on, its orange glow adding nothing to the interminable straight street, which eventually led me to the town centre.

A car with its bonnet propped open seemed to be swallowing a man whole. I said, 'Excuse me?' and he emerged unscathed, a sparking plug gripped between his teeth. 'What?'

'Is there a hotel here?'

'No.'

'Somewhere to camp then?' He shook his head.

A hundred metres further on I saw a sign proclaiming *Camping*.

The site was already wreathed in white mist that hid the wheels of peeling caravans parked with military precision. But something was wrong. No lights shone from the windows, and there were no cars. And no people.

The office, a glorified garden shed, was locked.

I sat down at a picnic table and watched my breath condensing. Stars were already twinkling in the east. It was going to be a cold night.

Suddenly a man materialised from nowhere. 'What do you want?'

'I want to sleep.'

'We're closed.'

'But the sign says open till October.'

He shrugged. 'We're closed.'

'There's nowhere else.'

'Try Nancy.'

'But I don't have a car.'

He noticed my rucksack. 'German?'

'English.'

'OK. You can stay.'

And so with my torch propped in a tree, spotlighting a patch of grass, I pitched my coffin-shaped tent and went in search of food.

Flavigny, like Toul, was closed – almost. A bar-cum-restaurant was open but its menu offered only veal, and even hunger could not assuage the squeamishness I have always felt at the thought of devouring dead calves.

I entered and asked the woman behind the bar if there was another restaurant in town.

'Down the street,' she said. 'Five hundred metres.' Restaurant Number Two was closed for the winter – as she must have known – and so, having added a kilometre to my day's trudge, I re-entered Restaurant Number One, ravenous for dead calf.

'You're too early,' she explained. 'We don't start serving till eight.'

'Anything'll do. Perhaps you could make me an omelette?'

'Impossible.'

The patron, a handsome man with a droopy moustache, wandered out from the kitchen.

'German?' he asked.

'English.'

'Get him an omelette.'

I thought I should press home my advantage. 'Maybe a salad too?'

'Get him a salad.'

I ordered wine and sat at a table while the woman failed to cook an omelette.

A fat lobster-pink girl wearing a miniskirt and satanic black eye make-up came in and fed the jukebox. She slouched in a corner and just managed to cross her legs. We both waited for her selections.

Someone screaming 'Pump up the VOLUME!' filled the bar with a cacophony that rebounded from the walls into my ears at the speed of sound.

Men on their way home from work drifted in and stood disconsolately at the bar drinking spirits. A mechanic wearing greasy overalls challenged the pinball machine whose name was PLAYBOY. Every so often numbers would flash like tumescent nipples across the busts of nubile bathing belles (circa 1959) although the mechanic's eyes remained chastely and obsessively riveted to the ball bearings whizzing beneath the glass.

Eventually my first experience of French cuisine was dumped in front of me: a salad comprising half a cylinder of tinned tuna, a pair of deformed lettuce leaves hidden under a dollop of Heinz salad cream, and a few cold tinned peas stacked like Lilliputian cannonballs.

It tasted extraordinary.

An omelette, I suspect, followed; milky white and as flat as a plaice with slices of wrinkled tomato at head and tail. But the bread was fresh and filled me with calories.

I ate every morsel and then, unwisely, complimented the woman on her bread.

Without batting an eyelid she charged me the full price of a five-course meal, but I was too weary to complain and limped back to the campsite, through deserted streets, miffed at having allowed myself to be ripped off on my first day.

My tent had been designed with Munchkins in mind, and so I squeezed in feet first.

I zipped myself in and, snug as a corpse in a body bag, drifted towards sleep, moonlight casting leaf shadows on the nylon just above my face.

I appraised the day. At least I had reached my objective, although I wondered if my physique would tolerate the equivalent of a marathon a day.

I had been disappointed to discover the people less than forthcoming, but perhaps they were merely victims of a history that had bred insularity. After all Alsace-Lorraine has been flung between France and Germany for centuries, and such buffeting must induce an innate distrust of strangers.

Perhaps the Swiss would be jollier?

My final thoughts were of my family, for although my muscles seemed to be coping well enough I was already suffering from acute pangs of homesickness.

Flavigny-sur-Moselle to Charmes

I was woken at 6 a.m. by a church bell tolling with the persistence of an infant demanding his morning feed.

To hell with getting up. I would lie in for an hour. But then I realised I was shivering. How could that be when my brand-new sleeping bag guaranteed survival on Everest – or at least on its lower slopes?

I turned on my side and my cheek was immersed in an icy puddle.

Directly above me water dripped from the grey roof like seepage in a limestone cave.

My tent, chosen for its revolutionary design, simply did not work. The ventilation was totally inadequate and I was lying in the liquid residue of my own breath. My sleeping bag and clothes were saturated and my fingers were corrugated with ridges usually associated with prolonged wallowing in bathtubs.

I was furious with the copywriter whose deft prose had duped me into buying such cunningly packaged tat; for my budget was limited, and I was relying on a tent to provide shelter for at least half my journey. However, this flush of anger did nothing to warm me, and so I set off, barefoot, in search of a hot shower.

My wooden legs ached, but at least I was able to walk even though my feet resembled an illustration from a chiropody textbook. Blisters had sprung up overnight like mushrooms around my heels, and my toes had become raw cocktail sausages. The moleskin patches had erupted into tender, pink domes which I dared not strip off for fear of breaking the bubbles beneath.

The shower was icy, although I persevered; for to stink of stale sweat would not endear me to the lusty country folk I was sure to meet en route who would doubtless invite me into their cottages to share steaming peasant broths and flagons of Brulé wine.

Outside the malodorous cubicle, where a flock of mosquitoes roosted, I sat on dewy concrete and tended to my feet while dawn spilled over the Moselle.

The eastern horizon was silky with cirrostratus, and the willows surrounding the campsite were outlined against a tower of hazy lemon light.

I festooned the shower block with tent, sleeping bag and clothes, and returned to the bar for a tepid coffee and a croissant, which I dunked and sucked like a patient in a geriatric ward while the jukebox implored me, once more, to pump up the volume.

The autumn sun failed to dry my camping gear, and so I packed everything wet, confident in the knowledge that I would be able to drape it over scalding radiators that night in the hotel I had promised myself as a reward for completing another thirty kilometres.

My itinerary was straightforward. Beyond Flavigny I would meet the Canal de l'Est, along whose delightful towpath I would wend my way to Charmes, which is the first town of any size in the Département de Vosges.

That was the theory, but when I reached the Canal de l'Est I discovered that there is no towpath.

I stood dejectedly on a narrow bridge and scanned the canal banks for any trace of a track but both slopes were thick with alder saplings right down to the black water in which archipelagos of yellow leaves, undisturbed by wind or current, looked permanent enough to map.

There was no alternative but to follow the N.57 trunk road which runs parallel to the canal.

Flat waterlogged fields stretched away to my left, and my boots became encased in clinging mud each time I was hooted off the road by convoys of trucks.

But soon the trees bordering the canal thinned and, crossing the road, I clambered up a levee where it was possible to push through tall grasses and between shrubs growing on a neglected path, which, in the past, must have been bald from the tread of heavy horses hauling barges full of iron and wheat.

The water, concealed from the sun, remained black and lustreless, although the gloomy atmosphere was alleviated by patches of meadow saffrons whose violet, crocus-like petals were supported by leafless stalks as thin and white as clay-pipe stems.

Coots, camouflaged by crape plumage, made forays from overhanging foliage and a mallard, caught napping, slapped into the air at an unlikely angle and fled towards the river.

Gossamer, trailing from trees and bushes, tickled my face although it was several minutes before I noticed the first spider crawling up a leg. I stopped to brush it off, then realised I was covered with the creatures. But spiders, unless they are hairy and venomous, do not perturb me and I allowed one to crawl on to my palm.

Its head was tiny, like an ant's, although its abdomen was absurdly out of proportion; plump like a puffball with curving lines of dots and dashes, like Morse, converging at its spinneret. And its entire body was coated with a ceramic glaze which transformed it into an exquisite piece of mobile pottery.

Taking the sensible precaution of walking with my mouth closed, I followed the deteriorating bank until my way was barred by dense undergrowth at a point where canal, road and river meet.

I consulted my map to confirm that this river was indeed the Moselle and not some minor tributary, but Belloc had been right. The sudden change was remarkable. Sparkling in the sunshine the Moselle now flowed fast and shallow between stony spurs; a river in early middle age, not yet wild and carefree like a mountain torrent, but not dull and stolid like the stretch south of Toul.

A family was picnicking.

The father, blubbery as a bull sea lion, sprawled on a sandbank while his wife and daughter flung pebbles at an antler of wood caught in midstream.

I should have followed the man's example and flaked out in the sun, but, like a fool, I carried on along the road, inhaling acrid clouds of carbon monoxide. If the day was to be salvaged then I would have to alter my plans.

A lane led off at a right angle towards the village of Tonnoy, and by following the river south from there to Velle I would be able to rejoin the canal at Crévéchamps where, with luck, a proper towpath would materialise. If not I would simply have to risk the appalling N.57.

The Moselle meanders here, and Tonnoy is built on its eastern bank, a couple of kilometres in the wrong direction across a featureless floodplain. But I did not regret having made this detour; for Tonnoy is a pretty red-roofed hamlet whose houses were garlanded with honeysuckle and climbing nasturtiums.

I was disappointed to discover that no footpath led south beside the river, but the little lane to Velle led through delightful woodland and pasture where fat cattle had arranged themselves like spokes around the hubs of tree trunks; for the heat was now intense.

A squirrel with charcoal fur bounded along the tiled ridge of a farmyard wall, and from force of habit I shouted, 'Squirrel!', a word guaranteed to release the wolf lurking within my Border collie. During our long walks in the Devon cleaves she goes berserk at the sight of a squirrel, and will leap through thorns or plunge into raging rapids in pursuit. She never catches one. If she did she would probably try to lick it to death.

How she would have loved this extraordinary walk. And how I missed her company.

The Moselle at Velle was clear and shallow. From the bridge I watched a triangular shoal of sleek red-finned fish facing upstream. I do not know what kind they were, but one would have been enough to feed a good Catholic family.

Another shadowless tramp over the floodplain returned me to the canal where my prospects looked more hopeful.

A white terrier tethered to the lock-keeper's cottage at Crévéchamps yapped at me, but its tail was friendly and I knocked on the door.

The affable lock-keeper, whose face and hands were burnt as brown as toffee, told me I could follow the canal without difficulty as far as Bayon.

I thanked him and popped into the village for a beer, but as I walked along the street an old man I greeted swore at me and spat. I can only think that, being relatively close to the border, he assumed I was German. Certainly he was ancient enough to remember both wars and both occupations, and who can tell what experiences might have caused him to react to a stranger in such a hostile way? But this is pure supposition. Perhaps he was merely a miserable old misanthropist.

Nevertheless I was reminded of how once, in Crete, my wife and I had camped in an olive grove close to a village on the south coast. There were two bars in that village. One was frequented by sullen out of season Australians we wished to avoid. The other, too basic to attract tourists, was the place we chose to drink our raki. And there, for the first time in many trips to Greece, I experienced mute hostility. The old men had thought that we were German and everything was explained when, on returning to our tent, we passed what we had assumed was an ordinary shrine on the edge of the olive grove. But on closer inspection we saw, piled behind the dusty glass, a heap of human skulls. As a reprisal against some act of resistance the occupying German forces had rounded up all the young men in the village and had murdered them. And this glass box was their memorial.

The clientele in the bar at Crévéchamps was friendly and garrulous and tried to persuade me to stay long after I had quenched my thirst.

'I really must leave now,' I explained after my third beer.

'Why?'

'I've a long way to go.'

'Where?'

'Rome.'

'By *auto-stop*?'

'By feet.'

Eyebrows arched. 'But why?'

'I'm not sure.'

A dwarfish man with yellow teeth tried to lift my rucksack with a bent finger, but could raise it no higher than his knees.

'You must be mad,' he said.

The canal south of Crévéchamps was a watery avenue flanked by limes whose grey-leafed parasols protected me from a sun now at its zenith.

Every few yards I disturbed basking lizards that scuttled into the dry undergrowth from which – believing themselves invisible – they watched me with beady amber eyes.

The canal widened into a pond where, in busier days, barges must have queued to go through the lock.

A large man and his larger wife sat statuesquely on the far bank, fishing. Their rods were not the ugly fibreglass sticks one sees beside the Thames but elegant wooden poles tapering to points from which threads led down to simple quill floats so still that they seemed embedded in the surface.

The entire scene was composed from slabs of colour like a canvas by Maurice de Vlaminck, and the tart smell of the water reminded me of countless summer evenings when, after school, I would cycle down to the River Wey to fish for roach and bream. Usually I only caught gudgeon, for I could not bear to impale worms on my barbs, and the bigger fish were seldom tempted by bait made from sliced white bread and saliva.

Someone had told me that fish feel no pain because their mouths are devoid of nerves, and so I had no qualms about angling. But when a perch swallowed my hook and coughed up blood I had been forced to bludgeon it to death and decapitate it with a penknife in order to extract the hook.

I felt so guilty that I confessed my crime to the parish priest who, having made some flippant remark about Christ choosing his apostles from fishermen, had dismissed me from the confessional without giving me even a single Hail Mary for a penance. But I had distrusted his theology, and, having exculpated myself by reciting an entire rosary, had thrown away my rod.

The canal between Crévéchamps and Bayon resembles one of those examples of perspective one finds in 'How to Draw' books, and although I walked briskly the vanishing point came no closer.

Hereabouts Belloc had found the walking dull and had relieved his boredom by varying his route between turnpike, towpath and fields. But 87 years later the turnpike is a super-highway and the fields are enclosed by barbed wire; which left me with the canal.

The trees no longer provided shade because the sun was now due south, and by the time I reached the next lock I was staggering under the weight of a rucksack full of bricks.

The lock-keeper was working my sluices to let a pleasure craft through.

I began to ask if I could continue along the towpath to Charmes, but the words stuck in my throat and I began to retch.

He was embarrassed and asked if I was ill.

My reply was definitive for I turned and deposited croissant, coffee and beer on to the towpath.

'It's far too hot to walk,' he said, averting his nose. 'You must rest.'

I took his advice and slunk away to sit under a poplar where, with my head in my hands, I vowed to eschew alcohol during daylight hours.

When I returned to the lock the boat was chugging out of sight. I should have asked for a lift for the lock-keeper assured me that the towpath was impassable.

Another detour; this time into Bayon, then south along minor roads to Charmes.

On the outskirts of Bayon a nave of horse chestnuts provided welcome pools of shade. The road and verges were glossy with conkers and I thought of how my sons would be baffled by the sight of such a crop going to waste.

A whiskery old man was working in his allotment beside the road and his harvest of pumpkins was meticulously piled into a cone. The largest formed the foundations; great golden globes striated with deeply indented longitudinal lines, while above these were smaller smoother varieties, pink and peachy.

At the pinnacle there was a solitary gourd as white and round as a baby's skull.

When the man saw me he straightened up and remained bent double. He would have to roll his pumpkins home.

Charmes was still fourteen kilometres away and for the next three hours I experienced what I imagine an aspiring commando must endure during the gruelling selection process, although I did not have the luxury of an NCO shouting obscene encouragement.

I could feel heat radiating from the white-topped lane through the soles of my boots, and during one brainnumbing section north of Chamagne, where the lane runs as straight as a fenland ditch, I discovered that some sadist had replaced the bricks in my rucksack with iron ingots.

I was vaguely aware of farms to the right and forest to the left, but distance was all that mattered. I counted my paces. One hundred; one tenth of a kilometre. Five hundred; half a kilometre. A thousand. Then begin again. Belloc had tried the same ruse, and it does not work. Try counting to 14,000 and you will understand why.

There was no traffic and the only sounds were the rattle of rusting corn leaves and the high-pitched squeaking of finch flocks.

In Chamagne I broke my vow by drinking a beer, and an hour later I limped across the Moselle into Charmes, where I collapsed on a bench in the town square. But I was not allowed to rest, for a persistent youth in neat pastel clothes insisted on practising his English.

Grumpy with fatigue I told him briefly about myself and then, without inquisitiveness, asked the usual polite questions.

He was an art student from Nancy who was 'doing very modern things with metal', and he sat so close to me that, in my uncharitable frame of mind, I assumed he was a genuine nancy boy in search of a bit of rough; for rough I certainly must have looked. And so I leered at passing schoolgirls, told him how much I was missing my beautiful wife, and soon he left.

I needed to relax.

The backstreet bar I chose was run by a podgy woman who might have been an off-the-peg madamè supplied by Central Casting. Her face was stony with foundation cream and powder, on top of which she had painted a mask which, far from rejuvenating her, only served to emphasise her haggardness. False eyelashes curled up into plucked eyebrows over which two pencilled arches spanned her forehead like a bridge. A cigarette drooped from shocking-pink lips, and her lacquered hair was carelessly bleached, its roots matching her ebony earrings. But nothing could disguise the dewlap dangling above her fussy blouse.

She looked me up and down as though I were applying for a relief barman's job.

When I asked for a beer she dumped a glass and bottle on the table and overcharged me.

Something was going on, and I was an unwelcome interruption.

A man, her husband I suspect, was pawing a compliant teenage girl in a clinging green dress that betrayed her lack of underwear. The man's ginger toupee clashed with his grizzly sideburns, and his T-shirt, cut away at the shoulders to accentuate freckled biceps, was streaked with sweat.

The girl, who was either drunk or doped or both, kept whispering to another man who stood protectively behind her like a pimp, his hands furtively hidden in the pockets of a pinstriped suit. His wrists were as thin and white as celery sticks while his jaundiced and cadaverous face suggested that he was the victim of some terminal disease.

And when bicep-man's hands cupped the girl's breasts a three-cornered shouting match began.

The girl slipped away into a back room, and between expletives the woman told me to get out.

I left, and will never know if I missed being the key witness of a *crime passionnel*.

The first hotel I tried offered three-star rooms, which would have consumed two days' budget, and so I set off in search of cheaper accommodation.

A run-down *pension* seemed perfect.

Its proprietor looked seven months pregnant, his grimy vest hanging like a miniskirt around elephantine thighs.

'You travelling alone?'

'Yes.'

'Then we're full.'

The pigeonholes behind the desk were clogged with dust, and all the keys were on their hooks.

'Not even a stable?'

'Very funny. Push off!'

Some things do not change. 'Charmes,' Belloc wrote, 'does not fulfil its name nor preserve what its forgotten son found so wonderful in it.'

Every hostelry I tried dismissed me with varying degrees of incivility, and I was beginning to feel like a fugitive from a chain gang.

Defeated, I strolled down to the Moselle, unpacked my dripping tent, and pitched it on the edge of the river.

At dusk I sat drinking Moselle wine and eating supermarket food, while the chameleon river changed its skin in tandem with the sky: rose, yellow, silver, grey.

I mopped the tent's interior with Andrex and slid inside my sodden sleeping bag, too tired to care.

I tried to read a novel picked at random from a bookstall in Bristol, but adulterous affairs in London and the inevitable recriminations seemed even less relevant in Charmes than they would have done in Devon, and having scanned the first few pages I lay back in the torchlight and watched my breath condensing efficiently on the roof.

Something hurled itself against the side of the tent. A cat perhaps?

I switched off the torch and tried to sleep, but the crackle of plastic in the porch fifteen centimetres from my head prompted me to sit up.

The wine had made me lazy, and like a fool I had left my food scraps outside rolled up inside a supermarket bag.

The uncorked wine bottle also lay outside, and I heard distinct licking sounds. A small tongue. A rat's tongue. And only a thin wall of nylon between me and it. Or them.

I switched on the torch, shouted, and slapped the sides of the tent.

Silence. I unzipped the door, grabbed the bottle and bag, and flung them far into the night.

Back in the tent I lay listening to my heart.

Then the wall beside me bulged and the bulge moved towards the end where only a synthetic mosquito net separated my feet from the fly-sheet.

I chucked my torch at the shape and heard a squeak. Silence again. And, thank God, the torch still worked. Then I heard scratching on the tent walls and I knew that *they were trying to get in*.

Almost immediately the roof sagged to within centimetres of my face as a rat clambered across. Instinctively my hands shot up and I punched something soft and heavy which plopped on to the grass.

It was the stuff of nightmares. Something from Edgar Allan Poe.

That is the trouble with tents. You cannot *see* anything. Everything is magnified and exaggerated, and in my mind's eye I saw ravenous beasts as big as capybaras with glinting eyes and guillotine teeth. And although I have camped in the wild many times, and have even had bears prowling around outside, I have never been so afraid as I was there, alone, beside the Moselle.

For the first time in my life I was aware of cold sweat trickling down my back.

What the hell was I going to do? There were still ten hours of darkness, and I was exhausted after the day's march. Perhaps, had I been fresh, I might have stayed awake all night and fought them off heroically.

Instead I fled.

From nakedness to being fully dressed took less than a minute, and grabbing only passport and wallet I ran from that awful ditch towards the neon-lit streets of Charmes where everything was wonderfully dull.

I went straight to the expensive hotel where the night porter, suspicious of my lack of luggage, stared pointedly at my unlaced boots.

He called the manager who would doubtless have turned me away had I not recounted my frightful experience in florid detail.

Perhaps he was embarrassed by the loutish behaviour of French rats towards an English traveller, or perhaps he simply wanted my money, but yes, he had a room. 'Only a double I'm afraid with TV and bathroom en suite.' And, 'I hate to ask, but would you mind paying in advance?'

Without hesitation I squandered two days' cash. In future I would simply have to walk a little faster and a little further.

Later, blanketed by bubbles up to my chin, I fell asleep in the bath and woke to wild applause.

On the TV a quiz show couple were rapturous with delight. They had won a major prize; a complete set of camping equipment.

Charmes to Epinal

At dawn I returned to the river.

Five tunnels led up through the damp grass from the muddy water. Big tunnels. And the rats had broken in.

In my haste to get away I had forgotten that food was stored inside the tent, and what little remained was strewn all over the groundsheet.

I turned my sleeping bag inside out, half expecting to find a nest of ratlets snuggling there, protected by their mother. But the attack was over, and somewhere under my feet, in their dank lairs, fat rats with hangovers were digesting smoked Parisian ham, Gruyère and an avocado pear.

That day my objective was Epinal, which I planned to reach by taking lanes along the eastern bank of the Moselle.

As I crossed the river I looked upstream to where a perfect blue crescent in the sky signposted the south.

Above me the sun was hidden by an inverted quilt of grey and purple clouds of the sort which, in the American Midwest, presage a twister. But in eastern France tornadoes hardly ever happen, and I set off through the dormitory village of Essegney in high spirits and with a spring in my steps, my rucksack suddenly lighter.

The road to Portieux reminded me that I was heading into the Vosges for the hills were higher now and becoming more frequent; easier going down, harder up.

Soon I was ambling along lanes with unfrequented forests on my left and the Moselle meandering on my right; and I was struck by the lack of a human touch in the landscape. Between villages it was rare to pass a farm, and the only living creatures I saw there were a flock of mute swans and a marsh harrier quartering the wild floodplain in search – I hoped – of rats.

At Châtel-sur-Moselle I was greeted by a pretty blonde picking windfalls from her farm orchard.

'I think it's going to rain,' she said like a true Englishwoman.

Since leaving home I had been so preoccupied with practical problems that sexual thoughts had not even entered my dreams. Now, faced with this tanned smiling woman in tight white shorts, I was reminded that there was more to life than blisters, guy ropes and map-reading. Like a Mademoiselle J. Hunter Dunn burnished by Vosgesian sun, she stood with her legs slightly apart and her breasts swelling under an unbuttoned tennis top.

I had eaten no breakfast, and thoughts of food were a perfect sublimation of – and substitute for – my other unassuaged appetite. Appetite! A word beloved by the black-cassocked priests who haunted my youth with their Lenten view of sex. But they were cunning bastards; for it is the word I have chosen.

A man in a boiler suit was standing in the garden of a large house separated from the street by tall metal railings.

'Where's the nearest grocer's shop?' I asked.

He grinned but said nothing.

I repeated the question, and this time he replied, 'Look at the flowers. Lovely aren't they?'

'Yes they are, but where's the shop?'

'Look at the flowers.'

A woman with perfectly balanced bags hanging from her hands was waddling along the opposite pavement.

When I asked her where I could find a shop she set down her bags and called me over. Pointing at the man she tapped her frizzy hair with a wrinkled finger.

'He can't tell you anything,' she whispered. 'He's mad.'

'Really?'

'They all are.'

She cackled and continued, web-footed, up the hill.

All was explained when I passed a brass plate attached to the main gate of the large house. It was a psychiatric hospital.

I found the grocery, and for some reason bought a bunch of bananas which I ate beside the river.

Swallows skimmed over the surface, drinking on the wing, while fishes, rising in the false midday dusk, sent concentric ripples across the inky water.

Once upon a time Châtel-sur-Moselle must have been a charming town. Not any more. Behind me the crumbling walls of a fortress were noisy with jackdaws, but instead of an ancient château rising grandly beyond these walls there was a keep of concrete flats (circa 1965), their balconies draped with socks and brassieres. And depressed by such vandalism I started along the clammy road to Vaxoncourt.

Something moved in the grass verge. It was a slow-worm, larger than any I have seen in England. I tried to pick it up but it squirmed out of my fingers and wriggled away into a copse of thistles.

Further on I saw an enormous squashed frog with skin like shrivelled bladderwrack and beside it the remains of a snake well over a metre long, its scalloped blue belly oozing entrails and its white fangs embedded like fossils in the viscous tarmac.

Walking in the centre of the road, well beyond the range of venom-spitting serpents, I approached a hillbilly sort of shack whose front yard was piled high with scrap iron that must have been gold in the owner's eyes because a guard dog, an Alsatian, bounded over a fence that would not have restrained a chihuahua.

There was no way of circumventing him, and so I approached at a brisk pace with my blackthorn holstered in my fist.

Like a sheriff with a trembling trigger finger trying to bluff a gunslinger I kept going, but the beast stood steadfast, like Cerberus, barring my way.

When I was only a few paces from him his nerve cracked and he began to wag his tail and whine submissively like a puppy.

Hercules, having just wrestled the fire-breathing bull, could not have felt more valiant, and I continued on my way brimming with confidence, my dread of hellhounds finally exorcised.

The village of Vaxoncourt, viewed from the north, is a marvellous sight.

Built on a hill, its church spire dominates the landscape for miles, and for the first time I could *see* my objective. Other towns had happened around bends or had suddenly sprung into view above hedges for they had been tucked away in coombes beside the river. But here, away from the Moselle, Vaxoncourt resembled a landlocked island, and I was reminded of Glastonbury Tor; for both rise above the surrounding countryside with Christian places of worship on their crests.

I climbed a steep lane to a leaf-strewn square where a thin boy was collecting conkers.

I picked up a splendid specimen and offered it to him, but he ran away as fast as his spindly legs could carry him.

Like so many picturesque places Vaxoncourt's allure was superficial.

Half-timbered houses bordering the street turned out to be dilapidated semi-detached farms. Romanesque arches, like cavern entrances, led into barns littered with neglected farm machinery, rusting cars, and rotting bundles of hay. Grubby net curtains hung behind the dirty panes of upper storey windows, and the few inhabitants I encountered seemed dejected and careworn.

I was reminded of certain nineteenth-century English paintings in which well-heeled artists had portrayed squalor through rainbow-coloured palettes. Find a peasant. Stick her in front of a cart or village pump. Add a cow or some geese. Light the scene with a setting sun (good for atmospheric shadows) and hey presto! A genuine evocation of rustic contentment. Cross her palm with silver and off to find another subject. A fisherman perhaps? Mending his nets. What a handsome sailor's beard. What piercing blue eyes reflecting the sea. What tosh! Give me Van Gogh's *The Potato Eaters* any day.

Gradually the landscape was changing.

Extensive pasture, no longer bounded by fences, stretched towards stands of beech and oak, and the lane I tramped was reminiscent of drives wending through English parkland.

Beyond Girmont my feet went on strike, their grievance shooting pains in the ankles caused by constantly walking on the steep-angled camber instead of the flat crown of the road.

And so, at a point where the Bois du Chenal abuts the road, I wandered into the forest.

Beech-mast crunching underfoot was the only sound, and having walked several hundred metres I offloaded my pack and lay down with a fallen bough for a pillow.

I tried to nap, but each time I began sliding into sleep I was jolted awake by twitching leg muscles.

No wind ruffled the treetops, and the silence was absolute.

Naively I had hoped to see birds unavailable in Britain – hoopoes, black woodpeckers, golden orioles, goshawks – but I neither saw nor heard any creature other than a purple beetle with feathery antennae crawling through the leaf mould.

Loneliness overwhelmed me and I craved human company.

'I talk to the trees but they don't listen to me,' the song says. Of course they don't, for they are mere objects, and only people who have totally given up on the human race can be content with nature.

When I left the south-east of England to live in Snowdonia I went solely for the landscape, and I would spend all my spare time scrambling up rocky ridges and musing beside gurgling mountain streams.

One sparkling day in winter, several years later, I kicked steps in steep blue snow leading to the horseshoe ridge linking Carnedd Dafydd with Carnedd Llywelyn. On the rim I stopped to look at the scenery. Green ice cornices overhung the precipice of the Black Ladders.

Promontories of rock rose above the swell of snow covering the summit plateaus. And suddenly I saw it for what it was; geology and frozen water. Nothing more. The legacy of a literary education incorporating Wordsworth, Keats, Ruskin, Yeats, and many others, had conditioned me into interpreting landscapes in vague anthropomorphic terms. But there, on the Carneddi, the scales had fallen from my eyes. And although I still spend much of my time in wild places I no longer see them through a stained glass window coloured by others' perceptions.

The trudge down into Dogneville was excruciatingly painful, and I stopped frequently, once to watch a Cessna taking off from a field called Epinal Airport. The plane headed towards Charmes, and I estimated that it would take only seven minutes to reach the point where my long day had begun.

Epinal occupies a trench where the Moselle has gouged deep into the hills.

The city's suburbs, having nowhere else to go, have been squeezed north along the valley, and it took me two hours to complete the final three kilometres; for my boots were full of killer bees, while the dead horse draped over my shoulders had contorted my body into a stumbling question mark. And for the first time I was forced to use my blackthorn as a genuine walking aid.

At junctions controlled by traffic lights I could never hobble fast enough, and would find myself stranded midway across while vehicles advanced like armoured divisions with orders to take no prisoners.

Apart from the physical discomfort, I enjoyed my stagger into town, which took me along tree-lined quays where people were strolling in the warm evening air.

I leaned on railings above the river, and a girl in a kayak waved her paddle in greeting, her luminescent orange life jacket and lemon helmet glowing fruitily in the gathering dusk.

How pleasant it was to be among sophisticated people again after the lonely lanes and forests, and how glad I was to melt into a crowd where no one stared at me as though I were a visitor from Mars as they had done in the countryside.

In the first hotel I entered I was welcomed with open arms, and from there I made my first phone call home.

All was well in England. The house had not caught fire. No crazy gunman was holding my family hostage. And after talking with my children I asked my wife to contact the tent's manufacturer and demand that a replacement be sent out to me.

'I'll try,' she said, sounding dubious. 'Where should they send it – if they agree?'

I tried to think of a city with an international airport reasonably close to my route. 'Bern,' I said.

'Bern?'

'Bern,' I confirmed.

Bats, weaving and diving like night fighters, were intercepting insects attracted to a floodlit fountain in the middle of the river; while in a dark harbour, away from the glare of reflected street lamps, the moon floated at anchor.

The original city was founded on an island, which is joined to the shore by many bridges, one of which I crossed. From this island, thronged with promenaders, I saw the surrounding hills stippled with lights, and I was reminded of Durham where I spent three dissolute years at the university; my only and inadequate excuse being that it was the sixties when promiscuity was compulsory and when musicians such as Thelonious Monk, Eric Clapton and Chuck Berry would play for us while we drank Newcastle Brown Ale at 1/10d a pint. We were naive then. Some of us even believed that Harold Wilson was a socialist.

The old city of Durham is built on an incised meander of the River Wear with its castle and unsurpassed cathedral dominating the rest of the town; and, like Durham, Epinal fulfils my main criterion for judging a city – that it be built among hills.

Fine architecture may grace flat towns, but Chester, Cambridge and York, despite their elegant buildings, merit only a B+ whereas Bath, Prague and Sand Point, Idaho, get straight As.

I was hungry, but few things are more dispiriting than sitting alone in a restaurant, for on such occasions the sole excuse for being there is the eating of food; an activity which – when devoid of conviviality – I have always regarded as a trifling necessity.

Fortunately the smell of grease wafting through the streets lured me to a mobile takeaway where all manner of junk food sizzled in vats of boiling oil.

In Britain the nouveau riche will not eat chips with their scampi, although French fries are perfectly acceptable. Here I was offered *frites Américaines* and I have seldom tasted such wonderful chips.

My body craved salt, and the serving-girl – possibly a medical student working her way through college – seemed seriously concerned by the blizzard I sprinkled on my mountain of chips, to which I had added a gigantic hot dog, comprising various toxic chemicals, and a huge helping of fried onions smelling of sour armpits. And with both hands laden with cholesterol I sauntered around the town, munching.

I was drawn by the sound of hurdy-gurdy music and joined a stream of people flowing to a riverside park whose main gate was lintelled with a sign proclaiming FÊTE D'EPINAL.

A boulevard lit by Chinese lanterns led me to a funfair.

It was not at all like those dismal affairs one finds in muddy English fields, but an entire ephemeral Emerald City erected in a grid pattern as regular as a small town in Kansas. And there was none of the latent violence one associates with English fairgrounds after dark. Whole families, from wobbly great-grandmammas to candyfloss-cheeked toddlers strolled together through the gaudy streets, perfectly at ease. And everywhere teeth were champing crêpes and toffee-apples.

Suddenly I saw a mouth I recognised. It was Mrs Thatcher's and she was eating balls.

Carved from wood, she sat beside Ronald Reagan, her ventriloquist's dummy jaw opening and closing mechanically while Epinal's gleeful citizens demonstrated their commitment to Europe by flinging missiles into her gape.

Such an opportunity was too good to miss and so I paid three francs for three wooden balls. But my aim was as ineffectual as my vote and when I left she was still staring crossly at the world and saying 'No!'

I popped into a bar for a nightcap and watched giggling men playing a variation of bar-skittles where, instead of employing a ball on a string to flatten the pegs, they were using a wooden spinning top.

I finished my cognac and was about to order another when I glanced at my watch. It was late. Already past eight. That is one of the major drawbacks of travelling on foot.

One is so bone-weary by the end of a day that all thoughts of spending a night on the town are unthinkable.

Epinal to Remiremont

I awoke to heavy rain pounding on my window.

At breakfast I studied the weather forecast in *Le Monde*. Concentric isobars spinning in from the Bay of Biscay promised worse to come.

In *The Path to Rome* Belloc wrote at length about the basilica in Epinal, and his book is illustrated with a sketch he made while resting his pad on an applecart in the marketplace.

Cocooned in anorak and overtrousers I took my camera to the precinct which must once have housed the market. Fruit stalls had been superseded by parked cars, and with Belloc's book open in my hand I tried to frame the church from the spot where he must have stood. My lens could not quite accommodate the base and so I moved back without bothering to look. Something fell to the pavement. It was a green apple dislodged from a display outside an *épicerie*. I replaced it and wondered if the shopkeeper might be the great-grandson of the cart-owner who had given Belloc three apples in appreciation of his artistic skill. But taking snaps requires no talent, and the man glared at me. Intimidated, I paid for the apple and left.

But this trivial incident of the apple served to remind me of the mainspring of this journey, which sheer fatigue had delegated to a subsidiary place in my scheme of things. Suddenly I was aware of Belloc's ghost beside me; though whether he was laughing at my presumption or encouraging me I did not know.

The interior of the basilica was still and sombre for the grey exterior light could scarcely penetrate the butterfly-wing windows. A few candles flickered in side altars, and from confessionals came indecipherable whispers, like palace intrigues echoed between the columns, filling every nook and cranny with adultery and theft.

Despite all its terrors confession is a remarkable invention, for it provides free psychoanalysis for every Catholic beyond the Age of Reason, which theologians, disregarding individual genetic and nurturing influences, set at seven. Or so it was in my day.

Look what you get: regular visits, the instant offloading of guilt, and a choice of analyst to suit your mood.

I think it is the reason why so many Catholics are such good company and such vehement debaters. For at the age when most primary school children are scooping up sand with yoghurt cartons their Catholic counterparts are engaged in a life or death struggle to save their immortal souls. Were those sins merely venial – meriting only the temporary fires of purgatory? Or were they mortal and deserving of eternal damnation?

I remember it well. All those sleepless nights. What did the Catechism – the junior lawyer's statute book – have to say about impure thoughts? Even murderers only go to prison for twenty years so why should God punish me forever simply for playing with my twinky?

And if my Mummy went to hell would I be happy in heaven?

And although I made my last confession at the age of fourteen I still value the habit of introspection it taught me. A sculpted *pietà*, its life-size figures half hidden by shadows, was extraordinarily moving.

Belloc did not mention it; but he was more interested in bricks.

Christ and the Virgin Mary, with Mary Magdalene, Nicodemus and Joseph of Arimathea in attendance, combine to portray a tableau of grief which is not surpassed by Michelangelo's *Pietà* in Rome. No doubt erudite art historians could prove me wrong but I would not believe them.

The sculpture, which is very old, had originally been painted, and faint traces of colour linger. But for the most part the flesh and drapery are bare and the better for it.

Such a peaceful atmosphere permeated the church that I remained there far longer than I should have; for each day was getting shorter and I had many miles to go.

My walk out of Epinal began beside the river along a boulevard umbrellaed by tattered chestnut trees.

The trees were soon replaced by factories and ugly windowless mills while all the while rain bucketed down, drenching me even though my deluge-proof garments repelled the water. If it rains one gets wet no matter what one does, for if the rain cannot get in then the sweat cannot get out.

A lane led into a forest where, every few hundred metres, blood-red skulls on notice boards commanded me to avoid the trees. MILITARY ZONE. ENTRANCE FORBIDDEN. DANGER OF DEATH!

I disregarded this advice, but only to pee, and failed to detonate a mine. But such warnings did nothing to lighten a mood already downcast by a ceiling of mist that stretched between the wooded hills like the grey capstone sealing a Neolithic tomb.

Taking one of his long short cuts, Belloc had clambered over a hill here, and I, having planned to superimpose my view of the valley upon his, was fortunate in finding the hill shrouded in mist. And so, with an unimpaired conscience, I continued along the road.

Again I found my map inaccurate, for a new highway has been constructed through the forest and I feared that my little lane would become a slip road leading on to this unwalkable stretch. But the lane meandered under a bridge and I continued towards Archettes with rain beating on my anorak hood like prolonged water-torture.

The super-highway, running parallel, became congested with a never-ending convoy of tank transporters whose flashing yellow lights were haloed in spray. As a diversion I began counting them but gave up when I reached a hundred. Perhaps Switzerland had declared war on France and reinforcements were being rushed to the frontier?

For the first time my road took on mountain characteristics, with a steep drop on one side and an overhanging outcrop on the other which reminded me of Harrison's Rocks in Kent where I used to go climbing.

Dispirited by the rain, I sought shelter in a cave and ate salami while a curtain of water cascaded between me and the road.

The cave had been formed in a peculiar red conglomerate in which globular stones resembling leather cricket balls studded the rock. And although such a simile may appear preposterous, I remember thinking that no one but an Englishman sheltering in this particular spot could ever experience it in quite the same way.

In the village of Archettes Belloc had found a cosy inn called Trout of the Vosges in which to eat.

My inn was as welcoming as an unemployment benefit office.

On opening the door I was greeted by a snarling Doberman pinscher whose muzzle I jammed in the gap. It yelped. Shouting ensued, the dog was led away, and I was allowed into a bare dun-coloured bar, which smelt of damp.

'Have you any hot food?' I asked, my breath condensing in the chill atmosphere.

'Sorry.'

'How about a beer?'

I was charged the price of two.

'Can I buy a bottle of mineral water?'

'Get it at the shop.'

'It's closed.'

After much deliberation in a back room I was grudgingly handed a bottle of Vittel at a price three times the going rate.

I left.

On the road to Eloyes I was delighted to find myself in an alpine landscape.

Chalets stood in clearings surrounded by pines through which a cold down-draught was clearing the mist in a disconcerting manner; the clouds resembling smoke filmed backwards. And for the first time I heard the tinkle of cowbells.

In Eloyes I rested by the war memorial and noticed that those slaughtered in the First World War are inscribed under the dates 1914–1919. Perhaps those who died from their wounds after the Armistice are included.

The church clock struck two, and on cue the school expelled children into the street, a proportion of whom were Jewish.

Apart from wondering why a Jewish community should have settled in such an out-of-the-way place I was reminded of an aspect of Belloc's personality which detracts hugely from his stature; his anti-Semitism.

Apologists have tried to excuse him by setting his prejudice in a historical context. After all, they argue, there was a lot of it about then. One only has to look at the host of contemporaneous literary and political figures who expressed similar opinions to appreciate that Belloc's views were merely a minor flaw.

But if you believe that then you will believe anything. The history of Catholicism is rotten with anti-Jewish sentiments, and Belloc was a staunch Catholic. Catholic Europe and its continuity is *the* thread stitching together *The Path to Rome* and woe betide all those who threaten this homogeneity.

Beyond Eloyes a white-haired agricultural worker, looking like Old Father Time, stood in a meadow honing his scythe.

'You won't get far like that,' he shouted. 'Straighten up!'

And, laughing, he rested his scythe like a Lee Enfield on his shoulder and marched up and down, whistling something by Sousa.

I saluted and tried to unbend my back, for his sake, but the driving rain had turned me into a tortoise, my anorak a carapace into which I had unsuccessfully tried to retract my head.

In the wooded hills beyond Eloyes I heard, then saw, my first mountain brook.

An ancient stone packhorse bridge, sprouting ferns, lay just upstream from the road-bridge, and I sat above the keystone of the former, my legs dangling above the swollen torrent, lunching on mineral water.

I remember the road to Remiremont as though through a glass darkly.

It was the perfect setting for a Bergman film; solitary farmhouses looming in the mist with pines stretching interminably into desolation. I saw no one mending fences or herding cattle, and can only assume that behind the rainlashed windows fornication and incest were rife.

EEC grants could not have done much to revitalise this area for later, advertised in estate agents' windows, I saw such properties complete with generous parcels of land going for around £40,000.

Marathon runners insist that each race is composed of two marathons: the first twenty miles and the final six. I have only completed one, and they were wrong. There are three stages: the first twenty miles; the six; and the final 385 yards.

The last stretch into Remiremont proved my theory, and like Jim Peters wobbling towards the tape at the 1954 Empire Games I lurched into town.

Realising that no hotelier would accept me if I fell across his threshold in my present state I hit upon the idea of going to the tourist office and booking a room in advance. In such inclement weather camping would have been a deliberate act of masochism, but I thought I should go through the motions and ask. What joy! The site was closed.

What can I say about Remiremont? It is pleasant enough, and in summer the pine-clad hills surrounding the town must add a semblance of prettiness, but I would not advise anyone to go out of their way to visit it.

Dutifully I made my Grand Tour gesture by trying the church door, but thankfully it was locked and so I stumbled along colonnaded streets towards my hotel.

The revamped old inn was superior to my status and I could not afford to eat there. Instead I shopped at a supermarket and smuggled my hermetically sealed supper up to my room where the radio provided a cabaret of fifties hits. And having gobbled cold sausage and swigged Médoc to the strains of Bing Crosby and Rosemary Clooney I lay fully clothed on the bed and sank into an oblivion that lasted 12 hours.

While I slept the bar downstairs was doubtless filling up with fascinating people but I never met the alcoholic ex-mistress of Emperor Hirohito or the only man in the world who knows how to square a circle.

And they never met me.

Remiremont to St-Maurice-sur-Moselle

The enclosed courtyard below my room had been transformed into an ornamental pond by torrential overnight rain, but instead of fish the only inhabitant was a drowned starling whose wings were spread-eagled like fins.

Were I superstitious I might have interpreted it as an ill omen, and stayed in bed, but the downpour was beckoning. Cashing travellers' cheques is usually a straightforward business. Not in Remiremont.

The slug-skinned man in the Vosgean Potato & Allied Vegetable Bank told me to wait, and so I waited. And waited. 'Excuse me,' I said timorously after ten minutes, 'but would you mind . . .'

'Wait!' He sipped coffee fastidiously from a paper cup, and fiddled with his pen.

'I'm in a hurry.'

'Well I'm not,' he replied.

Was he cracking up? Maybe he had awoken to discover an aftershave-scented billet-doux tied in pink ribbon hidden under his wife's pillow? Or perhaps working in a bank has that effect on everyone eventually?

The day was dripping away.

'I'll go to another bank,' I threatened.

'Please do,' he replied.

And so I did although my indignant exit was marred by a collision with a plate glass door; for in my anger I had confused *Poussez* with *Tirez*.

That day I planned to walk to St-Maurice-sur-Moselle where my first climb, over the Ballon d'Alsace, began, and where I would bid farewell to the river whose meandering course I had already followed for four days.

Remiremont is built at the north-western corner of a landlocked delta formed by the confluence of the Moselle and the Moselotte. And wishing to avoid the main road – Route 66 – I chose to take lanes across the delta and along the valley until compelled to join the highway near Maxonchamp.

Driving rain blurred my vision and I was forced to blink as regularly as windscreen wipers in order to see where I was going.

The steep pine-covered hills surrounding the sodden fields were veiled in mist, and I cursed the rain for depriving me of a proper evaluation of the landscape.

Vécoux clusters at the mouth of a valley leading into the Bois des Meules and I was reminded of similar villages in Wales; probably because of the persistent rain and deserted streets.

I was tempted to stop there for a coffee, but decided to press on for the day was dismal and I simply wanted to reach my objective. And something had happened to my body. Although my feet still hurt I was feeling fit for the first time. My rucksack was no longer an impediment but seemed an integral part of me and I realised that my muscles must be adapting to its weight.

Beyond Vécoux the valley narrows like an hourglass, and despite the rain I enjoyed the proximity of wildness and the promise of more challenging paths.

If all went according to plan I would be in Switzerland in two days and this thought brought a rush of adrenaline that made the weather seem no more than a minor inconvenience.

The Moselle, its flow halved above Remiremont, was no more than a stream, sluggish in parts, torrential in others, and seeing it like this was like stepping back in time. I was approaching its birth. Here it was simple and unexploited, and yet I knew what was to become of it. And it put me in mind of my children. I thought of how they were flowing inexorably towards adulthood and how, through this act of selfishness, I would miss a segment of their development. On my map of their childhood there would always be a section marked 'Territory Unknown'.

At Maxonchamp I took to the main road, which was not as dangerous as I had feared, for traffic was light. And striding towards Rupt I felt merry enough to sing. All my apprehensions concerning the following day's ascent of almost 4,000 feet had dissipated for now I knew that I would be able to cope.

The perspective was odd here and it took me a while to work out why.

The hills bordering the upper Moselle Valley are high, and although their tops were still shrouded in mist I could see a fair way up their flanks. Among mountains, colours usually fade in intensity, gradually becoming paler as distance from the observer increases; but here the opposite was true. And the reason was not – as I first thought – a trick of the light, but a result of natural vegetation.

Pasture rising from riverside meadows rolled up to meet deciduous forests whose beeches and birches provided a variegated band of mid-green foliage peppered with leaves that had already turned. Above them the blue-green of the pines drifted, getting ever darker, into clouds, which, with the rising ground still rearing behind them, were transformed into black cowls.

Alpine suburbia led into Rupt where I made my usual mistake of choosing the wrong bar.

Admittedly water guttered on to the floor from my anorak and overtrousers; but it *was* raining.

As I leaned my rucksack against a wall I intuited the barman's antipathy.

I asked for a draught beer, and as he half filled my glass he said, 'Are you a hippy?'

I had never looked less like a hippy in my life. My hair would have passed muster at Sandhurst, and I had even shaved that morning.

I asked him why he had asked, and in reply he pointed at my rucksack and said, 'No car.'

I was too weary to argue the fallaciousness of his reasoning, and stood at the bar staring at a jar of pickled eggs that reminded me of a collection of human eyeballs I had once seen while filming in a pathology museum.

Me a hippy? How absurd. And yet, like so many of my generation I had played at it. But we were not hippies. They came later. We were *beats*. We had read *On the Road* long before it became a Penguin Modern Classic. And with dog-eared City Lights editions of Allen Ginsberg's *Howl* and *Reality Sandwiches* poking ostentatiously from donkey jacket pockets we would listen to Chico Hamilton and Muddy Waters in darkened rooms with our arms draped around willing chicks who were always dressed in black.

I cringe when I remember how we addressed everyone as 'Man' – even the chicks. After a night of unbridled lust in Wimbledon or Esher I would turn to whoever it happened to be and drawl, 'Hey, man, how about hitching down to Brighton?' And although Brighton did not have the romantic ring of Des Moines or Denver we did begin to see a little of the world.

Hitching was a matter of principle. We never took buses or trains. And although, with hindsight, I can mock our pretentiousness it was a crucial period in our education; for we were privileged middle-class children who, through thumbing rides, came in contact with a cross-section of society we would not otherwise have met.

And hitchhiking took us abroad. We could go anywhere on a budget of a pound a day. But my disillusion with such a lifestyle came suddenly. I was in Istanbul, staging post on the compulsory Journey To The East.

Like migrating vultures, all the full-time beats would gather on the banks of the Bosporus, and it was there that I discovered how egocentric and ill-educated most of them were. With their brains befuddled by hashish they would sit in the pudding shops treating the waiters like lackeys. Real conversation was impossible for language and thought had been reduced to a short list of permissible phrases and cut-price ideas, all of which were punctuated with deeply meaningful looks.

I saw them for what they were: Conservatives in goatskin coats.

I left Rupt-sur-Moselle without regret and continued up the misty valley to Le Thillot, whose church, visible from some distance, lured me on; for it was a milepost informing me that St-Maurice was only an hour beyond.

By now the amount of traffic had been increased by fathers hurrying home to Pascal and Yvette and the last bendy kilometres into St-Maurice were fraught with danger. The road was wet, the light poor, and the near misses made me feel not only vulnerable but irresponsible. If I could be hurled off the road then Pascal and Yvette's papa could wrap himself around a tree.

On the outskirts of St-Maurice I saw a signpost: *Ballon d'Alsace 9 kms.*

Beside the signpost there was a small traditional alpine-style hotel with intricately carved gables and window boxes bright with geraniums.

In the vestibule a flustered chef hurried past with a bucket full of leaping trout freshly caught from the Moselle – I assumed – and about to go under the hammer.

The elderly manageress seemed severe, her hair swept back in a bun, but beneath this veneer there was a strong-willed and charming woman; the sort who – had I been a POW on the run in 1941 – I would have trusted with my life. Her attic would have been bursting with fellow escapees – John Gregson, Richard Todd, Richard Attenborough, Bryan Forbes – while outside Anton Diffring would have sped past in an armoured car on a wild-goose chase.

She escorted me to my room, and I was relieved to find that I had left the ubiquitous brown wallpaper behind. Walls, ceiling, floor and furniture were all made from pine. Even the TV was encased in knotted wood and I switched it on guiltily; for such decadence was out of keeping with my somewhat ascetic approach to the journey.

The weather forecast was discouraging. Snow was expected above 6,000 feet and although the Ballon d'Alsace is only about 4,500 feet high it did not bode well for the Alps where my route would take me above 8,000 feet. But the Alps were at least a week away and anything could happen before then. Meanwhile I had the Vosges and Jura to cross.

I phoned my wife.

Yes, the tent's manufacturer had agreed to send a replacement. Yes, it had been dispatched by air, express.

'Well done,' I said condescendingly. 'I'll pick it up in Bern in a few days.'

There was silence.

'Hello?' I said. 'Are you still there?'

'Oh God! I've told them to send it to Basel.'

'But that's nowhere near where I'm going.'

'I'm sorry, but they both begin with B and you were so angry on the phone I got confused.'

'Bloody hell!'

'Anyway, what does it matter? They're both in Switzerland.'

'But I'm on foot!'

'So get on a train!'

'That'll spoil everything.'

'Don't be so stupid. You're you. Not bloody Belloc!'

We declared peace before saying goodnight, and I lay back on the bed mulling over what she had said.

She had been absolutely right. I was not Belloc. I was following his route but that was as far as it went. From now on this path to Rome would be mine.

I switched on the TV without a qualm.

Lee J. Cobb was playing a tough Brooklyn cop in impeccable French. Switch. A game show. Switch. Commercials, which I watched with burgeoning nausea. Virtually all of them featured variations of the same stereotype: the chic, coquettish and decidedly unsexy woman with little-girl voice poutingly imploring the viewers to purchase everything from tractors to tampons.

Downstairs in the restaurant I ordered trout and when they arrived I wondered why fish are served with their heads on. Imagine a chicken with its head lolling over the side of the plate, its charred beak and singed comb flopping on to your fork. But the trout tasted of trout and I convinced myself that it was fitting to eat the fruit of the river whose meanderings I might never see again.

It was Friday night and the restaurant was beginning to fill up with the local bourgeoisie. I watched them eating. None seemed to be enjoying their meals although the range of complicated dishes looked wonderful to me. They picked at the food, holding up morsels spiked on forks for their companions to appraise; and a bad-smell-under-the-nose expression seemed de rigueur. For them food was like music and they were attending a serious concert.

I was reminded of the obligatory supping scenes in countless French films of the sixties and seventies, particularly Chabrol's, where no narrative seemed complete without the inclusion of a dinner party where the guests expend much time being non-committal about lobsters.

I left the restaurant by a different door and noticed a large glass tank that had been transformed into a millrace with trout swimming against a pump-induced current. And although their erstwhile companions now lined my stomach these live specimens were blissfully unaware that they were not in an aquarium but in a condemned cell, having been found guilty of being born fish.

I needed company but the only occupants of the bar were a young couple exchanging saliva. And so, after a glass of wine, I went to bed.

On the TV a frenetic report from the Seoul Olympics almost convinced me that only French competitors were winning medals.

I could have been in England.

St-Maurice to Belfort

My watch alarm woke me at five.

I lay still, listening for rain. There it was again, out in the darkness, challenging me to stay in bed. But the day ahead was going to be long and strenuous and so I flung off the duvet, packed, and crept downstairs.

The front door was locked and I fumbled behind the desk for a key. I found a jangling gaoler's bunch but none fitted.

Using my torch I tiptoed through the kitchen but the rear exit was also locked.

A clock chimed the half hour.

I sat down, wondering whether it would be wise to wake the manageress at 5.30 a.m., but where was she? I could not go knocking on all the doors.

I would simply have to wait.

In the restaurant the trout tank bubbled while above my head the clock ticked away precious seconds.

I shone my torch around the reception area. Something glinted: a solitary brass key on a hook. It worked, and like an absconding inmate I reached the wet pre-dawn street without triggering off an alarm.

The Ballon d'Alsace marks the south-western extremity of the Vosges, and the steep road did not allow me to begin the day gently. But, well practised in mountain walking, I set off at a steady plod past silhouettes of cuckoo clock houses and farms perched above hairpin bends.

The rain turned to drizzle and a dim light filtered into the valley. The undersides of the clouds turned purple, mauve, then pink, and I could see the Moselle's narrow shadowy floodplain stretching away to east and west, the cattle in its meadows as still as hayricks, sleeping as they waited for their later dawn.

Soon St-Maurice was lost beneath a bulge of hillside, and I entered forest.

Belloc wrote disparagingly about this road, and took great pains to describe how, in preference, he struck out into the wilderness. I suspect that he protested too much. He must have had an excellent map or remarkably good fortune for the trees are – and must have been – densely packed, with impenetrable underbrush between them.

A macho-man with a machete might force his way up such vertiginous slopes bristling with briars but I, being effete, was delighted by the little road that snakes up the great bulk of the Ballon.

The drizzle ceased and a hole in the clouds allowed a horizontal beam to spotlight the hillsides, transforming the wet leaves into a rolling wheel of silver.

Great spinnakers of cumulus billowed white above a cliff of stratus whose layering varied from lime-grey to graphite. And then, for less than a minute, the sun burst through completely, flooding the forests with shadows that imbued them with depth and grandeur for the first time.

I stopped at a cold clear spring to drink, and sat watching a faint rainbow forming in the west, while to the east the perimeter of sunlight disappeared, pursued by an eclipsing cloak of clouds.

I was about to set off again when movement in my peripheral vision prompted me to freeze. At first I thought the creature was a squirrel but it was far too big. It bounded across the road with feline grace, and indeed it was as large as a domestic cat, its fur a mingling of black and russet.

It spotted me, but instead of disappearing into the underbrush it leapt effortlessly on to a beech log and crouched there as though posing for a wildlife photograph.

I could see it better now. Its face was like a weasel's, and impaled between its thorny teeth there was a victim; a mouse or vole. The predator's body was lithe, tapering towards the neck, while its long fluffy tail hung like a feather boa over the log.

It stared at me with inquisitive black eyes, and then, more bored than afraid, glided noiselessly into the wild wood.

The road continued to rise at a steady angle, never taking short cuts but curling in and out of coombes where frost and torrents have eroded deep clefts overhung by rowans, bright with orange berries, growing from among mossy boulders.

No vehicles passed me, and the only sounds were of water, wind and birdsong.

At a hairpin where the trees had been thinned I came upon an unexpected vista of the Moselle Valley. The river, 2,000 feet below, was now a mere squiggle on a map, and I thought of all the kilometres I had tramped beside it and of all the kilometres to come. But I was not disheartened for I am happiest amongst hills.

My legs no longer ached and my leather boots, stretched by rain, now fitted my feet. At last I was beginning to enjoy myself, and singing a medley of songs from *Oklahoma!* I gradually gained altitude.

As I got higher the trees got shorter. The plump beeches, given to easy living, had decided to remain below, while rigorous birches and pines, nourished by acid soil, continued to accompany me.

I was eager to reach the pass from which I would be able to see the Jura Mountains – marking the Swiss frontier – rising beyond the Gap of Belfort. But towards the top my hopes were dashed by fog so opaque that a false night seemed to have fallen around me.

As I climbed I was the moving centre of a claustrophobic circle whose radius was no more than fifteen metres.

Trees vanished, and I was aware of grass swishing in a sudden cold wind that was already numbing my cheeks.

A rockface became a building; a monstrous ski-lodge, its locked doors and shuttered windows showing no lights. It was waiting for snow.

I heard creaking but its source was a mystery until a marshalling yard of metal gondolas materialised, swaying beneath steel cables around which the wind wailed like banshees.

A weather-beaten board displayed a topographical layout of the area, the ski-runs painted in varying shades of flaking brown. From where I stood I should have been able to see whale-back mountains stretching away on all sides but I could see nothing but fog.

I stood in an empty car park and donned balaclava and gloves, but the chill was so intense that I continued up the road with my teeth chattering.

I was desperate to see a person. Anyone. Even a driver in a passing car would have alleviated the intense loneliness. Where was the bloody top?

The fog was so thick that I almost missed a dim light glowing from a chalet which, on closer inspection, turned out to be a cafeteria.

Its capacious interior had been designed for coach parties and I was the only customer. I could have been in the Alpine Bar of a British holiday camp.

The owner was using the slack period between seasons to varnish a pine partition while his wife fed rusks to their blond toddler.

They were astonished to see me, but agreed to give me coffee.

'Is this the summit?' I asked, and it was.

A stuffed animal, a twin to the one I had seen, sat on a shelf. The taxidermist had arranged it with a snarling jaw that showed its lethal teeth to best advantage. I asked what it was, and the woman told me it was a marten.

'I've just seen one,' I told her enthusiastically.

'Oh.'

The windows rattled and the smoky fog persisted, but it was only 8.30 and I lingered, hoping that the sun might dissolve the gloom and present me with a vision of Switzerland. But after four coffees I shouldered my pack and set off into the murk.

At least it was all downhill now, and I walked quickly, anxious to rejoin the visible world again.

Cowbells clanked but I saw no cattle until, after several minutes, I came face to face with one standing in the middle of the road. Instinctively I glanced at its underparts. No tassel but teats and so I strode passed it without a care. But my pulse rate quickened when a spectral dog – like one of the whisht-hounds so common on Dartmoor – came at me from out of the mist.

Perhaps a combination of funk and fog exaggerated its size, but had it not been for its growl and lack of horns I might have mistaken it for a small white rhino.

Lord knows what would have happened had I not been saved by the cavalry. An army jeep, its yellow headlights blazing like an even larger beast, surprised us both, and the creature fled into the forest.

Soon I reached a junction where the eastern branch heads down towards Mulhouse and the Rhine.

My route led south, or rather it led south eventually, for here the road, seen on a map, resembles an anatomical drawing of the small intestine.

I had hoped to bypass the hairpins but the precipitous inclines between them invited a broken ankle and so I kept to the road, travelling north, south, east and west until, without warning, the fog lifted and the southern flanks of the Vosges were revealed all around me, their wooded slopes reflecting a milky sun.

I was among tall beeches whose leaves were greener than those on the northern slopes, and I could see the margin of the Belfort Plain far below although the Jura, thirty miles distant, were hidden by haze.

I rested for a while beside one of the many waterfalls splashing down from the western escarpment, and watched a pied wagtail bobbing from stone to stone through the foam.

It was not yet eleven o'clock and I had crossed the Vosges; but my contentment was marred by disappointment that it had been accomplished so simply. I had seen so little of this great range whose complex peaks and valleys extend north-east as far as the fringes of Strasbourg. I had merely gone up and down, and all those who know mountains know that the finest treks involve following the high ridges. Indeed there is a long-distance footpath following the crest of the entire range, but that would have to wait for another year.

Slowly I made my way down the steep-sided valley through pastures and past farms and rocky bluffs towards Lepuix where I did not stop, and Giromagny where I did.

Giromagny is built where the last foothills of the Vosges collapse into the plain, and the weather reflected its location. Here the sun shimmered while the mountain-tops to the north still shivered under a thin grey blanket of fog.

Belloc had found this little town seething with priests but I saw none, unless, being Saturday, they were in mufti.

The main street was packed with shoppers and so I chose a back lane to explore. The houses were brightly painted, their colourful shutters and wrought-iron balconies giving the place a southern air. Meals were being prepared and the smell of meat reawakened the carnivore in me. Someone was practising Mozart on a piano. A child fed a biscuit to her doll. People were getting on with their lives, and despite being the centre of my own universe I was acutely aware that I was an irrelevance to them.

A tallow-faced woman, wearing what I took to be the local costume, passed me. A silk scarf hid her hair, and the hem of her flower-patterned dress flapped around ankles encased in rumpled woollen socks disappearing into shoes covered with sequins. Her son, his black hair cut like a convict's, tagged along behind, a melon clasped in his chubby hands.

I chose a bar and, for a change, picked the right one. After the Wesleyan joylessness of the hostelries dotted along the Moselle Valley this place seemed almost Bacchic. The barmaid even smiled at me, and the customers parted to let me through. Someone helped me unload my rucksack and, to cap it all, the beer almost reached the rim of the glass.

Where had I come from? Where was I going? Why? Was I married? Didn't I miss my wife and children?

And there was no jukebox. No Sting, Prince or Michael Jackson; only an old-fashioned wireless broadcasting alpine folk melodies. 'Music to piddle by,' my mother used to call it, and although I have inherited her aversion to yodelling accompanied by concertinas and staccato brass it seemed appropriate, and I found that I was tapping my feet.

I bought fruit in an open-air market where I noticed more women wearing variations of the costume I had seen earlier. Perhaps it was traditional to dress up in peasant costumes on Saturdays?

It was one o'clock, and with Belfort only twelve kilometres away I sat on a wall, insouciant, sucking oranges and soaking up the sun.

Only twelve kilometres. I should have learned by now. The road was flat, straight, dull, and hairy; for without bends to slow them down the motorists were aping Grand Prix drivers.

The sun, which I had welcomed, now became my enemy, and I needed all my resolve to keep going.

That is the trouble with walking long distances; taking the rough with the smooth.

After two hours I thought I had reached the city but I was only in Valdoie, a ghastly suburb, and for a long time I plodded past grim factories and squalid houses, all the while inhaling the visible effluvium of exhaust gases.

I saw more women dressed like those in Giromagny but it was their male counterparts who showed me my previous error.

The women were Arabs, the wives of men who are euphemistically called 'guest workers'.

The men, who outnumbered the women forty to one, wandered the streets alone or in pairs like lost souls; the older ones with white beards and fur hats; the younger ones wearing woollen caps and ill-fitting chainstore clothes.

It was their weekend on parole from whatever filthy jobs they had been imported to do in the foundries and textile mills; and I surmised that they were walking aimlessly rather than spend hard-earned wages destined for their dependants in North Africa.

After the silence of the hills it was a shock to find myself surrounded by civilisation again.

Seldom have I seen so many cripples. Everywhere I looked there were amputees, and I was reminded of a story concerning L. S. Lowry. Someone had complained to Lowry that his paintings portrayed a disproportionate number of infirm people. Lowry had replied, 'Come with me and look for yourself,' and the two of them had walked the streets of Salford. After an hour the complainer had complained again, only this time he said, 'Your paintings are unrealistic. They don't show the half of it.'

Walk around any city and you will have these findings confirmed.

In the centre of Belfort, outside the entrance to a smart shop, an old man with a carelessly sutured stump was propped against a window that displayed titillating underwear. Around his neck was a scrap of cardboard with *J'ai faim* scrawled on it. When I put loose change in his hand a woman customer who was leaving the shop, laden with bags, turned on me and said, 'You shouldn't encourage that sort of thing.'

On the east bank of the Savoureuse, which flows through the city, I found a cheap family-run hotel in the old quarter. My room overlooked the cathedral square, and instead of collapsing on the bed I added insult to my injuries by going for a stroll.

The interior of St Christopher's Cathedral is heavy with baroque ornamentation, and the grand organ, gilded with cherubim, filled the incense-tinged air with Bach.

After benediction on Sunday evenings, when the church had emptied, my father would play Bach, beautifully. The organ was his throne where, briefly, he could be a king.

As a young man he had shown great talent as a musician and artist, and would have studied at the Royal College of Music had my grandfather agreed. But in those post-Edwardian days you did what your parents told you to do and he was forced into a stultifying life of business.

I had been conceived to celebrate the passing of war, and my father was forty-seven years older than me.

I never understood why he was always too tired to play football or cricket with me like my schoolmates' fathers, most of whom must have been in their thirties. He never accompanied me through the blue gate leading from our house into the woods. He was never Richard the Lionheart to my Robin Hood.

And when he died in 1960, four months after retirement, my mother was left with a pension which inflation turned into an indignity.

So much for the compassion of big business.

And seeing the grief caused by such squandering of natural gifts probably accounts for my decision to lead a precarious life. For, despite all its vicissitudes, at least I can be king for more than half an hour after benediction.

The sun was setting as I climbed the sandstone outcrop dominating Belfort.

This hill, which provides a commanding view across the Gap, is the reason for Belfort's existence.

During the Franco-Prussian War (1870–71) it was the scene of compulsory heroic resistance when the garrison, pounded by Prussian artillery, was ordered by its commander to hold out whatever the cost; which they did for over three months. The garrison only surrendered – two weeks after Paris had capitulated – when the French government insisted, and as a reward for such tenacity the Prussians – behaving with commendable chivalry – allowed Belfort and the surrounding territory to remain under French control while the greater part of Alsace-Lorraine was absorbed by the victors until the end of the Great War.

The siege is commemorated by a huge and hideous lion, shaped from red sandstone blocks, which squats under the fortress walls. It was designed by Bartholdi, best known for his Statue of Liberty, and its only memorable attribute is its size.

Entering the fortress is like descending into a labyrinth. Vast tunnels honeycomb the walls, and my footfalls echoed as I wandered alone through the dimly-lit warren.

A young Arab, half hidden in an embrasure, reached down to lift his striped djellaba, but instead of drawing a knife to mug me he pulled out his penis and pissed copiously against this symbol of French military prowess.

Back in the cathedral square a late wedding was beginning. Bells clappered while the groom, wearing a Ruritanian uniform, waited amongst the guests. Women in expensive dresses stood like mannequins beside best-suited husbands although no one was wearing a hat. Imagine an English wedding without hats. It is unimaginable.

Soon an open carriage, drawn by two snow-white horses, clattered into the square and drew up opposite the cathedral steps. The bride, whose veil could not disguise her homeliness was helped down from the carriage while one of the horses lifted a braided tail and deposited steaming figs on to the road. A bridesmaid giggled, but the official photographer was careful with his framing and no doubt in the year AD 2025 grandchildren will be shown figless photos of their grandparents' wedding.

Around midnight I awoke with tears streaming down my cheeks. I was a child again. My father, still alive, had handed me a Bach score and had asked me to play it on a piano.

'But I can't read music,' I had said, putting my arms around him, clasping him at knee-height. 'Look,' he said. 'I've invited all these important people to hear you play.'

And there, all around me, were well-known film stars. 'Why are you trying to impress me?' I asked.

'Because I want to make it up to you. For leaving. It was too soon.'

'Why did you never teach me to play the piano?'

'I was too tired. Always too tired.'

Throughout the rest of the night I lay awake waiting for dawn to dispel my resurrected resentment, each long hour ending with the chiming of the cathedral clock.

Belfort to Porrentruy

I followed a sandwich board man through Belfort's Sunday morning streets.

A large woman – or rather a blown-up photograph of a woman – bobbed ahead of me and I hurried to catch up with her. Victoria de los Angeles was singing in Belfort that night, but I would not be there to hear her. I would be in Switzerland.

There was still half a plain to go, and if the previous day had been anything to go by then I wanted to be done with it as soon as possible.

Outside the city there is an unpleasant junction where my road and the A36 autoroute unravel themselves. I took it at a trot, less concerned by the traffic than by fears of being stopped and fined by the police.

I should have chosen lanes further east, but flat is flat and I was keen to reach the frontier.

Factories, depots and used-car lots lined the road, their yards and buildings devoid of people, stark in their ugliness. Cold grey clouds, flecked with yellow, formed the dome above and around me, and the Jura were nowhere to be seen.

Belloc crossed the border just beyond Delle, but a woman in the Belfort tourist office had advised me to find some other route. Apparently the main road between Delle and Porrentruy – the first sizeable town in Switzerland – is fast, winding and dangerous to pedestrians. And so I planned to head east at Joncherey, just north of Delle, and take an unfrequented lane out of France.

Between me and Joncherey lay 15 kilometres of gently rolling land bisected by the Canal du Rhône au Rhin. And when I stopped on the bridge spanning the canal's grey cobbled surface I thanked fate that my route would not take me beside this oversized drain; for although the countryside through which I was tramping was unremarkable, at least I could not predict exactly what I was going to see for miles ahead.

I was in the land of storks although I saw none. By now they would be paddling with their offspring on the coast of Mauritania. Their nests remained like outsize crowns of thorns on steeples and gable-ends.

In Grandvillars parishioners were streaming into church to hear mass. Belloc would have followed them in – for in those days missing Sunday mass merited eternal flames – but I had no desire to break my rhythm; for I held an irrational belief that the weather would improve as soon as I left France.

At Joncherey I turned off the main road, and the ambience immediately altered. Clouds thinned and my faint shadow accompanied me. Farms replaced houses, and the smell of new hay and cowdung dispelled my memory of Belfort and its urban stink.

Beyond Eaverois where I saw – or thought I saw – an eagle, I went south along a thin reed-fringed lane, and went back 600 years.

Florimont is a hamlet where one could film a medieval story without having to change a blade of grass.

A cylindrical Rapunzel tower, its walls tressed with ivy, rises above half-timbered houses, and the ancient church is surrounded by farmhouses that are falling apart. Straw gusted along the street while hens, roosters, dogs and cats roamed at will. Collared doves scratched along cracked roof tiles, and I saw a woman in a white apron prodding a cow with a bloated udder into a ramshackle barn.

Taking care to avoid a minefield of olivaceous cowpats and a solitary dead rat I left this living museum and soon passed through another village, Courcelles, whose houses had been prettified by – I suppose – commuters. Like all dormitories its flowerbeds were well tucked in and its lawns meticulously vacuumed. No doubt Florimont will soon go the same way.

Switzerland was only a kilometre away along a pot-holed lane winding through dank woodland. As I approached a witch's house, overhung by trees, three wolfish Alsatians leapt at me, but they were restrained by chains and their jaws snapped air. Guard dogs used by border patrols I assume.

Soon I came across a rusting lollipop sign with INTERDIT painted in red above a list of restrictions I refused to read for fear of discovering that this obscure back door into Switzerland was closed. I was not prepared to backtrack all the way to Delle and resolved, if necessary, to cross the frontier illegally.

But my fears were groundless. A raised barber's pole marked the boundary between nuclear and neutral countries and I simply walked under it and into a green and pleasant valley bordered by pines. Swiss pines.

A stone bridge arched across a rushy stream where I took off my boots and socks, rolled up my trousers, and sat on the bank dangling my feet in the clear, numbing water.

The sun, having tired of its Sunday morning lie-in, threw off its sheets and filled the valley with afternoon heat. Apart from cheeping goldfinches feeding on thistles there was no sound and I felt wonderfully elated at having arrived in this country of incomparable hills and mountains. Suddenly the whole trip seemed worthwhile for I appeared to be coming to terms with being alone and was enjoying out-of-the-way places which no tour operator even knew existed. No coach would ever cross this delicate bridge unless it was pulled by a team of horses.

I wished that I could open a bottle of sparkling wine to celebrate but no amount of planning can anticipate such extraordinary moments.

Minnows darted from trailing weeds close to my feet which, lying white under the water like a pair of cuttlefish, had not failed me. Only one blister remained bothersome, but it was gross, resembling an ostracised four-in-the-morning fried egg congealing on the griddle of a motorway café. But it was a small price to pay.

I lay back in the grass and let the sun dry between my toes while I waited for nothing to happen.

Porrentruy, where I would regain Belloc's route, was only a few kilometres away and so I adjusted my pace to my mood and shuffled along to my first Swiss village: Lugnez.

Having crossed the frontier Belloc had found everything in Switzerland distastefully old and haphazard compared with the orderliness of France. Now the reverse is true.

Everywhere I looked I saw regularity. Even the bells around the necks of cattle in the riverside meadow seemed newly polished. And in contrast to Florimont, where the buildings were rotting, these just-over-the-border farms all looked as though they were awaiting a government inspection. Gleaming rakes, pitchforks and spades hung from allocated pegs on barn doors, tractor headlights sparkled, and even cow muck was sculpted into clever cones.

No dogs roamed the streets, for they were all chained up and sat sleekly outside architect-designed kennels. Even if one had broken loose and bitten me I would have had no worries, for every dog is vaccinated against rabies. What sensible people are the Swiss.

All the houses looked newly built and all the varnished window boxes sported compulsory geraniums. But after squalid Belfort and the drab towns between there and the frontier I found this reflection of wealth pleasing enough; although I wondered what action the local commune would take if a conservationist moved in and grew nettles to encourage tortoiseshell butterflies in his garden. Perhaps growing them in rows would make even nettles acceptable?

Needless to say, the first restaurant I found was a hymn to hygiene; all polished pine and starched gingham curtains. And ensnared by cleanliness I took extraordinary care to prevent beer dribbling down my glass on to the bandage-white tablecloth.

But the restaurateur was not at all starchy. My rucksack, which in the Moselle Valley had branded me as a peculiar person, was the object of expert scrutiny; for in Switzerland everyone owns one. I was obviously someone who loved to go a-wandering along the mountain tracks and, as such, I was perfectly acceptable.

A sophisticated couple with three flaxen-haired children asked me where I was heading. Their English was perfect. They did not think my journey in the least bit odd but warned me about the weather.

'You've left it rather late,' the woman said. 'There will be snow in the Alps.'

'I should just make it,' I replied, my optimism based on faith rather than current meteorological reports.

'But it's October already,' said the husband. 'What pass will you choose?'

'The Grimsel.'

They glanced at each other and their expressions were disconcerting.

'Perhaps you will be lucky,' she said.

Their youngest child, a toddler of two, had surreptitiously taken my blackthorn stick and was advancing menacingly on her brothers.

I leapt forward to wrest it from her, and knocked over my glass. Froth flowed on to the tablecloth where it remained quivering like spume on a beach. But instead of holding up his hands in horror the restaurateur smiled and said, 'May I get you another beer?'

I left Lugnez light-headed and walked through the contiguous village of Damphreux where, in an inn, piddling music was being played by an accordionist who had gone a beer too far. And feeling slightly the worse for wear myself I left the houses behind and strolled towards Porrentruy.

I was already in the Jura although these hills – half forest, half pasture – were as gentle as Dorset downs and gave no inkling of the high ridges to come.

Porrentruy was a name on a map, and for all I knew it might have been the centre of Swiss coal production. It was not.

I walked into a fairy-tale town built on a hill overlooked by an even bigger hill on which a Grimm castle stood, its tower taller and stronger than all the rest in King Grisly-Beard's realm.

There were several delightful hotels, but their prices were geared to Swiss gnomes and so I ended up in the Hôtel de la Gare, ten minutes' walk from the old town. But few trains trundled past and my room, overlooking a courtyard, was clean and warm. And, more importantly, the hotel was run by charming people.

At sunset I returned to the old town, passing under the medieval Porte de France, then up through leafy lanes where children in unscuffed leather shoes played demurely.

At the castle I did the usual things: climbed the tower, dropped pebbles down the well, and admired the architecture. And when I had performed these duties I stood on the ramparts and looked out over the town in search of the first great ridge of the Jura. But it was not there. A clear sky had encouraged mist and I could only imagine the high country through which I would be travelling for the next two days.

The Jura, unlike the Vosges, are not one long whale-back but several limestone ridges, roughly parallel, running east to west with deep troughs between. In my mind's eye I saw them as the earthworks of an Iron Age fort; ditch followed by palisaded bank followed by ditch, bank, and so on.

Belloc's task, and consequently mine, was to travel from Porrentruy on the north of the range to Solothurn in the south where another plain, similar to the Belfort Gap but on a grander scale, would lead me to the Alps.

With deep limestone valleys and gorges between the ridges there is no way of following a crow's flight between the two towns and so Belloc formulated a route which solved his linear obsession to his satisfaction. And when I had finally completed this section I thanked him for his eccentric plan, which had taken me into lonely and memorable places.

Alleys led me down to the town where elegant lamps hanging from wrought-iron brackets lit the streets with uncharacteristic Swiss inefficiency.

Fountains gushed while evening shoppers, all smartly dressed and cleverly coiffured, hurried between stores selling goods marked with outrageous prices.

Some of the vaulted cellars of the baroque burghers' houses bordering the street had been turned into dinky businesses and in one, a gallery, a private viewing was in progress. Local collectors, champagne glasses in hand, chatted with their backs to walls displaying dreadful Expressionist-style paintings. After a glass or two they would probably buy. It is the same in all provincial towns; mediocre artists providing the visually illiterate with mural conversation pieces.

I had eaten nothing – not even a Mars bar – all day, and so I decided to splash out on a cooked meal. The simple restaurant I chose provided a feast which any gourmet worth his salt would have flung back at the chef. But have you ever met a gourmet who has walked thirty-five kilometres on an empty stomach?

Thick vegetable soup, followed by potatoes, sausage and school cabbage fell down my gullet and lay like lead in my innards which, having grown unaccustomed to such bulk, rumbled their incapacity to cope.

I sat back, finished a carafe of red wine, and studied a map of the Jura.

A man in a brown suit was sitting alone at the next table, drinking brandy.

'American?' he asked.

'English.'

'Never mind. May I join you?'

I did not want to be joined, but my country's reputation was at stake and so I agreed for patriotic reasons. What had he meant by *never mind*?

His English was better than my French, although he must have been knocking back the booze all evening for his speech was slurred.

He was an engineer who had been sent over from Basel to do something or other about drainage.

Without any preamble he said, 'Why are your English football fans so violent?'

'Because they get drunk.'

'Why do they?'

'Everyone does only they're unhappy and badly educated. That's what makes the difference.'

'But they behave like barbarians.'

'Britain's a barbarous country.'

He laughed. 'But Mrs Thatcher is not a barbarian. She does much for everyone.'

'She does much for some.'

'But if you do not want her then the people can choose someone else.'

'No we can't. Not under our system. She was elected by a substantial minority. Thirty-two million people voted in the last general election but less than thirteen million voted for her.'

'Then change the system.'

'Governments in power don't change systems that suit them.'

'Switzerland is the finest democracy in the world. We vote about everything.'

'Including giving women the vote?'

'They have had the vote for sixteen years now.'

'Well it took you a hell of a long time to get around to doing them the favour.'

'They weren't interested. Running a country is man's work.'

He was beginning to get on my nerves, and when he slapped the table aggressively and demanded another brandy I told him that he reminded me of a soccer hooligan. He frowned. 'Why?'

'Because you're drunk and belligerent.'

He half smiled. 'Is this the famous British humour?'

'No. It's the British brush-off.'

I paid my bill and left.

Back in the hotel bar Nigel Mansell was letting the side down. He was failing to win the Spanish Grand Prix.

Porrentruy to the Gorges du Pichoux

Thick fog clogged the valley as I strode past dapper commuters hurrying to the station. I was impressed for it was only 6 a.m. but their pale faces were already etched with anxiety. Will I make the 6.03? What will Monsieur Verlaine make of my report? I bet that little runt Rimbaud's been given the Baudelaire account!

Monday morning blues must be the same the world over.

Along the road to Courgenay I used my torch as a headlight; not to see but to be seen. But despite this precaution I had to take evasive action several times, performing heavy *jetés* on to the verge.

Courgenay was still immersed in fog when I arrived amongst its ghostly houses, but by the time I reached the village of Courtemautruy, a little further on along a minor road, the sun was beginning to break through.

I sat by a fountain in the village square and nibbled chocolate, waiting for the day to clear, then set off between apple trees up a steepening lane, which soon brought me to the fringe of a forest.

Here I saw the Jura properly for the first time. Distant pines, high above me and across the valley, revealed themselves gradually as the mist, caught on a warm updraught, wafted between them like steam from a doused fire.

There was no detail; only the outlines of succeeding ridges whose edges were as jagged as swordfish jaws.

The sun was already hot and so I took off my sweater and lay beside the road, watching the day begin. In the distance dogs barked.

Something was crashing towards me through the undergrowth.

The deer leapt into the lane where she stood, shivering, her muzzle upturned, her nostrils dilating as she sniffed the air. I remained perfectly still, downwind of her, and she failed to notice me.

The dogs' barking was getting nearer. Farm dogs, I assumed, having a bit of fun at the deer's expense.

The deer, panic-stricken, jumped back into the forest, and that, I thought, was the end of that. But a minute later a pair of dogs ran out from the trees and snuffled around the place where the deer had stood. They were not farm dogs but some sort of beagle, bred for hunting.

Without hesitation they set off, yapping, in pursuit, choosing the exact spot where the deer had regained the trees. Twenty minutes later, when I was toiling up the steep lane, I heard a single shot; not the blast from a shotgun but the thwack of a high-powered rifle.

At a loop in the road I looked across a valley to Mont Terri, which Belloc had sketched. I dug out his book and compared his drawing with the actual mountain, which was a foolish thing to do for it confirmed my growing opinion that Belloc was a bit of a bullshitter who availed himself of every opportunity to exaggerate in a poetically licentious way. That is his charm.

Mont Terri is a limestone butte; a miniature Roraima rising distinctly above the surrounding slopes, but in no way as precipitous as Belloc depicts. But it is wild, its cliffs gleaming white in the sun while its topknot of Oxford blue pines bristled against a Cambridge blue sky.

At the crest of the ridge, at a farmstead called Sur la Croix, I decided to leave the lane and take a rough track to the isolated hamlet of Outremont through which, I suspect, Belloc passed although he does not mention it by name.

Even now no metalled roads lead to Outremont, and the huddle of wooden houses and barns must have looked much the same in Belloc's day.

Here I encountered my first Great Swiss Mountain Sheepdogs; the first to bark setting off a chain reaction along the crooked path I took between the houses. But they remained behind rickety fences while their owners, alerted by the pack, remained behind their windows, peering out, half faced.

Once clear of the houses I took an obvious path leading across a steep hanging pasture which I thought would lead me down to St-Ursanne in the Doubs Gorge far below.

At the furthest corner of the pasture the track ended at a strand of barbed wire nailed between trees. Thinking that this had been put there by a bloody-minded farmer – as so frequently happens on public footpaths in Britain – I crossed it and continued for some way along the semblance of a path leading into a forest. But after a few hundred metres the path petered out in steep limestone scree on which my boots slipped, sending me slithering down into brambles.

Apart from a few scratches I was uninjured, although the incident made me realise how vulnerable I was. No one knew I was there, and had I broken a leg I would have been unable to extricate myself. Any cries for help would have been absorbed by the trees.

And so, very carefully, I retraced my steps to Outremont where an old man hobbled out of his chalet to greet me. He spoke French but had not been taught by Father Ignatius at St George's College, and so we had some difficulty communicating. Instead I kept repeating, 'St-Ursanne?'

He gestured vaguely with his stick, which his Great Swiss Mountain Sheepdog interpreted as a defensive act. Baring its teeth it trotted towards me but was stopped in its tracks by a woman's bark.

This handsome woman and I were able to converse, and she agreed to put me on the path to St-Ursanne.

Here Belloc had also gone astray and had been shown the right path by a woman, and this was the first of several coincidences which linked my journey through the Jura with his.

With Rover at heel she led me across the hanging pasture and pointed to a spinney.

'You go down there,' she explained, 'and when you get to a little gate you will find the path to St-Ursanne.'

I thanked her and set off, digging my heels into the mud. When I reached the trees I searched for a gate but saw only pines clinging by exposed roots to a steep slope. Down through the pines I went until I found another barrier of barbed wire.

I was lost again, but the prospect of going back a second time was too humiliating. Besides, the hill was so steep that it would have taken an hour to clamber up the route which had taken only ten minutes to descend.

Panic. But then I remembered the lessons I had learned while researching a film about mountain safety. If in doubt follow the contours. And so I followed the lifeline of barbed wire, and eventually came to a gate – or rather a solitary piece of rotten wood dangling from a post.

Down the ravine I walked, rapidly losing altitude, clambering over fallen trees which barred this unfrequented and lonely path.

I had expected to see the Doubs sparkling below me but the encircling forest limited my vista to closely stacked pines and the occasional glimpse of limestone cliffs.

After an hour of solitude I came upon an old carpenter sawing planks on the outskirts of St-Ursanne, and without warning a G.S.M.S. (Great Swiss Mountain Sheepdog) lunged at me, its jaws snapping shut like a man-trap only inches from my genitals. Acting instinctively I leapt to one side and fell heavily, my rucksack frame thudding into my nape.

I lay there in a mild state of shock while the carpenter continued to saw biblically, in the style of Millais. His pet, thankfully restrained by a chain, stood on his hind legs, gnashing his teeth like a taunted bear.

'Call your sodding dog off!' I shouted, but the man was oblivious to my Anglo-Saxon, and slotted another plank into his vice.

I got to my feet and hobbled into the village, for my leap had caused something in an ankle to click.

St-Ursanne is a compact and pretty walled village named after a saint who had dealings with a bear. What exactly occurred I have been unable to discover, although canonisation suggests that their relationship was strictly above board.

Anyway, a rampant bear is carved in the arch of a gate leading into a leafy square where a strange man resembling Van Gogh was moving his fingers in the air, no doubt painting pictures with his memories.

A church offered sanctuary from the sun, and I sat on a pew trying to fill in the gaps between faded pastel patterns and portraits of saints on the walls and pillars.

The Gothic cloister added an extra patina of peace to an intense feeling of tranquillity with which the Jura, despite my minor mishaps, had imbued me.

In an inn opposite the church I drank two glasses of creamy local red wine. But knowing that the day was not yet half through I declined a third and went in search of the Doubs.

I found it under a bridge, flowing green and clear, and from its bank opposite the village I could see the deep horseshoe imprint of its gorge; rich pasture within the arc of its bend, cliffs and forest on its perimeter.

I returned to the square and, squeezing between an anarchic herd of cows, passed under the west gate.

There, before me, was Belloc's Terrible Bridge, a viaduct he had crossed in order to avoid an awful ravine.

To gain the bridge means taking a steeper route than that offered by the road curling around the rather picturesque little ravine. But I have to admire his courage for in his day there was only a single track with horrendous gaps between the sleepers. And it *is* high. Even now, when there are twin tracks and no gaps, I would have thought twice about tackling it, and I was glad that the constant buzzing of electric trains precluded an emulation of his feat.

Having successfully avoided the bridge I carried on up pretty lanes flanked by purple flowers and white thistles to Montmelon where two beautiful girls charmingly overcharged me for wine – although they filled my bottle with unchlorinated water for free.

Beyond Montmelon my map indicated a zigzag path leading up to yet another ridge, on the far side of which is Glovelier where I planned to sleep.

Somehow I missed this path and continued along a very steep lane running parallel to the rising ridge, thereby getting no nearer the top. Belloc describes how he clambered up the slope here, using hands and knees. My admiration for him grew, for to attempt this slope with 20 kilos on my back was out of the question. Already, like a Himalayan mountaineer, I was taking ten steps then resting to regain my breath.

Up I trudged until I saw two middle-aged couples sitting on a log pile, eating.

'Do you know the way to Glovelier?' I asked.

'Follow the road,' a sausage-munching husband advised.

'But this road doesn't go there.'

'Doesn't it?' Chomp, chomp.

'I think I'll head into the woods.'

'It's up to you,' he replied definitively.

Luckily a tractor pulled out of a farm and I asked the sub-teenage driver if I could reach Glovelier via the forest.

'There,' he said, pointing to a faint path. 'That's the way.'

Up through the trees I plodded at a snail's pace, my lungs rasping like old leather bellows.

At the top there was a locked gate wreathed with barbed wire. More of the stuff stretched to right and left, and I cursed its invention. No wonder there had been range wars.

Taking the utmost care – for a severed artery would be unpopular here – I climbed over the gate and found myself on a bald hill where a bull stood eyeing me with more than academic interest. Sweat swathed me. Bloody hell! All this *and* a bull.

According to my map there should have been a road here. Useless cartographers. And why hadn't they provided a symbol for places where bulls lurked? Horns or a gored rambler?

Crouching, and keeping to broom bushes, I skirted the well-hung beast and, having headed downhill for a while, saw a wonderful sight: the gunmetal grey of a crash barrier.

I had found the road, but getting on to it was another matter. A barricade of unclimbable wire separated me from the blessed tarmac, and I had no option but to throw my rucksack over and squirm under the barbs on my back through congealed cowpats.

A limestone gorge leads down towards Glovelier.

I could not find a path and headed blindly over fields towards the neck of the gorge where, beneath a great white cliff, I met cyclists.

A muscle-bound father and mother, wearing Tour de France gear, were succeeding in putting their two obese children off cycling for life.

Their bikes, slim racing models, must have been pushed up the slimy track all the way from Glovelier, and the children's cross faces were as wet and red as watermelons.

'Wonderful day,' said the man.

'Wonderful,' I agreed, 'but why on earth have you brought bicycles?'

'The ride down is very pleasant.'

'Is it worth the effort?'

'We all enjoy the challenge.'

One day, I thought, when you are old and grey, your children will drag you up here in a wheelchair – and then let you go.

I was enclosed within the claustrophobic gully for an hour with only the occasional tapping of woodpeckers to relieve the silence. But when I reached Glovelier and daylight I was disappointed, for the town straggles along a shallow valley and its buildings are as unpleasing as any you might see in Billericay.

It was only four o'clock but all the ups and downs of the day had tested my legs to the limit. I approached the first person I saw and asked her, in French, where I might find a hotel.

She did not understand a word I said, and answered me in German, a language as foreign to me as French was to her. But how could this be? Over the hill rising behind us they spoke French, and although a line on a map can separate languages I could not fathom why, in a country with four official languages, every child was not taught at least a smattering of her compatriots' tongues.

My thirst was intense and I bought a bottle of lemonade. Outside the shop I took a swig, then dropped the bottle on the road where it shattered into a hundred pieces although the neck stayed intact. A group of sullen onlookers gathered around the scene of my accident and watched as I tweezered the splinters into the upturned neck. No one offered to help.

Smeared with bullshit and clutching a jagged bottle I entered a hotel where silence fell like snow on the beer-swilling customers. I asked the barmaid for a room.

She hurried away and was replaced by a man of Paul Bunyan proportions who, on seeing me, puffed out his barrel chest aggressively.

Belloc had had trouble with an ox-faced man in Glovelier, and perhaps this bovine hotelier was a descendant.

'Yes?'

'I'd like a room please.'

'We're full.'

It was Charmes all over again. 'Are you sure?'

'It's my hotel,' he said, advancing towards me. 'And if I say it's full then it's full!'

'OK, but would you mind getting rid of this bottle?'

He disarmed me and I set off briskly for Undervelier where I felt confident of finding a more welcoming reception.

'Glovelier,' Belloc wrote, 'is a place of no excellence whatever.' I concur.

A road bordered by a suburb of wood-mills led across a floodplain to Berlincourt, where I entered an umbrous valley of pines and bluffs through which La Sorne river wriggled, cold and grey.

Undervelier, a village constricted in a gap between the previous and ensuing gorges, boasted a hotel across whose threshold I dragged my feet.

The interior was sombre with fat women wearing fir-green alpine bowlers and stetsons. They were eating cakes seriously; cream sandwiched between fluffy pastry capped with strawberries.

'Good evening,' I said to the woman who confronted me.

'What do you want?'

'A room please.'

'We're closed.'

'I'll happily pay for a double room.'

'We're closed.'

'But it's almost dark and I need a place to sleep.'

'We're closed.'

'I'll pay double.'

'I think you'd better leave.'

Close to despair, I used the last weapon in my armoury: lies. 'I'm a journalist writing an article about the Jura for a British national newspaper. Just think of the publicity.' But she did not believe me. Why should she? After all, journalists drive sparkling hired cars and smell sweeter.

'Then what do you suggest I do?'

'It's no concern of mine.'

Belloc, as constricted by his Catholicism as Undervelier is by its restrictive valley, had seen this place as a symbol of Catholic continuity. When the church bell tolled he had watched the entire population flocking into mass; but instead of viewing such a herd instinct as the epitome of conformity he had construed it as a metaphor for the power of the Faith. Deeply impressed he 'considered the nature of Belief' but 'not without tears'.

Bounced from the hotel and close to tears myself – of anger – I wondered what to do. Night was near and I had the options of sleeping rough or walking through the night.

Rain was falling as I set off into the Gorges du Pichoux, which, objectively, presented a splendid landscape of precipitous limestone cliffs. But with darkness descending and my legs feeling woodenly subjective I experienced no Turneresque visions beneath the beetling crags.

I passed a grotto with an iron cross outside. So what? Who cared if some peasant, dying of boredom, had imagined a Virgin or a Bear Saint there? A gurgling river: H20. Perfect bowls of rock beside the river: the inevitable result of corrosion by water-borne particles. The sky: vapour. A hotel: wooden beams and bricks. A hotel!

There it stood at the southern gates of the gorge, offering sanctuary, its porch light casting a yellow welcome mat on to the wet ground.

In the empty interior chamber music filled the room with serenity.

I was determined to avoid a third ejection, but I need not have worried because the owner of the Hôtel de la Couronne, though diffident at first, was charming, and led me past his slobbering English bulldog – imported from Devon – to a room reflecting exquisite taste.

'Mind your rucksack,' he admonished kindly as I threatened to stain hand-printed pink wallpaper with mud.

It was a room for a honeymoon, and had I possessed Faustian powers I would have conjured up my wife there and then.

I bathed and caught sight of myself in a full-length antique mirror. Who was this person? Years of accumulated flab, which no amount of jogging and avoidance of fried food had succeeded in dispelling, had vanished. My body was twenty years younger, my stomach firm and flat again for the first time since my teens. And those wobbly bits above the hips which

Americans euphemistically call love jugs – had turned to perpendicular muscle.

There you are, middle-aged readers. If nothing else in this book interests you then you can, at least, accept it as a formula for losing weight. *The Slimmers' Path to Rome*: guaranteed to work when all else has failed. Simply go to Toul. Walk south. Eat little. Carry much. And after a week or so you will appear the man, or woman, you used to be.

Downstairs I realised I was the only guest, although the owner and his wife encouraged me to offload the cold helmet of solitude which I had become accustomed to wearing.

They fed me and talked to me, and later, while I was jotting down notes about the day's occurrences, I showed them the sketch of the gorge which is printed in Belloc's book. They were, to my surprise, unsurprised. During the previous summer two travellers from Belgium had shown them the same picture. They, too, had been following Belloc's route, and I wondered who they might be. Academics from Bruges perhaps, checking details for the footnotes of the definitive biography? Or simply kindred spirits? But whatever their motives their passage comforted me, adding a living companionship to the ghost of Belloc who always managed to nip behind a tree whenever I glanced over my shoulder.

Wine, conversation and Mozart prepared me for sleep.

I opened a window in my room, undressed, and slid under a duvet as light as a cloud.

In the forest and rocks surrounding the hotel owls were hooting, while on the stairs outside my door the bulldog snored like a friendly jailer.

Gorges du Pichoux to Solothurn

Hot croissants melted like communion wafers in my mouth, and tanked up with litres of freshly ground coffee I was ready for another day.

When I had paid my bill the owner thrust a package into my hands.

'Take this,' he said. 'It will help you on your way.'

I unwrapped the paper and saw a work of art: a slab of pâté framed by curlicues of pastry.

'It is made from a recipe handed down by my grandmother. There is nothing like it. You will not find it in any cookbook. You will enjoy it.'

'I will. Thank you.'

He led me outside into an unsettled day and pointed to a track which even my efficient Swiss map neglected to show. 'Take that path,' he said. 'It will save you climbing those hills and it is prettier.'

And trusting his judgement I shook his hand and set off along the lonely path with limestone cliffs to my left and silent woods to my right.

My itinerary for the day was simple: east to Moutier and Crémines, then south-east over the final spur, the Weissenstein, and down into Solothurn where the plain between Jura and Alps begins.

Mist spiralled from the little stream, the Tschaibex, whose secret valley I followed to the hamlet of Les Ecorcheresses, my only companions rabbits, who, unused to humans, remained in Disneyesque poses as I passed.

From Les Ecorcheresses the road descended gradually through forests and fields towards Moutier.

Immense black clouds pillowed up above the rugged southern ridges and I thought I was in for a thunderstorm, but the sky uncluttered as I approached Moutier, and with an escort of cackling jays I followed a stream towards a town Belloc thought detestable.

Perhaps ill humour coloured his perception of Moutier. It is not detestable, merely nondescript, although its setting is fine because its northern wall is a limestone escarpment where stands of coppery beeches and blue firs alternate with Gothic spires of white rock. A spectacular gorge, reminiscent of the Samaria Gorge in Crete, slices through the mountains here, but it leads north, and my way led south.

I telephoned the main post office at Basel but my tent had not arrived.

'The English are very slow,' the woman in Basel explained.

'There has been a postal *strike*. You know? A strike?'

She made it sound as though the Black Death was ravaging the anarchic little island across the sea. But I suppose strikes are rare in Switzerland. Come to think of it they are fairly infrequent in Britain now that the government, with union assistance, has returned collective bargaining to a nineteenth-century footing.

A pleasant enough road following the valley to Crémines took me past dairy farms whose pastures swept up to a great wall of limestone cliffs. And having travelled east all morning I finally turned south again, gradually gaining height as I strolled through fields and forests towards Gänsbrunnen, where the climb to the crest of the Weissenstein begins.

In a field of feathery grasses I saw three hinds grazing. Each faced outwards, forming the points of an equilateral triangle – for defensive reasons presumably. And when one of them scented me they bounded away, their white scuts rising and falling in splendid disunion until they were lost amongst their dark kingdom of pines.

I filled my water bottle from a spring, passed through a miniature gorge, and began the long ascent, through tidy fields at first, then forest.

I passed a sign: ACHTUNG! WILDSCHULTZ. I had no idea what this meant but, prone to pessimism, assumed that it was warning me of danger from wild boars. And so I headed up through the trees, glancing to left and right, half expecting to glimpse inscrutable porcine eyes or the glint of wicked tusks. The pine boles, I noted, were bare of branches and consequently unclimbable. If attacked by frenzied pigs I would simply have to wrestle them to the ground.

The sun beat down mercilessly, turning the air sticky with the smell of resin and, stripped to shorts and T-shirt, I left a trail of sweat that a blind boar with flu could have followed.

There are boar in these forests but later I was to learn that *Wildschultz* means 'poacher'. But ignorance had lent excitement to an otherwise purgatorial ascent.

Two hours from Gänsbrunnen, and 2,000 feet higher, I finally reached the top. And despite being close to exhaustion I felt euphoric because from here I would be able to see the Alps for the first time. But as I passed a sign proving that I was exactly 1,284 metres above Brighton beach I was hit by a squall. A black wall of cloud enveloped me and the temperature dropped dramatically.

Shivering like a shorn poodle I trotted downhill until, on a grey and blustery alp just below the crest, I found an inn.

Here I faced a tricky choice: soup or beer.

Both would have been best but the price of Swiss hotels was reducing my pack of travellers' cheques drastically. Soup would have been sensible but I chose beer.

Swaddled in sweaters, and still shivering, I sat and sipped the beer in the certain knowledge that the alcohol was lowering my temperature even further. Lord knows how many pilgrims, dragged from snowdrifts, have been killed by brandy dangling from St Bernards' necks.

I was writing in my notebook when I became aware of a man, wearing a funereal black coat, standing over me. Tall, big-boned, and in his sixties, he smiled and said, 'Excuse me but I couldn't help noticing your accent. Are you British by any chance?'

'I am,' I admitted reluctantly, half expecting a diatribe against soccer thugs, Thatcher's regency or our record export figures for acid rain.

'Then please allow me to pay for your beer.'

'Why?'

'Because you're thirsty.'

His accent flummoxed me. His English was perfect but I could not pinpoint its origin: German but with half familiar vowel sounds constricted at the back of the palate.

He held out a strong hand, like a carpenter's, which shook mine.

'Let me introduce myself. My name's Murdoch. I was born in Northern Ireland.'

Murdoch is a Presbyterian minister who, after fifteen years of missionary work in the Far East, had found his true vocation in Switzerland where he has lived for a decade.

'People usually laugh when I tell them I'm doing God's work here but there's a terrible need. On the surface it's all sweetness and light but despite all their material possessions there's a poverty of spirit among these people.'

'Have you been in Britain lately?'

'No. My work is here.'

'Well if you do go back you'll find the same poverty there. And the material kind.'

He introduced me to his elderly Swiss wife, a sprightly woman with white coconut-matting hair and eyes surrounded by laughter lines like wrinkled appleskin. They had met at a mission in Bangladesh.

'My husband is the finest pastor in all Switzerland,' she said, squeezing his hand.

'She's prejudiced.'

'Wives should be,' I replied.

'But it is true,' she affirmed. 'When he is preaching the churches are full to bursting.'

'And when he's not?'

She shrugged. 'The word of God needs passion, and we Swiss are not known for our ardour.'

Murdoch, naturally modest, changed the subject.

'Where are you going?'

'To Rome.'

'On foot?'

'If my feet let me.'

'Well isn't that something? And what were those notes all about? Are you planning to write about it?'

'Yes.' He touched the side of his nose conspiratorially.

'Well, if you do, then for Pete's sake don't mention me by name or my parishioners will be up in arms because I bought you a beer. They don't approve, you see.'

'Don't worry,' I said. 'I wouldn't use your real name.' And I haven't.

When he and his wife had gone the waitress brought me a roll and a steaming bowl of soup in which circles of sausage were floating.

'But I didn't order soup.'

'The gentleman did.'

May this Good Samaritan's church always be full to the rafters and may he not go to heaven until all the heathen Swiss have given all they own to the poor – provided they can find any.

Outside the inn the gale still howled as I began the 3,000 feet of descent. But mountain weather is fickle, and within ten minutes I walked under the curtain of cloud into brilliant sunshine.

Far below I saw a vast hazy plain with the meandering River Aare lying upon it like a sleeping silver snake.

With precipitous slopes all around me the plain seemed tilted, like the lid of a school desk, and this optical illusion made the river appear unnatural. Why didn't the water spill over and flood the fields at my feet?

I looked up towards the south where I saw black paper cut-outs of the pre-Alps, including the Brienzergrat, over which Belloc's bizarre route would take me. At least it was free of snow. But above this, disappointment. Where the High Alps should have filled the sky with blue pyramids of snow and ice I saw only clouds.

From here, on a crisp day, I would have seen the entire range paraded before me from Austria in the south-east to France in the south-west. I would have seen the Bernese Oberland, the tips of the Pennine Alps, and even the Italian slopes of Mont Blanc.

But the next valley and the one after always seem more exciting and I contented myself with my surroundings. Buzzards traced helices above impressive limestone faces falling towards the lowlands where, far, far away, in the world of men, a car's windscreen flashed like a moving heliograph.

I heard children laughing but the forest was deserted. Ghosts? And then I saw them, high above, sitting in a chair suspended from a cable. They waved to me and I watched them as the spar supporting them lurched over a pylon. One clunk and they had gone.

On a heathery knoll a blond youth with acne was lying with his head resting on a coil of orange climbing rope, his Sony Walkman churning out heavy metal music at a volume even I could hear.

Presumably he had been climbing on one of the cliffs, solo, using a back-rope for protection, for he was obviously spaced out on some illegal substance and no climber in his right mind would have accompanied him.

'*Guten Tag!*' I said flawlessly, but his eyes were incapable of focusing and his fishy lips formed silent o's.

A white Mercedes swept past, and through the rear window I saw the beaming Murdoch waving like royalty.

Evening sunlight shafted through the scented pines as I reached Oberdorf, a smart dormitory of Solothurn, where Belloc had seen water wheels – their purpose to drive machines for sawing planks – attached to many of the houses. I saw only one water wheel – its function a feature of a surburban garden.

Oberdorf became Langendorf, which coalesced into the outskirts of Solothurn.

After the stillness of the hills the traffic was intolerable. A car, driven on the right, screeched around a corner and narrowly missed me. Everywhere there were traffic lights, traffic cops and signs in German forbidding everything. *Verboten! Verboten! Verboten!*

Behind me the Weissenstein rose sublimely, its top now clear of cloud, while all around me people were hurrying home from work like wealthy refugees escaping a financial catastrophe.

Within the walls of the old town I asked passers-by where I might find a hotel, but their reactions were uniformly hostile. It was true that I looked a bit of a tramp but it had been a hard day. Had the telltale symptoms of plague erupted on my face? No. Were my flies open? They were, and an ambiguous pink pouch – ambiguous if merely glanced at – was clearly visible, protruding from my shorts. Closer inspection would have revealed C&A's best red underpants but I cannot blame the citizens of Solothurn for treating me as a pariah.

Well zipped up I followed signs to the tourist office opposite the cathedral.

'I have a list of prices here,' the woman told me. 'What does sir wish to pay?'

'Not more than twenty francs.'

An intake of breath. 'I am afraid sir will be unlikely to find accommodation for under thirty-five francs.'

But something at the bottom of her list had caught my eye. 'There. Eighteen francs.'

'Sir would not like it,' she informed me.

'Sir will love it.'

'But it has no running water in the rooms and young people use it . . .'

It took me a while to find the hotel, tucked away down a side street beside a theatre.

It was obviously the rendezvous for the town's subversive element; students and intellectuals. The bar looked like a German–American movie mogul's concept of a Left Bank café in the fifties. A Parisian film set with steins. Men with carefully trimmed beards, black sweaters, and pipes sat amongst Juliette Greco lookalikes. Heads nodded sagely and expressions of concern flickered across faces taut with angst.

A bowl and ewer, impersonating a still life, stood beside my simple bed but there was a communal shower and also a communal kitchen where I cooked a dinner of four eggs fried in butter, much to the disgust of a willowy young man who was preparing a complicated but geometrically stunning salad.

When, having mopped up the grease with bread, I put two more eggs in boiling water in preparation for the next day's march, his disgust turned to contempt.

'You like eggs?' he asked, attempting irony.

'Not that much but every so often I get a craving.'

'But think of the cholesterol.'

'I'm not looking for immortality.'

'But you want to live?'

'Not if life becomes nothing but a perpetual salad.'

'I do not drink alcohol. I do not smoke. I do not eat meat or fish. I do not eat eggs. And look at me.'

I looked at him and escaped downstairs for a glass of wine before taking a stroll around the town.

The Aare flowed fast and green like all Swiss rivers. The fountains spouted like all Swiss fountains. The goods in the shops were chic and expensive like the goods in all Swiss shops. But the town – objectively beautiful with its alleys, fine houses and impressive cathedral – was beginning to get on my nerves. Not a toffee paper littered the streets; not a paving stone was cracked; not a hair was out of place. There was no evidence of human frailty or excess. No evidence of life. The town was a morgue.

Even in the restaurants and bars, through whose windows I peered, the customers were sitting woodenly like children on their best behaviour.

After only three days in Switzerland my affection for it was waning fast. The sense of order and cleanliness which had seemed so appealing after I crossed the border from Belfort now struck me with a sort of terror; for it epitomised the kind of society to which many in Britain aspire.

I had gone out on a date with Switzerland, but at the end of the evening I had been left with an ice maiden who had contributed not one original thought to our conversation. Her clever make-up and exquisite clothes had seduced me, but it was the superficial allure of a beauty queen. Miss Switzerland, despite all her curves in the right places, was not for me.

I was going to walk out on her, but it was going to take me a while.

Solothurn to Burgdorf

After two days of climbing in and out of Jurassic troughs I had planned an easy stroll – which was just as well, for rain, driven by a cold southerly wind blowing off the Alps, was destined to make the mere twenty-five kilometres to Burgdorf forgettable in a memorable way.

I stopped for coffee in the Solothurn Co-op, then headed out through dreary suburbs, and by the time I crossed the River Emme I was feeling thoroughly fed up. My only consolation was that Belloc had also found this stretch mindnumbing, and only a foolish sense of duty kept me going; for it was not merely the dismal rain but also the anticlimactic surroundings that crushed my spirit.

'I had,' Belloc wrote, 'experienced the ebb of some vitality . . .'

No wonder. Switzerland, in the collective unconscious, is a land of ravines, glaciers, lakes and peaks, and here was I heading into a gale through country as flat and unappealing as a tombstone. There was not even the magnetic lure of distant peaks to attract me since the horizon was draped with mist.

Deserted rainswept villages followed deserted rainswept towns, and as I crossed the plain I imagined myself as a figure in a landscape glimpsed by a farmer's wife from the comfort of her kitchen. What would she think? If she had gone to evening classes in Utzenstorf or Kirchberg (Shakespearean Tragedy For Beginners) she might have seen me as Edgar in *King Lear* wandering the highways as a Bedlam beggar. Or perhaps Banquo on the blasted heath.

I saw no hags but something equally frightful.

When driving I frequently see dead dogs which turn into plastic bags. Here, on the verge, I saw a black plastic bag that turned into a black dead dog. A mob of carrion crows was strutting around it and were loath to leave at my approach. Like flapping fylfots they hovered untidily while I passed, then returned to their meat.

A windbreak of pines interrupted the desolation, and I sought shelter amongst them. It was as comforting as a crypt. The ground was spongy with fungi while above me the foliage moaned like the dying.

With difficulty – for my fingers were trembling – I peeled my two boiled eggs and ate them.

Swallowing cold eggs alone under saturated pines during an autumn squall on a bleak plain was not something I had anticipated when planning the trip in my centrally-heated house. Where were the lusty milkmaids with rosy cheeks and blonde plaited hair shining like corn? Where were the jolly peasants who ceased scything to share their Emmental cheese and fruity local wine? Not here. That was for sure.

In Kirchberg there is a church, and near the church a bar where I drank a cup of warm water flavoured with a tea bag. And having crunched three paracetamols for dessert I left the sodden town, my socks squelching audibly at every step.

My map showed white lanes, like spirogyra, squiggling between low hills to Burgdorf, but I needed no persuasion to change my plans and take the quick main road. Lorries with their headlights flashing did their best to blind me while those coming at me from behind hooted irately, their drivers' field of view swamped by the torrential downpour.

It was only 3.30 when I reached Burgdorf but any vestige of resolve had been drowned. All the kingdoms of the world laid at my feet would not have induced me to paddle a cubit further across this rainy desert.

The prospect of fifteen hours of enforced inactivity did not appeal but I chose the first hotel I saw, a gloomy edifice with dripping plastic chairs stacked up on the terrace.

Yes, they had a room available, a double of course.

I emptied the water from my brown boots into the washbasin, lay on the brown coverlet, and scanned the brown wallpaper in search of inspiration. There was none.

Drowsy, I tried to snooze, but heavy lorries trundling past the window kept me awake.

This, I told myself, will not do. All over the world people would give their eye-teeth to be transported magically to Burgdorf with its thirteenth-century castle and Late Gothic church and there was I moping like a malingerer in a school infirmary. At least I could play the tourist.

In the old town people were employing a wonderful invention; the umbrella. I had not thought to buy one and decided against doing so now, for this Welsh weather was an aberration. By dawn the sky would clear and there would be sun all the way to Rome.

I could not find the castle even though postcards proved its proximity, and now I will go to my grave without having seen its fine collection of halberds. That's the way it goes.

Instead I sheltered under ancient stone arcades and watched the narrow streets flow by. Later, by chance, I found the church, but its entrance was caged by scaffolding and entry was *Verboten*. At least I had tried.

On the way back to the hotel I saw an extraordinary sight. Tucked away under the town walls there was a tin box, the size of a confessional, which at first I took to be a passport-photo machine. It was not. Here, in ultra-conservative German-speaking Switzerland, was a public wanking booth. *SEXY VIDEOS* a dayglow sign proclaimed in Esperanto, and I wondered if the solid citizenry actually availed themselves of its sleazy eroticism; for Burgdorf is a smallish town, not an anonymous city.

All the restaurants were far too expensive, and so I entered my first Swiss supermarket whose prices exceeded those of a Knightsbridge delicatessen. An apple, a wedge of Emmental no bigger than a doorstop, bread, a tomato, butter the size of an ice cube, and the cheapest flip-top bottle of wine cost me half a single British youth's weekly state benefit. And secreting this feast about my person I mounted the hotel's mock-marble stairs and locked myself in my room for a spot of alimentary self-abuse.

The Swiss cannot read. I do not mean that they are illiterate; merely that reading cannot be a regular habit. Not one bedroom in Switzerland was equipped with a reading light. There were bedside lamps but they were decorative, with thirty-watt bulbs encased in opaque shades, usually pink, designed to make middle-aged flesh more appealing.

And so, like a naughty child, I read by torchlight until the regular rumble of passing lorries rocked me to sleep.

Burgdorf to Konolfingen

I woke in the small hours and looked out.

The sky was sparkling with stars and I drifted back into sleep confident of a day's pleasant rambling along the Emme valley *wanderwegs*.

Swiss maps are a delight to read. They are similar to Ordnance Survey maps but show footpaths even more clearly: red *wanderwegs* like veins coursing all over the country's physique where the going is easy, and *bergwegs*, differentiated by broken lines, where things get tougher.

At dawn I woke to fog but that was a good sign. By eight it would lift and I would be walking through country as pretty as posters.

My optimism was premature. By seven the fog had gone, but I stepped out into the smell of snow.

The sky was the colour of unripe plums; pale green at the horizon darkening to faint purple directly above.

Snow was the last thing I wanted, for in two or three days Belloc's route would take me over the Brienzergrat, an 8,000 foot ridge. In summer conditions it would be no more serious than a scramble over a Lakeland fell, but the southern slope is very steep, as Belloc found, and to cross it alone in winter conditions without ice axe and crampons would be inviting trouble.

Weighed down with doubts I wandered out of Burgdorf and finally saw the *Schloss*. *Schloss* sounds exactly right, for the word 'castle' conjures up stark towers, battlements and portcullises; whereas Burgdorf's *Schloss* had all the appeal of a kitsch Beverly Hills theme home, its leonine coat of arms emblazoned like a studio logo on its grandest tower.

I pride myself on my map-reading ability, and confidently choosing a *wanderweg* I headed for the Emme. My path ended in a factory yard. I should have turned left. I turned left and came to impassable railway tracks. I should have stayed in bed.

I gave up and returned to the road.

Floodplain fields led to Hasle where luck led me to the river.

The path took me behind modern semi-detached houses whose living rooms – clearly visible through fish tank windows – were as soullessly decorated as anyone might find in Britain: TV as shrine; four books; blue-glass Bambi and school photographs perched on veneered display cabinet; smoked-glass coffee table with neat stack of magazines; mirrors but no pictures on the walls; playpen with toddler, like a pet, safely confined and threatening no mess on the freshly shampooed carpet; perfectly normal young housewife staring out through the glass like the inmate of a soft asylum.

The Emme, bordered by firs, was in spate. Slabs of glacier-grey water rushed between high banks and I could hear the noise of boulders grinding along the riverbed.

The Swiss must take their walking very seriously for at one point, only a few hundred metres from a perfectly good stone bridge, a suspension-bridge has been constructed specifically to link one path with another. Made from steel, it must have cost a fortune, and as I bounced across its narrow walkway, with the river racing beneath, I suffered an attack of vertigo.

In mountains I can sit astride a knife-edge ridge without a qualm, but add water and my knees turn to jelly.

In the woods before Lützelflüh I found further evidence of the Swiss taking their pleasure stringently.

Pictures, like Stations of the Cross, were nailed to trees along a riverside jogging track: a man touching his toes, and beside the figure the instruction x 20; a woman doing press-ups, x 10; a child leaping with arms raised, x 5. And between these pictures were ropes dangling from branches (for climbing); a metal bar wedged between trees (for pull-ups); and railway sleepers arranged in chevrons on the ground (to balance on). No doubt I missed the illustration explaining how, in order to walk, it is necessary to place one foot in front of the other.

Beyond Lützelflüh the river cambers between shaly bluffs. The path plunged into a dark wood in the middle of which there was a cage, far from habitation, where a score of undernourished white doves perched, as still as porcelain. Only blinking upside-down eyelids indicated that they were alive. What they were doing there was a mystery and finding them as disquieting as a Magritte painting, I hurried on towards Langnau and less surrealist surroundings.

The delightful path follows the river all the way, alternating between narrow strips of woodland and pasture full of Emmental-uddered cows. And all around there are gentle hills capped by firs.

Despite cold drizzle I enjoyed the exercise, for I was feeling fit, although I met no one apart from a man with a shotgun leaning on a tree beside the Ilfis, a tributary of the Emme.

There was an air of wealth about him. His shirt was cleaner than a farmer's and his green-lapelled jacket looked made to measure. He also spoke French.

'What are you hunting?' I asked.

'Nothing in particular.'

'What is there here?'

'Not much. Some ducks.'

'But you don't have a dog.'

My French was imperfect, and so was his. He misunderstood.

'Why should I shoot dogs?'

'No. I meant that if you shoot a duck you don't have a dog to retrieve it.' I mimed a doggy paddle.

He shrugged. 'What does it matter?'

'Then why shoot them?'

'Why not? They're not people.'

In Langnau I went straight to the tourist office to get a weather report.

The man at the desk was pessimistic. 'Not very good I'm afraid.'

'But I need to know precisely. I'm planning to climb the Brienzergrat on Saturday and I must have an accurate forecast.'

'I can phone the air force meteorological office if you like?'

'Please.'

When he replaced the receiver the corners of his mouth were downturned. 'It's bad. Snow down to 1,000 metres clearing by Tuesday perhaps.'

Today was Thursday.

'Heavy snow?' I asked.

'Heavy. Light. It makes no difference. There is wind also. You have companions?'

'I'm alone.'

'Then you would be foolish to try it.'

I thanked him and went to a bar for a glass of wine and time to think.

I had planned to spend Friday night in the village of Schangnau and go over the top on Saturday, but the route to the Brienzergrat was a cul-de-sac and if the forecast was accurate I would have to retreat, adding at least two days to my journey.

Should I risk it? I ordered another wine and weighed the pros and cons.

Having lived in Snowdonia for ten years I knew how snow and ice could turn the simplest mountain ramble into an alpine expedition. If I found myself in white-out conditions or lost my way in cloud – for there are no paths in snow – I could easily come to grief. And no one would know I was there.

Had I been twenty and inexperienced I might have decided to take a chance, but I had children to consider, and before setting out I had promised my wife that I would not risk my life.

And so, regrettably, I decided to take my own route to Brienz, on the far side of the Brienzergrat, by way of Thun and Interlaken. It was longer but safe.

It was already early afternoon and there was no hope of getting to Thun by nightfall. But with the extra mileage my decision had added I decided to abandon my planned overnight stop in Langnau and head south at once.

For the first time since leaving Toul I tasted the bitterness of defeat, and no rational argument could sweeten my sense of failure.

Like a spoilt child who has just been told that his trip to the pantomime has been cancelled, I walked sulkily towards Konolfingen. The valley was charming but the gently rounded hills only served to remind me that beyond them lay the first real mountain chain whose rocky ridge I would probably never tread.

Far to the east I heard the rumble of thunder – unless it was Belloc taking time off from hectoring St Peter to give vent to a resounding belly laugh at my expense.

I reached Konolfingen after dark and found all the hotels, except one, full of drunken army officers, ostensibly on manoeuvres.

My attic room – all cock-eyed angles like a set from *The Cabinet of Doctor Caligari* – was delightfully seedy with peeling wallpaper and tepid water flowing from both taps. Downstairs the bar was the nearest thing to a pub I had found during the entire trip, and, sitting under a candelabrum made from antlers, I drank an excellent draught beer served by a laid-back waiter who marked my coaster with a biro in lieu of cash.

The clientele comprised three distinct groups: the Nogood Boyos, all long hair and earrings, drinking beer around the pinball machine; working men slapping their playing cards down with gusto between generous slurpings of wine; and a smart table at which the male bourgeoisie, drinking gins and vodkas, were conversing heatedly about some local political issue.

After a while one of the last group, well into his cups, spoke to me. I explained that I only spoke phrase-book German but a ginger-bearded friend, who spoke French, asked me to join them.

And with Ginger acting as interpreter we spent the next couple of hours talking about all manner of things, most of which I forget, for the beer was strong. One subject, however, I remember with clarity.

A young man with bifocals asked me, point-blank, why the English hated children.

'I'm English,' I protested, 'and I love my children.'

'But we keep reading in the newspapers about the terrible cruelty in England. The torture of babies and the sexual abuse.'

It is axiomatic that travel forces one to face one's country as others see it, and I had no defence.

'Well? It's true isn't it?' he persisted.

'Yes, but I've no real experience of the subject. I don't know any child-abusers.'

Possibly it was true but if statistics are anything to go by then I probably do, only I do not know who they are. But I have seen the contempt with which so many parents treat their children.

'In England children are often seen as an inconvenience.'

'Then why in God's name do people have them if they don't want them?'

'Because of many things. Ignorance, poverty, history.'

'Poverty! In Italy there's terrible poverty but they worship their children. And history? What on earth has that got to do with it?'

'Queen Victoria and all that. Children being seen and not heard.'

'But she's long dead.'

'Ah – but her legacy lives on. A lot of people who can afford it still send their children away to boarding school at seven.'

'But why?'

'To make them self-reliant.'

'At seven? What for?'

'It's an excuse. Nothing more. The English rich are a selfish and emotionally bankrupt load of swine.'

'All of them?'

'No, of course not. It's a generalisation, but as I get older I believe more and more in generalisations. I see so few exceptions.'

'But it's terrible.'

'The only answer's education and the parents aren't educated. Not in the important things. Neither are their children.'

'But you have good schools in England?'

'It's not in the government's interests to educate most of the children beyond a certain level. Even our so-called socialists didn't do all they could when they were in power. It's dangerous to have an electorate that can think for itself.'

And so it continued until alcohol made us even less articulate.

As I lay down to sleep I saw an image of Britain floating in an old grey sea; a cold bed of slate on which a million children tossed and turned trying to erase the memory of Daddy and his sickening love.

Konolfingen to Interlaken

At six I looked out of my window and watched a squaddy stumbling like a drunk under the weight of pack and rifle as he completed an all-night route-march. On the steps of the hotel opposite he collapsed and was half dragged inside by an officer who doubtless spouted the Swiss equivalent of, 'Well done, lad! That's the spirit!'

Never, outside Turkey, have I seen so many soldiers per capita as I saw in neutral Switzerland.

Even when on leave they are armed to the teeth in case of a sudden national emergency. 'Quick, Heidi, pass the ammunition. There's trouble with Liechtenstein.' And they are a rum lot.

At Crewe Station one sees soldiers en route to Aldershot or Catterick but there is a homogeneity about them: crop-haired, moustached, 5 foot 8 inches tall, muscular, with dead fish eyes. But in Switzerland they come in all shapes and sizes from 5-foot gnomes with beards and rimless glasses to stick insects of 6 foot 6 inches who carry their automatic rifles like conductors' batons.

In Britain they are professional. In Switzerland they are compulsorily drafted. Everyone. Like ants they swarm around bus and railway stations. But what can one expect from an ant economy?

The only positive attribute of the Konolfingen to Thun road is that it is more or less downhill. Yes, it was raining, but if I were to dwell any more on precipitation then these pages would become too waterlogged to read. But as I walked through nondescript towns and villages I could not help noticing one positive aspect of Swiss society: a desire to disguise the industrial efficiency which has made the country the capital of capitalist aspirations. Depots storing gas and fuel were camouflaged with green paint that made the storage tanks as anonymous as Swiss banks.

Thun was a shock for it was there that I encountered my first tourists.

Until then I had been in places other travellers do not reach. But in Thun's busy streets I came rucksack to rucksack with International Youth doing Europe on $25 a day.

It was like going back twenty years: the same gauche American girls, with orange nylon backpacks, looking lost in perpetuity; Australian women, coarser and beefier, with their harsh *I've been everywhere and learned not to get screwed by these bastards* look; the Japanese and South Koreans with optic luggage and bland smiles; Canadians sporting mapleleaf logos to disassociate themselves from their unpopular cousins south of the 49th Parallel.

It was my Englishness, I suppose, that disposed me to walk straight through Thun; a snobbish desire to distance myself from a generation just old enough to have been my own unrecognised offspring. And to tell the truth I felt somewhat silly. All that had gone before – the Moselle, Vosges, Jura – had already become a memory. Now I was just one tourist among many. Or was I? Tourists do not walk the entire length of the Lake of Thun. Tourists, clutching guidebooks, traipse in crocodiles around castles and go on excursions accompanied by multilingual guides. I was a traveller for whom such things held no interest. And feeling superior I strode out of Thun along the banks of the

Aare where dripping trippers were queuing for lake steamers.

After walking a kilometre I reached a lakeside park; but why were the gates locked? I rattled them and only the appearance of a growling Doberman convinced me that I was trying to break into a private residence.

Back in Thun I began again and chose a *wanderweg* that seduced me up a steep hill and through geranium-bedecked suburbs before depositing me back in more suburbs beside the lake. To hell with *wanderwegs*! I would choose my own route.

Beyond the houses the Lake of Thun spread its wares before me. Aquamarine water, solid as glass, fringed the lee bank and led my eyes across the choppy centre, where sailing boats heeled, to mountains rising above the far shores.

Contorted rock peaks, 4,000 or 5,000 feet high, were grey with a dusting of snow, while clouds shaped like Zeppelins floated above them. But the High Alps, which should have been visible rising beyond these outliers, were hidden by storms. No Wetterhorn, Schreckhorn, Eiger, Mönch or Jungfrau, although at Oberhofen I sat on a jetty beside a miniature castle and watched clouds falling like avalanches down the flanks of the Stockhorn.

The steep south-facing slopes above me were rusty with vineyards whose harvest had already been plucked. They were invariably covered with acres of blue plastic anti-bird netting although the number of sparrows and blackbirds trapped underneath had turned each vineyard into an aviary.

Beyond Merligen, a pretty village perched below a headland, the lakeshore is too precipitous for a road to squeeze between water and cliffs, and my way led me up and away from the green *See*.

Thinking the route straightforward I had not bothered to buy a detailed map of this stretch. Later I learned that *wanderwegs* lead around this section but I was ignorant and pushed on along the road, which took me into a series of short but scary tunnels which were not indicated on my map of Western Europe; not surprisingly, for Switzerland is only five centimetres wide.

Here it was a question of listening for traffic at the tunnel entrances and then running like billy-o towards the glow of daylight at the far end. The road between the tunnels was also perilous, its crash barriers – designed to stop vehicles plummeting into the abyss – preventing me from escaping from the tarmac when lorries swept by, spraying me with mud.

Interlaken, approached across a grassy plain ringed by mountains, induced a severe case of culture shock. If Thun had been a landlocked equivalent of Morecambe then Interlaken was Coney Island. There were hotdog stalls, cinemas, discos, a casino, and everywhere interrogative thoughts voiced by elderly Americans.

'Is this the station?' a woman asked outside the station as a train screeched to a halt beside her.

'Say, d'you think we can get a hamburger here?' said a man beside a stall with HAMBURGERS displayed in neon above his head.

Fiacres pulled by funereal plumed horses and driven by pissed off men in feathered hats bobbed by, their passengers mainly septuagenarian women whose blue rinses were crushed beneath see-through plastic rain gear. Air-conditioned coaches, complete with comfort stations, crawled behind them, their not-quite-so-affluent but equally elderly passengers staring out through smoked glass designed to diminish the sun's glare. In the drizzle the world, seen from within, must have seemed in the first throes of The Last Judgement. Interlaken is a centre for excursions, the most famous being the train ride up to the Jungfraujoch which, at 11,333 feet, involves a sudden yank into rarefied air. How many heart conditions, I wondered, were diagnosed by sudden death? And what did they do with the bodies? Airlift them off by helicopter or stash them in the luggage van?

Aged sixteen, and inspired by Heinrich Harrer's *The White Spider*, a friend and I had hitched to Interlaken, walked up to Alpiglen and camped under the Eiger's North Face. Innocent of all dangers we had climbed up the *firn* at its base but had been forced to retreat when we realised that stones, having fallen a vertical kilometre, were thudding like shrapnel into the snow all around us.

That night I had endured the second most terrifying alpine storm of my life – the worst, by far, being 10,000 feet up on the Gornergrat in a tent with my wife. There the earth had moved even though we had been in separate sleeping bags.

Below the Eiger lightning bolts had struck all around us, but despite discomfort we survived. On the North Face things were more serious. The next morning someone had lent me binoculars.

'See those two climbers up there?'

I had scanned the face and found two bright specks, like ladybirds, on an ice field.

'Yes, I see them.'

'They're dead.'

The man in the Interlaken tourist office had gone far beyond surliness. He was cracking up.

'A hotel room? Alone and you want a *hotel* room? You must be joking unless you've 100 francs to spare. There's the *Judendherberge* at Bönigen for people like you.'

I had not joined the Youth Hostel Association since my twenties but with my children in mind I had taken out family membership that spring. Luckily I had remembered to bring my card.

'How do I get there?'

'Take bus X. It runs every hour.'

Bus X was disappearing into the evening traffic, and so I walked the four kilometres to Bönigen, a village on the west shore of the Brienzersee.

Surging tourists, like a mob without a cause, blocked the pavements. Singed offal from hamburger joints scented the streets, while souvenir shop windows glittering with clocks and watches tempted the naive into buying highly dutiable mementoes.

The English must take much of the blame for initiating such vulgarity.

The Victoria-Jungfrau Hotel gleams like a monument to all the Grand Tourers who flocked to the Bernese Oberland with sketchbooks, wet-plate cameras and journals in which to record their impressions of the Reichenbach Falls and the peccadilloes of their fellow travellers. And their example is my excuse for recording what I saw as I walked to Bönigen.

I glanced up at the great U-shaped gap of the Lauterbrunnen Valley and watched mist scudding beyond its black cliffs. Suddenly I was aware of a stationary cloud stretching across the upper reaches like an immense white dam. But this dam was rent by horizontal cracks which became – as my eyes grew accustomed to the light – crevasses.

The Jungfrau was performing a dance of the seven veils, and after the final layer of gauze had been teasingly discarded I saw her naked. Her face and shoulders were delicately rouged by the setting sun while below the sun's reach she was as frigid as the Snow Queen, her flanks and hollows an inviolate desert of ice.

Although fifteen miles away the mountain filled my field of view, and despite *breathtaking*'s relegation to the basement of descriptive words it is the one which describes, perfectly, my physical reaction to this extraordinary revelation. Yes, it was only frozen water and rock, but on such a scale that I felt joyous.

I do not know why such sights can lift the spirit. It happens without warning like a child suddenly being hoisted aloft by his father. All I know is that it occurred.

Lower, and to the left, I saw the Brienzergrat, its blue ridge speckled with snow like albinotic splodges on a shark's back. Tomorrow would have been the day I tackled it and I was peeved to find it so seemingly accessible. The weather forecasters had exaggerated.

The youth hostel was run by a humorous chain-smoking matriarch who was the antithesis of all those prim wardens who had run the hostels of my memory with rods of iron.

As I queued to sign in a beautiful Japanese girl giggled like a geisha, a hand held like a fan over her mouth in an attempt to disguise her impoliteness.

'Why are you laughing?' I asked.

'Your socks,' she said. 'They look funny.'

Boots and shoes were *verboten* and everyone had to slot them into racks before treading the hostel's parquet floors. My socks were odd; blue and red.

'It's perfectly logical,' I explained. 'My left foot is slightly larger than my right and so I wear one sock on the left and two on the right.'

'Ah . . .'

I visualised a delightful evening stretching ahead of me; a shared fondue, sparkling wine, and a reappraisal of Kurosawa's films. But her boyfriend joined her and my fantasies crumbled.

I was assigned to a small dormitory where, on the bunks, five young steak-fed Americans were sitting like inmates in a penitentiary.

'Hello,' I said.

'Hi.'

And having dismissed me as an old fogey they continued a fundamental conversation based on their bible: a students' guide to Europe.

'I vote we go to Vienna the day after tomorrow.'

'OK, but let's take in Munich the day after.'

'Why?'

'*Oktoberfest*, you dummy.'

'OK. Vienna, Munich. Then where?'

'Amsterdam's cool. You can get grass no problem and it's legal.'

'How long've we got?'

'Flight leaves Gatwick on Monday week. That's what? Nine days?'

'OK. Vienna, Munich, Amsterdam. Then where?'

'Copenhagen maybe? I met a guy said the hostel's really neat.'

'I'd just love to visit Stockholm. You know what they say about Swedish girls.'

'Yeah. We could grab a student flight to London from there.'

'OK, but what about tonight?' Flicking of pages.

'It says here there's a real great disco.'

'Great! I'm gonna take a shower.'

'Me too. I'm tired of jerking off. I want some real action for a change.'

'Never know who you might meet.'

'More Americans?' I suggested.

'Whatsat?'

'Doesn't that book take you to places where you only meet a load of other Americans who've also bought it?'

'Yeah, but it's cool for a quick screw. Hell we don't speak no foreign crap and it cuts out the foreplay if you know what I mean.'

'Why are you all in such a hurry?'

'Gotta see it all, friend. Don't know when we'll be back.'

'What've you seen so far?'

'Italy, Greece, Yugoslavia.'

'Did you like Greece?'

'Mykonos was great. And Ios. One long party. You been to Mykonos?'

'Yes, before it was put in your book.'

'Say – you're English aren't you?'

'Yes.'

'No one's perfect.'

I have not attempted to differentiate one from another. Apart from varying hair colour and physiognomy there was nothing to choose between them. They spoke as one.

While cooking supper I was cooped up with a Manitoban who kept punishing the side of his head with vicious slaps.

I should have known better than to ask him if he was all right.

'You want to hear about my ears?'

'Well . . .'

'I don't mind talking about them. It's otitis. It's killing me and the medication's no damned good.'

'I'm sorry to hear it.'

'I'm supposed to be taking my daughter up to some goddamn hotel in the mountains tomorrow and I'm deeply concerned about the effects of altitude.'

'How high are you going?'

'A couple of thousand metres.'

'How old is your daughter?'

'Ten.'

'Then she should be all right.'

'Not her. Me! And there's snow forecast.'

'Go somewhere else then.'

'I promised her.'

'But if it's going to ruin your trip.'

'I'm not going to let my goddamn ears rule my life.'

'Put it off for a day or two.'

'That'd spoil our schedule. Anyway, I've already booked the goddamn room.'

'Why not see a doctor?'

'You kidding? Swiss doctors don't know shit.'

I pointed out that his pork steaks were burning. It was not meant as personal criticism but he turned on me.

'I'll cook the goddamn meat any way I choose. Any damned fool knows you can't take chances with pork.'

I lapsed into silence but he needed to talk.

'Where're you headed?'

'Rome.'

'Rome stinks.'

'All of it?'

'Take my word for it. Goddamn Italians. The country's falling apart.'

'You don't seem to think much of Europe.'

'Damn right I don't.'

'Why not go home?'

'Go home? I told you. We've got a schedule.'

In the dining room his gawky daughter sat alone with a can of Pepsi, her sad eyes staring back at her from the window.

Earlier I had phoned Basel. The elusive tent had finally arrived and I had decided to collect it. It would be my first rest-day since leaving Toul although the prospect of returning so far north filled me with unease. It would take only two hours for the train to whisk me to a point beyond the Jura; almost as far north as Belfort. Six days in 120 minutes.

As I lay on my bunk I wondered how things might have been had I stuck to the original route. I would have been in Schangau with the Brienzergrat ahead of me. Perhaps it was not too late? Why not fetch my tent, return to Langnau, and get back on Belloc's route? And with this plan in mind I fell asleep.

Interlaken to Interlaken

I woke to a strange yellowish light shining through the dormitory window.

Climbing down from my bunk I stepped over a snoring American who had fallen on to the floor, rubbed a porthole in the condensation, and looked out.

Overnight there had been a heavy fall of snow to within 200 metres of the valley floor.

I dressed quickly and walked across a meadow to a lake white with reflections. Not a ripple disturbed its surface although spindrift was blowing from the ridges of the Brienzergrat which had been magnified threefold, its steep slopes as impressive as the Jungfrau had seemed the previous evening.

My decision to bypass this mountain had been justified, for only a fool would have attempted it alone in such conditions. I would not be returning to Langnau.

But my complacency was short-lived; for this myopic way of travelling confines one's concentration to immediate problems. I had been so concerned with the Brienzergrat that I had forgotten all about the Grimsel Pass which would lead me towards Italy. Would it still be open?

But there was nothing I could do about the weather, and meanwhile I would take a day trip to Basel.

Back in the hostel the Manitoban was pouring muesli. Bottles of vitamins were arranged in a row, like spices, beside the bowls.

'Goddamn snow. I just phoned the hotel and they said don't try it. They said there're cliffs and we could go over.'

'Your daughter must be disappointed.'

Daughter, obviously relieved that her route-march had been cancelled, was looking as blissfully happy as any child with her father could.

'At least you won't have to worry about your ears.'

'Didn't sleep a wink all night.'

He looked wonderfully rested.

'What will you do instead?'

'How the hell do I know? Take a boat ride maybe. Christ, I wish I was back in Winnipeg.'

I found it hard to believe that anyone would return voluntarily to Winnipeg, which is nothing but an oasis of concrete in a Sahara of wheat. The city fathers have turned a rubbish dump into a mountain 100 feet high which the more adventurous citizens can drive up at night to observe the street lamps not so far below. And when this palls they can cruise the poorer quarters and watch the pathetic remnants of indigenous Indian tribes falling down drunk in the gutters. Mind you, Winnipeg is not as bad as Medicine Hat. Nowhere is as bad as Medicine Hat.

The extraordinary railway carriage I boarded had been converted into a playground complete with uniformed nanny. Everything was painted in primary colours. Toddlers hung like monkeys from a climbing frame, slid down a spiralling slide, or cuddled soft toys, while outside they had a fairy-tale landscape to watch.

Accompanied by children's laughter I sped along the southern shore of the Lake of Thun, and while we followed a long curve I looked back and saw the entire Bernese Oberland, as white as dogs' teeth, rising from a jawbone of icy outliers; the canine Eiger, Mönch and Schreckhorn, and the pitted molar of the Wetterhorn.

But their position at the bottom of a vast page of blue sky diminished them, and en masse they seemed no more impressive than a fold-out panorama from a guidebook.

How luxurious it was to sit in a comfortable seat and watch the world passing at one and a half kilometres per minute.

Across the lake I could see memories of yesterday's route, which had taken me half a day, and I realised that by taking a train from Basel I could be in Rome by midnight.

I dozed, and awoke an hour later as we pulled into a sunny station. A magnificent castle was gleaming on a hill. What a shame, I thought, that I had not passed through such a delightful place. And then I read the station sign. I was back in Burgdorf.

A tunnel burrows under the Jura and I entered Basel suffering from severe train-lag.

Basel must have much to offer a tourist but I only saw the street leading from the station to the post office and back. This day trip had been a mistake. It had altered my perception of time and distance and my only desire was to return to the simplicity of rambling. For a day I had become like the Americans in the hostel. I had seen everything but nothing and longed for slow movement.

From the train forests had been forests. On foot they were a beech followed by a chestnut followed by a birch. From the train I saw no birds. On foot I watched woodpeckers and buzzards and finches. On the train I stopped only at stations. On foot I could stop anywhere I wished.

And so, clutching my new tent, I took the first train back to Interlaken, where I spent the entire afternoon lazing in the sun by the lake, watching cloud shadows sliding up the snowy slopes of the Brienzergrat, feeding bread to fishes, and listening to the wake from passing steamers slapping against the shore.

That night the hostel was silent with a score of South Korean students.

Back in the dormitory I found one of the Americans excavating his toenails.

'Hi,' he said.

'Hello. Good day?'

'Yeah. Took the train up the Jung-Freud Jock.'

'Tell me about it.'

'You mean you haven't been there?'

'I can't afford it.'

'It's only $100.'

'How was it?'

'It was great.'

'In what way?'

'Really great. You know?'

'I don't know. Tell me.'

He simulated thought for a moment. 'Like it's real high. You know?'

'The Empire State Building's very high but it's not the Jungfraujoch.'

He studied the pile of green toenail dirt on a Kleenex and said, 'You know something? You snotty English can really get up my nose.'

At least he was finally expressing an opinion.

During a six-month stay in North America I came across a major social problem: niceness. Everyone was so nice to me that I left without knowing who had liked me and who had loathed my guts. I have a tendency – some would say a flaw – to speak my mind, and I would become infuriated when, having vehemently disagreed with someone during the course of a conversation, he or she would revert to stock phrases such as 'Maybe you've got a point there' or 'Everyone has a right to his opinion and I respect that' instead of defending their points of view.

That is why I made no enemies in America, and few friends.

Interlaken to Handegg

As I walked out of Interlaken I heard church bells echoing across the Lake of Brienz whose southern shore was still pencilled with shadows.

An old couple, dressed in their Sunday best, parted to let me squeeze past them on the narrow path. The man raised his hat, and the woman, who moved arthritically, smiled gracefully. A well-thumbed missal, which she clutched to her bosom, was wrapped in a sandwich bag while her wooden rosary was wound like a bracelet around a claw-like wrist and hand.

Belloc might have made much of such a meeting: each rosary bead a symbolic drop of Jesuit martyrs' blood or the Virgin's tears as she interceded on behalf of all God-fearing European Christians.

I saw it differently.

When young I was forced to recite countless rosaries which, for me, epitomised the sheer boredom of repetitive Catholic ritual. Litanies came a close second. And as I grew older even the mass became nothing more than bad theatre. The acting was invariably lousy, the costumes garish, movement minimal and wooden, and the script, in Latin, incomprehensible.

For years I was a spear-carrier in these productions, and with various cues to follow my concentration was confined to getting through to the final curtain without making a hash of things. But as soon as my altar boy days were over I joined the audience.

I had always been a secret admirer of doubting Thomas, and like him I was more concerned with the tangible. It was not the mass but my fellow onlookers who interested me, not least the pretty parishioner with whom, aged ten, I fell madly in love. I am not the first, nor will I be the last, to thank Catholicism for inculcating a humanistic approach to the world.

And so I did not see the old lady and her rosary as Faith personified. For me the encounter only served to highlight the power of Rome and its manipulation of those who, by accidents of birth, have been press-ganged into accepting the Pope's shilling.

When I read of missionaries successfully spreading the Gospel According To Our Interpretation it always amazes me how they got away with it.

Imagine John Smith, fresh from his seminary and feverish with zeal, paddling his kayak into unexplored jungle and meeting the chief of a tribe who, hitherto, has had no contact with the White Man.

'What exactly do you believe?' asks Smith, having miraculously picked up the Twala language as quickly as an apostle in a shuttered room.

'Well,' says Chief Ignatius (having been provisionally baptised by Smith's cunning ruse of accidentally spilling water over the Chiefs forehead during a meal of *tzungo* – human brain – which Smith, inadvertently high on *psombe*, has confused with *tsungo* which is hyena liver), 'our basic beliefs are simple. The world was created by the Great Spirit Zd whose Being we see in every Living Thing – from the great elephant to the humble penguin-louse to Man himself. Zd lives on Mount Zhwbswi, far across the savannah, and when we die our ancestors welcome us to the fertile Valley of Ozim where we dwell under the protection of Zd who ensures that there are always enough bison to provide us with meat and always sufficient snow with which to build our igloos and always *bhwzi* wood to make our boomerangs. There!'

Smith, filled with righteous indignation, replies, 'Now you listen to me Chief! And listen good! There is no Zd. There's only God. G-O-D. God! And He, or rather they – for there are three of them in one including a Holy Ghost – sent His son who is – was – one of them into the world, born of a virgin, where he did all sorts of amazing things like walking on water and raising the dead. And then he was killed but didn't die and so he ascended into heaven – which is a little like your Valley of Ozim only different. And when you die you'll go there too – but only if you're good. If you're bad you'll burn in eternal flames in a place called Hell, which is run by an ex-angel called Satan. Now then! Doesn't that sound altogether more reasonable?'

The Chief thinks for a moment, then says, 'My Zd! What a fool I've been all these years! No more will I speak with a forked tongue, *bwana*. Death to Zd! Long live God!'

And donning a pair of Y-fronts supplied from Smith's Gladstone bag he leaps into the kraal and persuades his people, by sheer force of argument, to embrace Christianity.

Or something along those lines.

Chestnut leaves crackled underfoot as I followed paths, then the road, along the northern shore of the Lake of Brienz.

Scenically it was hardly different from my stroll along the Lake of Thun although today the sun was shining, the sky was blue, and I was full of renewed vitality after my day of rest. And when I reached Brienz I had the added encouragement of knowing that I was back on Belloc's path.

Sitting on a tombstone I glanced up at the Brienzergrat's gleaming roof of snow and felt glad to be alive and amongst men, for although Brienz is a tourist town it is a pretty place with a promenade beside the green lake where families strolled prior to eating an early Sunday lunch in one of the waterside restaurants. I was a figure in a postcard and content to be nothing more.

Belloc's route has many disadvantages, the main one being that at no point does it touch the sea. But sitting in the churchyard at Brienz I could imagine I was beside the ocean, a fjord perhaps, with the Faulhorn range rising majestically above the far shore.

Haze hid the highest peaks but I did not mind; for sheer wilderness can be dreadfully dull, and generally I prefer landscape where the human touch is evident. When camping in the Rocky Mountains I had found them uninspiring despite their objective grandeur. All those billions of trees; a world before or after mankind. A world custom-made for misanthropes.

Forgetting to eat, I followed the curve of the lake and then took a road beside the Aare which was now little more than a stream rushing between levees. And although the mountains rose steeply all around, my way was level and took me through the little villages of Unterthis and Unterthat whose houses were still bright with flowers despite the cold autumnal nights. No doubt the windowsills inside were already nurseries for geranium cuttings in preparation for the following spring.

At Meiringen the road begins its climb to the Grimsel Pass, and as it was not yet two o'clock I decided to continue for a few kilometres more.

The sun still shone although there were mares' tails in the southern sky.

In the main square I saw a bus station and entered the office to check the weather, since my map told me that the pass was closed from October to May.

'Is the Grimsel open?' I asked.

'It is today, but heavy snow is forecast for tonight.'

'Will it be open tomorrow?'

The man shrugged. 'Maybe, but I cannot guarantee it. The post bus leaves for Andermatt at 2.30. You had better take that.'

'But I want to walk over.'

'You're too late. Winter is early in the mountains this year.'

I weakened. Was it better to choose the bus and at least see the Grimsel or risk having to take a train through a tunnel into Italy?

'You want a ticket?'

The people in the square were casting black shadows but I knew that alpine weather is unpredictable in a predictable way.

'All right. A ticket to Andermatt.'

If the weather held I would at least be able to walk from Andermatt over the St Gotthard into the Ticino Valley. I remembered Belloc and his defeat on the Gries Pass when, in June, a blizzard had forced him to retreat. But it was small consolation.

With the bus ticket burning a hole in my pocket I sat outside a bar and ordered beer. I remembered my wife's words. 'You're not bloody Belloc. You're *you*. You

166

mustn't be a slave to what he did.' But it was no good. I felt belittled even though I had not made Belloc's solemn vow – which he broke – to 'take advantage of no wheeled thing'.

At 2.20 I sauntered back to the square where my bus awaited, its smartly uniformed driver standing stiffly beside it like a waxwork figure.

Then I saw the tourist office. Clutching at straws I went inside and asked their opinion.

Yes, there was snow forecast.

'When?'

'Tonight.'

'Could you phone and ask for an exact forecast?'

'If you insist, but it's a waste of time.'

The minutes ticked by, and through the window I could see the driver getting into the bus, but eventually the man got through to the meteorological office.

'There's a chance,' he said. 'There's a possibility that the snow won't arrive until tomorrow afternoon – but only a slight chance.'

It was all I needed. I ran across to the bus station. 'I want to change my ticket.'

'To where?'

I glanced at my map. Two thousand feet below the Grimsel Pass there is a place called Handegg. If the snow held off I would get up early and use the weather window to walk over the pass. 'Handegg, please.' And with seconds to spare I boarded the bus.

The road rose immediately, causing my ears to click, taking me past pine-clad crags and into a claustrophobic black valley where the sun can seldom shine. The villages were no longer pretty but functional; the homes, I suppose, of those involved with forestry and hydroelectric schemes.

The sudden ugliness jarred, reminding me of similar towns in the English Pennines where the exploitation of natural resources has created similar little hells amongst the hills.

I recalled Gerard Manley Hopkins' poem 'God's Grandeur', particularly the lines:

'And all is seared with trade; bleared, smeared with toil;
And wears man's smudge and shares man's smell: the soil
Is bare now, nor can foot feel, being shod.'

Above Guttannen the Aare was a raging torrent and the cliffs rose so vertically that I could not see their tops. It was wild, wild, country and I looked forward to arriving in Handegg; for a community built so high in this desolation must certainly be a singular place.

The bus stopped in the middle of nowhere. No doubt some farmer would get off and tramp through the stunted pines to a hut built high among the rocks. But no one moved. The driver turned.

'Handegg,' he informed me.

I descended, retrieved my rucksack from the hold, and watched the bus disappearing beyond a crag.

Where was Handegg? A track led up to a large building. Handegg must lie beyond. Shivering, I followed the track to the edifice, which became a hotel. Beyond there was nothing. No village. No road. Only mountains.

Vans were parked outside, and men were loading them with boxes.

In reception a girl seemed surprised to see me. 'Yes?'

Although the hotel was obviously way beyond my means I thought I should go through the motions and ask the price of a room.

'There are no rooms. We're closing in half an hour.'

'Why?'

'Snow. The season's over.'

It looked as though I would have to camp, and I was just about to ask if she could recommend a site when she said, 'I suppose you could always stay in the hut.'

'Anywhere.'

'You'll have to pay in advance. I'm leaving.'

Thinking Handegg would have a shop I had bought no food. 'How about dinner?'

'Impossible. No staff.'

'Breakfast?'

'I suppose we can leave you something.'

She gave me a set of keys and told me where to find the hut. My accommodation, reached by crossing a pasture where dwarfish horses grazed, was the musty, windowless, upper floor of a byre converted into a climbers' dormitory. Shelves, separated by wooden partitions, provided stalls on which bare mattresses were laid. None were occupied.

I dumped my gear and returned to the hotel where I persuaded a waitress to sell me several bottles of beer. And clutching my clinking dinner I returned to the empty hut. Outside, logs had been arranged around open fireplaces, now piles of wet ash, where mountaineers must have spent jolly summer evenings carousing. Again I was left with evidence of how things might have been, and I sat swigging beer while a breeze caused a nearby clump of pines to swish and creak.

I went for a stroll, choosing a *bergweg* that meandered along a cliff edge overlooking the valley. The way was marked by parallel red and white stripes, like war paint on the cheeks of boulders, and I wondered how walkers could possibly find their way in snow.

But in the golden evening light snowfall seemed an abstraction, even though, to the east, I could see green crevasses slitting the Aerlengletscher spilling from the ridges of the icy Ritzlihorn.

I sat on a granite seat in the gods of a great theatre. The stage was a perfect setting for *Prometheus*, with colossal slabs rising, unbroken, 600 to 900 metres from the bed of the Aare. Such smooth rock, I thought, would be impossible to climb, but I was wrong. There, on these burnished west-facing slabs, were several infinitesimal figures, so far away that the ropes linking them were imperceptible.

It was far too late to complete a climb, but they must have been using the face merely for practice, for as the shadows rose they began to abseil on their invisible threads, stopping every so often at pitons before continuing jerkily like spiders down a wall.

I hoped that they might join me later but they must have been weekend climbers, bank clerks from Bern or secretaries from Thun compensating for their five days of deskbound mortality with two of fire-stealing insolence.

Later, beside the road, I found a notice board with the *bergweg* leading to the Grimsel Pass marked on a crude map. I copied it into my notebook as best I could, and returned to my hut, passing a hotel without guests or a glimmer of illumination.

An icy windfall was already pouring from the glacier, which, in the feeble starlight, looked as white and wrinkled as a frozen corpse.

By seven I was asleep, but haunted in nightmares by climbers who had spent their last nights where I slept. Dreams that are enacted in the place where the dreamer sleeps are the worst, for the edge between reality and make-believe is not blurred by displacement.

Faces, hideously injured, stared down at me with dead eyes and I could feel their blood seeping through the sleeping bag on to my skin.

I woke up and the undead shuffled to their beds where they continued to stare at me malevolently. A head, cleanly severed, lay on the pine floor, its mouth moving, oozing gore.

I woke up, grateful to find that dawn had broken, although the door would not open. I kicked it down and saw that it was raining and that the rain was blood.

I woke up and heard rain battering on the roof.

It was only 11 p.m. but all thought of returning to such dreams persuaded me to remain awake.

I opened the door but cold driving rain lashed my face and the pines moaned in the wind.

I stayed awake all night, my nerves on edge. In the dark corners of the hut I imagined movement, and shone my torch, but there was nothing there.

At around 3 a.m. a noise like a rock avalanche prompted me to rush to the door, and as I opened it lightning flashed off the glacier above me.

The storm increased in ferocity, and I lay like a child with my sleeping bag pulled over my head while the thunder echoed across the valley. At least I could not see the lightning, and by 5 a.m. I finally succumbed to sleep.

Belloc had spent a night in a 'very expensive' hotel somewhere in this vicinity; possibly the same one, for there is no other habitation nearby. And these upper reaches of the Aare had had a disquieting effect on him too, for he had awoken twice, 'suddenly, staring at darkness . . . and I was full of terrors'.

A coincidence? I suppose it must have been.

Handegg to Airolo

Beep-beep-beep-beep-beep went my watch alarm at six.
Outside, in the pre-dawn light, I saw snow plastering
the rocks only about 60 metres above me while the slabs
where I had observed the climbers were awash, the
gullies bordering them having become waterfalls many
times the height of Niagara, the upper ledges marbled
with snow.

William Wordsworth wrote a poem about the
Handegg waterfalls; not those I saw, but the ones that
form a permanent feature of the Aare below this face:

'From the fierce aspect of this river throwing
His giant body o'er the steep rock's brink,
Back in astonishment and fear we shrink . . .'

And so it continues without flowing any more smoothly,
putting me in mind of another poetic William: William
McGonagall.

I had not eaten for twenty-four hours, and I made
my way past bedraggled horses to the hotel which I
entered via a side door. By torchlight I searched the
dining room, which was empty although racks of wine
and a selection of brandy had been left in place for next
year's itinerant clientele; for this was no ski chalet, the
slopes around being far too steep. The bottles could
have been mine for the taking but theft is not a habit of
mine, and I continued along a dark corridor to the bar
where I found food awaiting me like a meal on the *Mary
Celeste*.

Having eaten cheese and jam, and having drunk coffee from a thermos, I slipped away from this hotel whose crew had already taken to the lifeboats.

My path seemed clear enough, but as it rose I met wet snow and became confused. I could not see the telltale marks on the rocks, and with only my rough sketch to guide me I lost my way.

Above me I could see white cliffs rising into a yellow sky, and I watched as a squall, trapped in the ravine, came at me.

My anorak and overtrousers flapped like sails as I turned my back on the horizontally driven snow and at that point I decided to retreat, following my footsteps back to the hotel which remained just below the snow-line.

A timetable on a post told me that a bus was due at 8.30, and although I doubted its arrival I waited, for the only alternative was to return to Meiringen.

Men with less imagination and a surfeit of testosterone might have taken to the road, but in spite of wearing every stitch of clothing I possessed I was already shivering uncontrollably and nothing, apart from companionship, would have induced me to attempt it.

At 8.30, to the minute, the post bus arrived and I bought a ticket to Andermatt.

'You'll have to change at the Grimsel,' the driver told me.

'Will the bus get through?'

He tapped the steering wheel. 'No problem.'

I sat adjacent to the only other passengers, an elderly man and woman sitting forward nervously in their seats.

'You English?' the man asked.

'Yes.'

'Well hi! I'm Louis and this lovely lady's my wife Pattie.'

We shook hands.

'Excuse me for asking,' asked Louis, 'but where the hell did you come from?'

'I spent the night here in a hut.'

'Well isn't that something?'

Louis and Pattie had stepped straight out of a canvas by Grant Wood. They were from some small town in Illinois and were staying at Meiringen. That day they had decided to take a bus over the mountains and then catch a train back.

'We've got a pass which means we can go anywhere for free,' explained Pattie, 'but I've got to admit we're a little worried about the weather. D'you reckon this bus'll get us over OK?'

'I'm sure they wouldn't risk it if there was any doubt.'

They seemed reassured, but as the road rose around snow-encrusted hairpins I began to share their concern. At every blind corner the driver slowed to walking pace and hooted his klaxon while his windscreen wipers, going full tilt, could hardly cope with snow which had suddenly become a blizzard.

The Räterichsbolensee, the lake around which my path would have taken me, was a desolate stretch of flinty water flecked with whitecaps, and the far shore – where it was visible between squalls – was a featureless white wasteland where verticals and horizontals had become indistinguishable. Had I attempted it in such Antarctic conditions then I might, like Captain Oates, have been gone some time.

The Grimselsee is hidden from below by a hideous dam. Dammed valleys are invariably ugly, their natural features arbitrarily sliced by a plane of water. And because the level rises and falls at the flick of a switch there is always an intertidal zone, like scum around a bath, where nothing can grow.

Postcards tell me that on a clear day the snout of the Unteraargletscher would have been visible, but in my album of memories there is nothing but a grey picture with a grey frame on a grey page.

Only one passenger boarded the bus at the Grimsel Hospice; a soldier with an automatic rifle and a silver crucifix dangling from a pierced ear.

More hairpins took us up to the pass, where the full force of the gale hit us, causing the bus to veer.

The driver halted outside a restaurant and told me that I should change here for Andermatt.

I asked where he was going.

'Airolo.'

'Via where?'

Louis explained. 'We're supposed to be going over the Nufenen Pass, but it's a thousand feet higher than this one.'

'Can I use my ticket to Airolo?' I asked the driver.

'No problem,' replied the driver who went in search of a coffee, his nonchalance just a little too showy.

I followed, not for a coffee but to see what lay outside, for the windows were opaque with driven snow.

It was awful. Apart from a couple of bleak bars there was nothing to see but snowdrifts and a terrible stretch of black water into which the swirling snowflakes hissed. The Totensee, the Lake of the Dead, would appeal enormously to necrophiles – and here I am using

176

the word as Erich Fromm does, to differentiate such people from biophiles, or lovers of life. But for me it was as seductive as a cadaver. They should run trips on this lake – get an old man to dress up as Charon and ferry tourists to an Underworld theme park on the other side.

Louis tapped me on the shoulder. 'Lake Michigan can be pretty damn depressing, but I've seen nothing to beat this.'

He was wearing slacks, a tartan shirt, and a pair of slip-on shoes. His socks were already saturated and his silver hair made the snowflakes settling on his head look dingy.

'Would you do me a favour?' I asked. 'Would you take my picture?' I thought I should have evidence.

'Sure,' he said, and with his back to the wind he snapped me, his bare fingers already blue with cold.

'You'd better get back in the bus,' I said.

'I guess I better had at that.'

I enjoyed our descent into the Rhône Valley. The drops were frightful but fun, and this ride was the nearest I have come to flying on land. There was nothing I could do but trust the pilot and so I might as well enjoy the view.

He took the hairpins wide and I could look straight down into the next loop 30 metres or more below. At least there was no chance of a collision, for no one else was foolhardy enough to be on the road.

The temperature had drawn a green contour on the mountains. One moment it was snow, the next rain, and we continued to wind through firs and pines until we met the torrential Rhône and a succession of riverside ghost villages; their shutters closed, their streets brown puddles, and even their geraniums reduced to stalks.

At Ulrichen, a dismal railway town, the soldier sloped off and disappeared into the downpour. No one took his place. The driver swivelled in his seat and said, 'Usually we stop here for food but with the weather the way it is I think it would be wiser to carry on.'

As we began to climb again I chatted to Louis and Pattie. He was a retired salesman, his field agricultural machinery. Pattie had taught in school, before having children, and had not returned to the profession.

'We come here every year at the same time,' he explained. 'It's cheaper out of season,' added Pattie, 'but we've never known it quite so cold before.'

'Why Switzerland?'

'You been to Illinois?' asked Louis.

'Once.'

'Then you'll know it's as flat as a floor.'

'It's the mountains we come for,' said Pattie.

'And the people?' I asked. 'How do they strike you?'

'Oh they're nice enough,' said Louis, 'but a little, well . . .'

'Uptight,' supplied Pattie, using a word probably added to her vocabulary by grown-up children.

'Have you ever been to England?' I asked.

'Hell, no!' said Louis, laughing. 'It's always raining there.'

Waterfalls fell, streams streamed, and the gusting rain returned to snow.

For some kilometres the road followed a treeless, V-shaped valley resembling a Scottish glen. This isn't so bad, I thought, but then we took to the air, zigzagging up a series of hairpins that made the Grimsel seem like

Primrose Hill. Perhaps the Nufenen is little used and consequently undeserving of funds, but with uncharacteristic inefficiency the Swiss have neglected to install safety barriers.

A snowplough, its yellow beacon flashing like a crash tender's, was the only vehicle we saw for an hour or more. And as we ascended in the unpressurised bus this second sudden change in altitude made me feel woozy. Pattie was not looking too bright either, but no oxygen masks popped out of the luggage rack – even at 8,000 feet – and we sat limply in our seats while we descended through clouds towards our landing at Airolo.

At one point we were only three or four kilometres from the Italian border. In summer a pleasant stroll would have taken me over the Gries Pass into real Italy instead of the Canton of Ticino which is a hybrid, hanging like an udder from Switzerland's underbelly.

Snow and fog filled the barren Bedretto Valley as far as the outskirts of Airolo, where, to the north, the roofs of the St Gotthard road snake down the mountainside like ugly ribbon development.

I said farewell to Louis and Pattie by the monument erected in memory of the men killed during the construction of the St Gotthard Tunnel.

'You really sleeping here?' asked Louis.

'Why not?'

Louis cast his eyes around the rainy town and its reservoir. 'Rather you than me.'

European station buffets are good places to eat if you want quantity rather than quality, and using basic German I asked the waitress in Airolo for a menu.

She frowned and, to my surprise, answered in Italian. That is the trouble with travelling on wheels. Of course

I should have realised that the Nufenen Pass had crossed a stony wall separating German from Italian Switzerland, but I had arrived too quickly and was unprepared for this cultural shift. Nevertheless I was cheered by this change, for I had finally encountered the last of the three languages paving my route.

As I drank wine and ate pasta I listened to customers conversing, and found their southern timbre to my taste; lilting strings and woodwind after the brass and percussion that had accompanied me all the way from Glovelier in the Jura. But my pleasure was short-lived.

The doors were flung open and The North gusted in.

The two middle-aged German men epitomised health, wealth and self-confidence.

The first, Protein, dumped his rucksack, stripped off his anorak and overtrousers, and stood like a still from *Health and Efficiency*: his hands on his hips; his bronzed thighs and calves all rigid sinew and muscle; his shorts tightly belted around a concave stomach.

His companion, Vitamin, was stockier with powerful shoulders and a bald head as brown as leather.

They sat opposite, ordered mineral water charmlessly, and studied a map on which Protein marked their route with a biro.

After a while Protein glanced at me; or rather at my boots and rucksack.

'Guten Tag!' I said.

'English?' he asked.

Of course he and Vitamin spoke perfect English. They were professional men, a dentist and an accountant, walking from Locarno to their home in

Freiburg. They had just arrived from Biasca, the town I was hoping to reach the next day.

'It's terrible weather for walking,' I said.

'If you don't like rain then you should stay at home and watch TV,' Protein advised.

Obviously I had missed the whole point of walking. Its aim was not to enjoy but to endure.

'Are you planning to walk over the Alps?' I asked.

'You don't think we would take the tunnel?' said Vitamin.

'There's been a heavy fall of snow a little higher up the valley.'

'What do you expect in the Alps?' said Protein. 'Palm trees?'

Vitamin thought this remark hilarious, and flashed his perfect teeth.

'I simply thought I'd mention it.'

Protein blew his nose and examined his snot for omens. Fortunately I had finished my meal.

'Where are you going?' asked Vitamin.

'Rome.'

'By train?'

'On foot.'

Vitamin rose and lifted my rucksack with ease. 'It is much too heavy,' he informed me.

'It's not illegal, is it? I mean, I'm not breaking some weight restriction, am I?'

'No, but it is stupid to carry so much. It will slow you down.'

'I'm not in a race. Besides I've got used to it.'

'You tourists are all the same,' said Protein. 'You cannot bear to travel without all the comforts of home.'

Vitamin said something cryptic in German and they laughed.

'So where have you come from?' asked Protein.

'Narvik.'

'In Norway?'

'Is there another?'

'On foot?'

'Every step of the way.'

'But it is north of the Arctic Circle. How long has it taken you?'

What, I wondered, would sound unreasonable but feasible? 'Three months.'

It worked. The supermen lapsed into silence.

I paid my bill, picked up my rucksack with one hand, and said, 'How much further are you going today?'

'We are staying here tonight,' answered Protein.

'But you've only come from Biasca.'

'Only?' said Protein. 'It is over thirty kilometres.'

'I suppose thirty kilometres will seem a long way to me one day,' I said. '*Auf Wiedersehen!*'

Belloc praised Airolo for its wine and songs, but that evening, as I tramped from bar to dingy bar, I found no songs; only a succession of TVs with the same blaring film stifling all conversation.

A Rambo lookalike was busy slaughtering lemmings played by oriental extras. It was a truly international film for there was no dialogue, merely grunts, groans, and screams – and that was the music. But the producer was no fool. He knew that even morons would switch off if the killings and maimings continued for more than 20 minutes at a stretch, and so, like a composer varying the mood of a concerto, he had slipped an *adagio* in between the *con furores*: a rape scene shot in slow motion.

Certain idealistic politicians continue to strive for a United States of Europe, but in many ways it already exists in social and political terms. Everywhere is the same. Only the architecture is different. Even the diversity of language loses its importance when words, written and spoken, are becoming redundant.

Why go to all the trouble of reading or listening when comic book culture, living in outer space, can be enticed into houses via clever dishes? Pictures are immediate, and the media people do not have to worry about confusing the average viewer; for there is no such thing as a polysyllabic picture.

I happened to be in Airolo but it could have been almost any small town anywhere in Western Europe. Certainly anywhere in Britain on a rainy autumn night with a spot of sex and violence on the telly.

Once I was in a shop when a man brought in a hired video. The cover displayed sections of female anatomy in the style of the photographs one finds in books about meat cookery. The video was called *Famous Bums and Tits* (really) and the man caught sight of me perusing it:

'What's the matter, mate?' he said. 'Don't you approve or somefink?'

'It's entirely up to you what you watch.'

'Too right. It's a free fuckin' country.'

Of course he was wrong, but he knew his rights.

Airolo to Bellinzona

Rain from a broken gutter splashed on to the balcony below my room, and the headlights of lorries on the *autostrada* were the only non-monochromatic items in my field of vision.

Many alpine valleys have been ruined by modern transport requirements, and the upper Ticino Valley, known as the Leventina, is a case in point. Three routes vie for position; the old road, the railway, and the *autostrada*. There is an alternative: the high level route, a footpath linking villages perched on the northern slopes. Had the weather been fair I would have chosen this way, but the prospect of struggling through fog and heavy rain did not appeal, and I took the old road that Belloc had followed.

A tunnel led me out of Airolo and into the valley where I expected to find charming Italianate villages. But all the places through which I passed were unattractive little towns dominated by factories and timberyards, their wooden houses run down and streaked with damp.

Two sodden hours brought me to Rodi-Fiesco, a town perched on a shelf in the valley. At least the walking had been downhill although the constant rumble of traffic on the *autostrada*, never far away, had become as irritating as an inaccessible itch.

Beyond Rodi-Fiesco a long tunnel burrows through a bluff. Galleries, cut every few hundred metres, overlook the Ticino as it plunges through a wild granite gorge, but I did not linger in these galleries for the combination of carbon monoxide, claustrophobia, cold, and a desire for daylight lured me on towards the exit at whose mouth I stood, shivering, watching a curtain of water falling on to the road.

Hairpin bends led down towards Faido, and here I fell ill. I was not merely cold and wet but saturated, and my shuddering became as regular as the bleeps on a cardiograph.

Sheltering in the lee of a boulder I waited for the rain to ease but it became even more intense, the drops rising like miniature fountains from the road below me. My hands were shaking so violently that I could not open a side-pocket where I had put a Mars bar, and when I began talking to myself, trying to calm my fears, I realised that my speech was slurred. This, I knew, could be a symptom of hypothermia. I had to find warmth, but how?'

Walk fast. Find a barn, a bus stop. Anything. Anything to get out of the rain.

It did not even occur to me that the solution – tent and sleeping bag – was on my back.

Retching like a dog I strode along the road, and when I heard a vehicle approaching I broke a vow and stuck out a thumb, but the lorry accelerated and I cursed it with every expletive I knew.

Large Swiss cars, empty apart from their drivers, swished by, and for a while I imagined I was in Wales, which is the worst country in the world – apart from Bulgaria – for hitchhiking.

My legs were beginning to wobble when I saw a tiny orange Fiat approaching, its unsynchronised windscreen wipers conducting different tunes.

I raised my thumb and the car screeched to a halt. It had Italian plates and was driven by an elderly man with his rotund wife sitting beside him.

'Get in!' she said, and I scrambled into a rear seat designed for dwarves where I sat with my rucksack wedged between roof and knees.

'Thank you,' I said. 'Are you going to Biasca?'

'Yes. You are English?'

'Yes.'

'I speak English too. My sister is a chaperone in England. Chichester. Very important family. Very big house. Very rich. I stay there one month.'

'Where are you going now?'

'Home. To Como. You want to go there?'

The temptation was intense. 'Biasca will do fine.'

'Why do you want to go to Biasca? There is nothing in Biasca. Como is much better. A beautiful lake. Sunshine. Good food. Good wine.'

'No. Really. I want to stay in Biasca.'

'OK. If you want.'

My sponge-like presence had already fogged up all the windows by the time we unexpectedly swung off the old road and on to the *autostrada*. I could see nothing but spray through the windscreen and I wondered how the husband could drive at 120 k.p.h. without aquaplaning us into oblivion.

Ridiculously soon we passed the slip road to Biasca.

'Biasca?' I said.

The woman admonished her husband who took his hands off the steering wheel to remonstrate.

'Will Bellinzona be OK?' she asked.

Accident had deprived me of half a day's march; but what the hell? If I was going to be seriously ill then I wanted a place with serious hospitals and seriously trained doctors. Bellinzona would do fine.

I did not want to talk. I wanted to die. But the kind woman insisted on chatting.

She continued until we reached the Bellinzona turn-off where the husband braked sharply, almost causing a pile-up.

I said goodbye to these generous people, and just as I was about to close the door the woman thrust a tube of sweets into my hand.

'*Ciao!*'

'*Ciao!*'

'*Buon viaggio!*'

A toot and they were gone.

Slopping through rain I passed the Bellinzona Municipal Camp Site; a large brown puddle occupied by a rusting Bedford van with GB plates. An awning had been improvised over the rear doors where two men, wearing khaki shorts and shaggy beards, were cooking something – baked beans probably – over a Gaz stove. I was not tempted to pay them a visit.

It was only one o'clock when I reached the town centre, but as soon as I found a room I crawled into my sleeping bag, covered myself with a duvet, and lay flapping like a flat-fish on the deck of a North Sea trawler. In England I would have called a doctor, but I was too exhausted and feverish to move and soon, nursed by an overdose of paracetamols, I fell asleep.

It was still light – just – when I awoke and although I was still feeling queasy I put on dry clothes and went out into the town.

Even the torrential rain could not detract from Bellinzona's charm, and I walked its ancient arcades searching for the ornate doorway which Belloc had sketched while sipping vermouth outside a drinking booth. The booth has long gone, but the red stone doorway has not altered, its lugubrious lions and intricately carved balcony still overlooking the narrow street now filled with cars instead of carts.

I am no artist but I snapped its picture in the half-light and ambled at random until I found La Collegiata, a church with a splendid Renaissance façade, which I entered for purely secular reasons: to shelter from the rain.

The doors swung shut behind me, and like Pinocchio in the whale's belly I groped my way into a vast interior lit only by a sprinkling of candles. Organ music echoed between the walls although I could not discern its source.

I sat on a pew, waiting for my eyes to grow accustomed to the gloom, but nothing materialised apart from the vague shapes of pillars and a hint of statuary. The candlelight was too weak to reach the ceiling and this lack of solidity affected my senses. I felt as though I were floating.

The music ceased and I was left in silence, or so I believed until I became aware of almost subliminal sibilance. No doubt in some dark corner of a side chapel a mortal woman was whispering her prayers, but I found the anonymity disconcerting, and decided to leave. But the door was wrapped in darkness and it took me a while to find it by fumbling along the wall. Nothing horrid scuttled over my feet or breathed icily on my neck, but the whispering continued to unnerve me and I was immensely relieved to regain the street.

Bellinzona, dominated by three castles, guards the routes going north and east into the Alps, but it is not a true mountain town, and this may account for the shape of the people. Something must. The women, I noticed, were elegant and willowy compared with those I had seen in the high country. And there was an air of sophistication about them, not only in their clothes – which money can buy – but in their entire demeanour.

It is my habit to look strangers in their eyes, and, as a rule, I am disappointed by their responses. Eyelids fall like the hinged tops of children's desks. They do not want me to see inside. But in Bellinzona the women returned my gaze, and often they smiled.

And the shutters did not fall with the coming of night as they did in the hills. Shop lights and electrical displays turned the wet streets oily with colour. Bright umbrellas bobbed along the pavements, and delightfully unsuitable high-heeled shoes splashed through puddles. I was the only person wearing boots.

When Belloc was in Bellinzona he begged a glance at a map, and I did likewise for I was unsure of the following day's route to Lugano.

The jolly staff in the tourist office formed a committee to help me.

Was the road walkable? No, they said. It wound through the hills and was too fast and dangerous, particularly in rain.

But there was an alternative, I hoped, for at least part of the way where Belloc had walked through a chestnut forest. They spread out a large-scale map and I spotted a foot path meandering through the greenery.

'There,' I said. 'Can I take that path?'

The committee consulted a printed sheet covered with dates and hieroglyphics. 'No. It's not possible.'

'Why on earth not?'

'You could end up with a bullet in your head and that's not good for promoting tourism.'

'There's hunting there?'

'It's the military. They are using this area for manoeuvres. You would not be allowed in.'

'Isn't there some other way of getting to Lugano?'

'Of course. It's only twenty-five kilometres. Do what everyone else does. Take the train.'

Bellinzona to Lugano

Had there been a yellow brick road leading all the way to Lugano I would not have taken it; for the following morning the black clouds over Bellinzona were incontinent.

How pleasant it was to lie in bed making bets with myself as to which raindrop on the windowpane would reach the sill first; how luxurious to stand under a hot shower for longer than it took to wash myself; how hedonistic to savour cup after cup of coffee without having to glance at my watch.

Leaving my clothes at a launderette run by a Gina Lollobrigida (as she appeared in *The Hunchback of Notre Dame*) I took little lanes up to the Castello Grande whose towers and battlements overlook the old town. Two more castles were visible. The higher, Castello di Sasso Corbaro, was half hidden by a fringe of fog that also denied me a view of the surrounding hills, although I could see the swollen Ticino rushing across the flat valley floor on its mission to fill up Lago Maggiore.

By ten I was soaked again and I took refuge in a backstreet bar where coffees and brandies warmed blood turned to water. How good it felt, after the furtiveness of the mountains, to find myself amongst vivacious people who shouted when they were angry, laughed when amused, and used their bodies uninhibitedly as outward signs of inward emotions. They might pay their federal taxes to Bern but in spirit they are Italian.

After several brandies I fell head over heels in lust with a gazelle-eyed glass washer who kept standing on a chair to replace the glasses on a shelf. Each time she reached up she exposed bare brown thighs that ascended provocatively into a skintight miniskirt. And for a while I was reminded that I was not a travelling machine but a man.

But like all good Englishmen I flung such Latin thoughts aside and concentrated instead on priorities: the launderette. However, I had not forgotten the delectable Gina, and with fantasies of female flesh taking precedence over geography I walked stiffly up to the station.

The local train rose steeply, providing unmemorable amateur snapshots in its window frames: the racetrack of a road, all spray and madness; the rain-washed alluvial valley leading to Lago Maggiore, its green fields infected with a rash of industrial estates; the blackness of tunnels.

Lugano's station is high above the old town and I took a funicular down to the centre.

Rain still fell but there was a new softness in the air that transformed the wetness into a mere inconvenience rather than an all-pervasive nuisance. And added to this southern scent there was the smell of money.

My route had not taken me through the other wealthy lakeside cities of Switzerland – Lucerne, Lausanne, Zürich, Geneva, Montreux – but here, just in time, I came across the dream to which so many in Britain aspire.

In Via Nassa, the main shopping street, the arcades resembled a strange mammalian aquarium. Display cases made from sledgehammer-proof glass were locked to the pavement while inside, dead animals – mink, sable, chinchilla – waited to be petted by shoppers too well-heeled to be mere browsers. Limousines –

purchased, not hired – lined the street while their owners paraded, their affected boredom printed on their faces like numbers on plastic charge cards.

Lugano is an amphitheatre with a lake for its stage, and I went to the front row of the stalls: the esplanade where, under a marquee of dripping leaves, I ate salami, bread and cheese.

Water taxis bucked across the choppy lake whose shape – roughly like the three-legged emblem of the Isle of Man – is incomprehensible at water level. To the north-east lay Italy. To the west, Italy. To the south, Switzerland.

Directly opposite Lugano, on the eastern shore, is the Italian town of Campione, which is entirely surrounded by Switzerland. It is an enclave where those who cannot lose their money fast enough in Lugano's Kursaal – where stakes are strictly limited – can flee by launch to fritter away their soft-gotten gains in the casino where only the sky is the limit. A hotel room in Lugano would have cost me a fortune, and so I decided to stay at the youth hostel. But like all institutions it had restrictions. It did not open until five o'clock.

And so, like a tramp, I killed time by walking in the park where palms, unaccustomed to rain, stood stoically erect like giraffes in English zoos.

Beyond the cabbage-water lake, green mountains rose steeply, their forested crests the watershed where the rain on its far, invisible, slopes splashed down towards Lago di Como which occupies a basin exhibiting true Italian plumbing. The overflow system simply does not work and so it floods, frequently. In Switzerland, even in Ticino, such periodic inundations would not be tolerated.

Having been ushered across a road by a policewoman wearing a cowboy hat I passed a hotel where aproned waiters, with little to do between feeding times, stood disconsolately on a covered terrace.

A gaunt middle-aged lady sat sipping tea, a notebook on her lap, and having read *Hotel du Lac* I immediately pigeon-holed her as a forlorn Edith Hope.

And my Edith pointed to one of the problems of literature. Frequently, instead of achieving what the author sets out to do – describing individuals as individuals and setting them apart from the general mass of humanity – a book merely adds to the list of stereotypes to which one has access.

The hostel, in a leafy suburb, is an old and spacious villa set in a palmy garden. Flowers, untouched by frost, bloomed in summer splendour although the swimming pool betokened autumn, its surface brown with reflected leaves.

A school party of rowdy German youths, all acne and bum-fluffed chins, were checking in ahead of me, and when it came to my turn I asked the woman at the desk if I could avoid their company.

Alone in my cramped dormitory I opened a bottle of Chianti I had smuggled in, and sat reading by a window overlooking the pool where martins winnowed over the water. But my privacy was short-lived.

Ben, from the USA, and Izaak, from Israel, both in their early twenties, were affable and respectful of my advanced years. It was a shock to realise that I was old enough to be their father.

'Oh great!' said Ben, throwing down his kitbag. 'You're English. I haven't spoken English in days.'

Izaak joined in, and with the Chianti lubricating our under-used vocal cords we became temporary friends.

Ben was from New Mexico and I asked him what he did there.

'I'm a writer,' he said.

'Of what?'

'Short stories mainly.'

'You can sell short stories?'

'I've had a couple published.'

'But you don't make a living from it?'

'No. Journalism's what brings in the bucks.'

'You work for a newspaper?'

'Kind of. I'm studying journalism.'

'So you're a student?'

'Yeah. Journalism and creative writing. I'm on a kinda sabbatical.'

I asked the question most writers – with justification throw back at their interrogator. 'What do you write about?'

But Ben was eager to answer. 'Everything. You know? Like Ernest Hemingway. You heard of him?'

'Yes.'

'Well, I try to write like him. That's why I'm in Europe to experience the kinda things he experienced. I'm on my way to Spain right now to see some bullfights. He wrote about them. You know?'

'Do you think it's wise?'

'What?'

'Modelling yourself so closely on someone else.'

'He's the best.'

'Perhaps, but shouldn't you be doing it your own way?'

'I know what you're getting at, but there's still plenty of time. Hell, I know so little and if you want to be a writer you've got to make things happen. I mean you can't just sit on your ass in a one-horse town waiting for D. H. Lawrence or someone to call in for a root beer.'

'You could write about one-horse towns.'

'It's been done. So what do you do?'

'Sit on my arse in one-horse towns mainly.'

'So why're you here?'

'The same reason as you. Making something happen.'

'How do you make a living?'

I decided to forget my scribbling. 'I make films when people let me.'

'Features?'

'Would I be staying in a youth hostel if I made features? No. Documentaries.'

'About what?'

'Everything. Like Hemingway.'

Ben laughed, and I liked him for his openness and complete lack of pomposity.

'Can you still make documentaries in England?' asked Izaak.

'Of course.'

'I've read that your government's stopping anything controversial being done.'

'Only things that show them up in a bad light. Other than that we're as free as birds.'

'Jailbirds?' suggested Ben.

'England's an open prison. We can go anywhere, do anything just so long as we don't breach its own definition of security.'

'It sounds a little like Israel,' said Izaak.

And so, as always happens in the company of Israelis, the conversation turned to Israel and its neighbours.

Izaak was no adherent of Halacha but he tried, successfully, to make me appreciate the Israelis' chronic and constant xenophobia.

'Surely you must sympathise with our problems?' he said, having delivered an erudite speech in defence of Israel's position.

'Of course I do, but I'll tell you something that changed my attitude towards Israel. It was when your army invaded Lebanon. I watched a report on TV and saw a hospital full of dead babies. I was so angry I rang the Israeli Embassy in London and said, "Look, I'm just an ordinary person, but I've got to speak out against the killing of innocent children." And do you know what the spokesman said? He said, "What right do you have to criticise us, when your bombers destroyed Dresden?" I said I thought that the bombing of Dresden was a war crime but I couldn't understand how that exculpated Israel from murdering children. I tried to point out the terrible irony of a people decimated by the Holocaust indulging in similar acts of terrorism, but all he said was that they had to fight the PLO by whatever means were available. I said, "Including the slaughter of babies?" He told me I didn't understand, and slammed the phone down.'

Izaak was silent.

'And then,' I continued, 'there were the massacres in the refugee camps. And the shooting of Arab children in the occupied territories. And the torture.'

'You're right,' said Izaak sadly. 'The dream has become a nightmare. No one in Israel will ever forget the camps at Chatila and Sabra. In 1967 and 1973 everyone was behind the government but not any more. There are many Israelis who are now ashamed of what has been done in their name.'

The bottle was empty and the wine had turned us melancholy.

We walked through the rain, found a restaurant, and like sailors on shore leave we got disgracefully drunk.

Two Scandinavian girls at an adjoining table came over and the conversation drifted – by design I suspect – towards a subject about which I had not the slightest knowledge; contemporary pop lyrics. And although – so close to T-shirts studded with nipples – I was feeling far from avuncular, I saw myself through this quartet's eyes. It would not have been fair to remain and so, making my excuses, I left.

I turned to glance at them as I opened the restaurant door. Already they looked more comfortable. Ben's choice was the prettiest and I imagined her asking, 'Who was that old fellow?'

'Just someone we met in the youth hostel.'

'But I thought youth hostels were for youths?'

Brimming with self-pity at being past forty I swayed through the undulating streets towards my metal bunk, cursing God aloud for not existing; for when you are drunk who else can you blame for scheduling our absurd journeys from cot to coffin?

I awoke to the clatter of Ben and Izaak stumbling into the room.

'Hey, man, why d'you leave?'

'Four's company. Five's a crowd.'

'It's not like that anymore,' said Izaak. 'People don't screw around like they did in your day. We're too afraid now.'

'AIDS?'

'Damn right,' said Ben. 'Fucking AIDS!'

'AIDS no fucking,' said Izaak.

'You shouldn't've gone, man,' said Ben. 'Mai said you were real interesting to talk to.'

Interesting? I suppose I should have been pleased but the word was a double-edged knife and I fell back into sleep with its hilt protruding from my back.

Lugano to Como

The road south from Lugano follows the lake's western shore, then crosses a causeway and bridge to the eastern edge, where it continues towards the frontier at Chiasso.

A woman in the tourist office told me that it was not possible to walk this stretch, but I had resolved to take no more trains and, ignoring her advice, I set out along the promenade, having passed a chic sports shop whose name was either intentionally camp or a dire mistake. It was called Athlete's Foot.

Avenues of trees beside the bay acted as umbrellas under which despondent queues of off-season tourists waited for excursion boats beside floating jetties slopping in a gentle swell.

Swans paddled through the green water, while above them a halo formed around a sun doing its best to burn a hole in the clouds.

On the outskirts I passed a string of hotels, including a genuine Hôtel du Lac. An air of desolation emanated from them all. Drained swimming pools, like elderly women without make-up, were displaying their cracks and blemishes. Windows had been permanently shuttered for the winter. Car parks were empty. Plastic sun-loungers lay stacked on rain terraces.

I sat on a bench to rest and enjoy the view, but I was accosted by a pretty young man dressed all in leather. I asked him to go away but he persisted and so, shouldering my rucksack, I departed. Perhaps he thought I looked interesting?

As the busy road rose around a cliff the pavement became concrete slabs no more than a metre wide. But it was walkable even though the road, perched on pillars, overhung a considerable drop whose void I could see through the cracks.

I glimpsed the bridge and I sang as I walked for the rain had stopped. Watery sunlight had turned the lake to silver and my jollity was augmented by the knowledge that in three or four hours I would be in Italy.

Without warning the concrete slabs contracted into a kerb only a boot wide along which I had to balance, turning as the traffic approached, my rucksack resting on the crash barrier above the drop. But I continued, determined not to be thwarted so close to the bridge, now less than a kilometre away.

Then there was not even a kerb. Drivers hooted and flashed their lights at me; and, squeezed between rockface and barrier, there was no place to hide. A man, having nearly hit me, stopped his car and shouted abuse before speeding away like a rally driver with his tyres screeching and his horn blaring.

Reluctantly I turned and walked all the way back into Lugano.

Kismet. There was nothing I could do apart from deciding on the most pleasurable way of reaching the southernmost shore of the lake.

The serried seats on the boat to Capolago were as thinly peopled as the stalls of a provincial theatre during a matinée performance of *Krapp's Last Tape*.

As we smoothly sped out into the bay I stood at the stern and watched the perfect reflections of Monte San Salvatore and Monte Brè wobbling in the wake.

We glided beneath the cliff along whose rim I had just walked. Was it any wonder that I had met only two other walkers during the past 500 kilometres? This was far easier. The equation was simple. Money = ticket = movement.

The bridge was a border separating two distinct climatic zones. To the north the sky was grey, to the south lapis lazuli.

I strolled to the bow as we slid into the pretty village of Melide with its pink and yellow houses and sunny backdrop of steep forested slopes. The water was deep and clear, and Melide reminded me of Hydra in the Aegean, where the houses, built by Venetian merchants, display the same Italianate features.

As we cruised into the south-eastern leg of the lake I realised that I was seeing the last of the Alps. Beyond these outliers, where solitary church steeples pierced the trees, there was nothing but flatness all the way to the Apennines whose ridges would lead me down into Tuscany.

At Capolago the rest of the passengers headed for the rack-railway that would hoist them up to the summit of Monte Generoso while I walked into the village, a kilometre from the quay.

I bought red wine and fruit and sat by the lakeside for a long time, absorbing the sun, overjoyed to be in the south at last; for although the frontier was still several kilometres away I was already in Italy.

Everything around me was Italian: the fat pasta-fed women dressed in black, hanging extraordinary underwear in their courtyards; brightly plumaged songbirds in wooden cages suspended from wrought-iron balconies; youths on mopeds skidding around the village square while girls carrying schoolbooks pretended not to notice; stucco; malodorous drains; and the blessed heat.

Shady alleys lured me up to a yellow-domed church, the Tempio di Santa Croce, which I had spotted from the lake. Two small doors flanked a huge weathered wooden door, as solid and impressive as the main gate of a Norman castle, on which lions are carved. All three doors were open, and as I approached the church a flock of birds flew out like bats from a cave.

The damp-smelling interior was lit only by the sun. Faded religious paintings hung on peeling walls, their frames soiled with bird shit. There were no seats and I leaned against a chilly stone pillar, savouring the silence and wondering why this magnificent building was being allowed to fall into disrepair.

Each church I visited on my journey provided temporary sanctuary from making decisions, and I stayed in Santa Croce for perhaps half an hour. No one else entered, but when I turned to leave I saw that the birds, sparrows mostly, had returned. They stood on the floor like a congregation waiting for mass to begin. I cannot think why they chose to assemble there unless the church provided respite from difficult avian decisions.

A squiggle on my map, like a vein on an old man's temple, indicated a lane leading south that would take me to Mendrisio, a little before the frontier, avoiding the main road.

I left Capolago with regret. There is not much there to attract tourists, and I am sure that it is little visited, but for me it was intensely memorable. Every house and every shadow is indelibly catalogued under my hair. Why? Because it was a place of transition.

To the north lay the frigid mountains separating the warm Mediterranean from the cold Baltic and North

Seas. To the north the people have subjugated themselves to an internal world of immutable certainties. To the south uncertainty – and therefore hope – still remains. There, volubility is not an aberration. It is an acknowledgement of our vulnerability and our humanity.

And although I am not an economist or a politician, I can only say that if circumstances allowed me to live with my family amongst these intemperate southerners instead of amongst the New Britains (who inhabit a barbarous little island off the coast of Gaul) I would choose the south.

A bizarre valley, combining vineyards and factories, led me to Mendrisio and on to Chiasso, both ugly towns ringed by industrial mess and dreary blocks of workers' flats worthy of Belgrade or Sofia.

My Italian Indian summer had reverted to monsoon and the crossing was an anticlimax. An obese customs officer, destined for a coronary thrombosis at fifty, flicked through my passport with nicotine-stained fingers, then waved me into Italy's groin; for if, like most schoolchildren, you visualise Italy as a leg then that is exactly where I was.

The streets of Como, despite the rain, were a delight.

Cars breed like rabbits in Italy, and every road is a warren. Fiats parked bumper to bumper blocked all the pavements. In Lugano they would have been towed away. No, in Lugano, where there is great respect for the law, they would not have been parked there in the first place.

Family businesses bordered the backstreets, and through open windows I saw a woman hunched over a sewing machine; a cobbler with silver nails protruding from his lips; a sign writer speckled with paint; a baker sculpting dough. And there was not a hint of orderliness anywhere; by which I do not mean that these craftspeople were incompetent, merely that neatness was not a prerequisite of efficiency. There were no rubber plants, no filing cabinets, no anaemic limited-edition prints on the walls, no clever furniture. Just people getting on with their work as they have done in Italian towns for over 2,000 years.

Grand mansions, their foundations rotting in water, line Lago di Como, each with its private canal leading to Romanesque-arched boathouses where no boats float; for the wealthy have fled to new steel and concrete palaces in the hills above the city.

These crumbling edifices are now municipal offices or sanatoria or private schools but there was no evidence of occupancy, for although evening was approaching not a single light shone from their windows.

Steamers with empty decks chugged across the lake. They were distinctly Italian. On Lake Lugano each vessel had looked newly commissioned; its hull glossy with new paint, its brass fittings massaged daily, its ropes coiled like wheels, its life-rafts wrapped in cellophane. But here the tourist boats resembled tramp steamers. Rust bled from their anchors, their paintwork suffered from eczema, and their wooden cabins had forgotten the smell of varnish. But they looked reasonably lake-worthy and I have heard of none plunging to the bottom. In Italy it is sufficient to get from A to B and back. The rest is cosmetic.

Economy preluded a hotel, but there is a hostel in Como and I waited for opening time in the gardens of

Villa Olmo, an eighteenth-century *palazzo* on the west shore.

People, alone or in groups, isolated by so much space, wandered about the formal gardens like extras in a Resnais film. And I, like every solitary traveller, merely added myself to the cast.

The picture was the same for all of us although our scripts lacked continuity.

A toddler was throwing gravel at pigeons eating crumbs supplied by his mother but she did not intervene. A Giacometti woman, in pain, crossed a waterlogged lawn, her stick sinking through grass into mud, causing her to stumble. A couple cuddled under a palm. A middle-aged man, looking lost, leaned on his rucksack.

The hostel was managed by volatile people whose extended family came and went carrying musical instruments in preparation for a birthday party the following night. No mandolins or concertinas but a drum machine, a computerised keyboard and electric guitars. The amplifiers, positioned like monoliths on each side of an improvised dais, would have filled the Hollywood Bowl.

The family outnumbered the guests. We were four: a Tunisian who spent the entire evening shaving and applying cologne to armpits and crotch; a depressive Dane who lay on his bunk groaning; Jamil, a Pakistani; and me.

Jamil and I talked while I drank beer and he sipped tea. He was from Hyderabad and had spent six months guest-working in West Germany prior to attempting the almost impossible: entry into Britain, not as an immigrant but as a short-stay visitor; what we, in the

West, usually refer to as a tourist. He had relatives in Yorkshire with whom to stay, but was having difficulty understanding the complexities of Form 1M2/A which had been supplied Free of Charge by the British consulate in Munich. It was in English only, and although Jamil spoke better English than most Englishmen I know the pseudo-legal jargon was incomprehensible to him. And to me.

Britain is officially non-racist. Anyone can holiday in our green and pleasant land but some incomers are more welcome than others. Although colour of skin is officially immaterial, if you are a white Pakistani there should be no problem.

Perhaps I am being unfair, for I am ignorant of our laws. Doesn't everyone have to supply evidence of annual income before breaching the white cliffs of Dover? Don't the Swiss have to give details of hosts/sponsors in the UK? Don't Swedes have to provide a pre-arranged list of hotels where they will be staying along with the dates?

I helped Jamil fill in his Form 1M2/A although certain sub-clauses in the Helpful Notes (provided free) made me suspect that its writer – I use the term loosely – was being deliberately perverse.

It made me angry. The British had printed the atlas red. They had preached justice and – eventually – democracy. No country could exist without the rule of law. And there, in my hands, was a piece of paper, concocted in my name, which espoused the principle of guilt until innocence is proved. And not for the first – or last – time during my comparatively short journey I felt ashamed. And my apologies were inadequate.

Jamil and I had dinner together. We both delved into wallets to display photographs of our children. We made each other laugh. But there were aspects of his character that set him apart from me. He was better educated. He had read more, travelled more widely, spoke several languages fluently, and possessed wisdom far beyond his years.

I imagined him confronting an English immigration officer. Jamil would say too much. Make a thorough nuisance of himself. He would question the logic of illogical rules, or worse, try to conduct a rational conversation. And he would be branded as a troublemaker, for there is nothing that raises the hackles of a semi-educated Englishman more than a foreigner demonstrating superior intelligence.

I tried to explain all this to Jamil.

'But I only want a bloody holiday!'

'Pakistanis don't have holidays in Britain. There's always an ulterior motive.'

Jamil laughed. 'You're joking of course?'

'I wish I was.'

And I wished I was.

Como to Milan

In the morning I said goodbye to Jamil, wished him luck, and headed for the centre of Como, where – like Belloc – I found floods.

Walls of sandbags, carelessly arranged, had failed to prevent the lake inundating Piazza Cavour. Policemen, blowing whistles randomly, like referees in a game without rules, were unable to stop drivers spraying passers-by, including me, with liquid souvenirs of the lake; not that it made much difference, for it was raining.

Armed robbery must be, after Vatican banking practices, the most lucrative means of making a living in Italy, for in Piazza Cavour I fell victim to Italian security.

Cashing travellers' cheques required strenuous efforts. The first bank I tried had a cylindrical electrically operated airlock into which I and my rucksack would not fit.

'Leave your luggage outside,' the gun-toting guard advised, but I refused, fearing street crime.

The second bank's airlock was more capacious. A green light flashed and I just managed to squeeze through although a guard immediately leapt forward and divested me of my rucksack.

Security was followed by bureaucracy. I could not simply sign a cheque, show my passport, and collect. Forms had to be filled. What was my mother's maiden name? Had I ever been a member of the British Conservative Party or ever associated with anyone who sought world domination via monetarist policies? And

my next address had to be divulged. Milano, I wrote
naïvely.

'Where exactly in Milano?'

'I don't know.'

'You must write something.'

Hôtel Splendide looked credible.

'Now go to desk 4.'

'Sign here,' said the man at desk 4. 'Now go to desk
7.'

The woman at desk 7 perused my machine-printed
passport photograph – which resembles an overexposed
fibreoptic snap of an embryo – and for some inexplicable
reason seemed satisfied. And feeling guilty for collecting
my own cash I left the bank and sought shelter in the
cathedral from the downpour outside.

There are red-light districts in Como's cathedral.

Each vacant confessional displays a red lamp which
the priest switches off while judging venial
misdemeanours and capital offences. There is no
privacy. The recidivists kneel in full public view, their
whispered crimes amplified by the fourteenth-century
nave.

Mass started in a side altar and I sat beside a dwarfish
hunchback in the shadowy back row.

When we reached the embarrassing bit where the
members of the congregation display a sign of peace to
their neighbours the hunchback shook my hand. His
fingers were small, like a child's, but as brittle as a
starfish.

I was the only person to refuse communion, although
for a while I suspected that the hunchback shared my
secret understain of mortal sin. While the rest of the
congregation poured from their pews to eat Christ's

flesh (for that, make no bones about it, is *exactly* what belief in the doctrine of transubstantiation entails), the dolphin-nosed little man remained knee to hassock. Only when the priest had fed the penultimate communicant did the cripple leap like an athlete into the aisle and scuttle to the rail. Like all public acts in his life this one had to be accomplished quickly and efficiently. To queue would have made him visible and therefore risible. This way he was there and back in less time than it takes to receive a plenary indulgence – if you know the right prayer.

Belloc, short of cash and faced with a dreary march into the suburbs of Milan, asked God to decide whether or not he should break his pilgrim's vow by taking the train. It was an ordeal by fire. He chose two candles burning at a shrine in Como's cathedral and waited to see which would remain alight the longer. If the left flame lived longer then he would walk all the way, but if the right won then he would go as far towards Milan as his cash would allow. The right flame won by a short neck and so he took the train. Miraculously he had exactly the amount of change to take him into Milan.

With this precedent to justify my own weakness I decided to put myself similarly on trial; not by fire but by water. I had been in the cathedral for an hour. This, I reasoned, was ample time to allow Apollo an opportunity to evaporate the clouds. If, when I stepped out into the Piazza del Duomo, people were still scurrying about under umbrellas, I would take the train. If their umbrellas were folded I would walk.

The Piazza was a rainbow of umbrellas and so I went straight to a grimy little station near the lake and bought a ticket to Milan. But as I waited on the platform I was aware of guilt nibbling away like a rat at my conscience. That is the trouble with a Catholic upbringing. As one gets older one can throw away dogmas like so many ill-fitting shoes but no amount of rational thought can entirely extinguish the insidious little flame of guilt kindled by nuns and priests when one is too young to distinguish fact from opinion. Even the simplest decisions tend to be seen in terms of black and white. But my life is not completely determined by this early conditioning and so I chose a grey solution. I would take the train halfway and walk from there.

I looked at my map. There was a town called Séveso which fitted the bill, and so I changed my ticket. The name Séveso seemed familiar although I could not think why.

An inspector jostled his way through the strap-hangers, demanded my ticket, then informed me that in order to reach Séveso I would have to go to Milan and take another train north.

An elderly man wearing a frayed suit asked me why I wanted to visit Séveso.

'No particular reason,' I replied.

'Séveso is not a place for people like you.' His expression was not friendly.

'Why?'

'You don't remember? *Séveso*?'

When recalling such moments people frequently say that they wished the ground had opened up and swallowed them. I felt a shiver run down my spine and was aware that I was blushing. All around me people stared.

'Many, many people suffered tragedies in Séveso.'

'Now I remember. I'm sorry.'

212

'There is nothing there for you to see.'

'I had forgotten. I won't go there.'

He smiled, just. 'That is good. Milano is better.'

Had I met a tourist on his way to Aberfan I think I would have reacted in precisely the same way as this man who, for all I knew, may have lost relatives or friends when the cloud of poison gas had shrouded the town with death.

Tears of rain blurred the windows and I was only vaguely aware of flat muddy fields and ditches passing by. So this was Lombardy which Belloc described, with uncharacteristic succinctness, as an alluvial plain.

Agriculture gave way to industry as we trundled into the outskirts of Milan.

Seldom have I seem such ugliness; factories and high-rise slums separated by roads flagged with plastic and paper bunting which the wind had wrapped around every rusting fence and derelict shed. Everywhere there were groups of children, careless of the weather, playing amongst the squalor. Each patch of muddy waste ground was an imaginary stadium where expectant forwards and goalies were hoping, perhaps, to be snapped up by passing talent scouts from AC Milan. Girls with prams practised motherhood. And above them all the concrete towers glowered like wicked uncles.

'Milan's the most dangerous city in Europe,' Jamil had warned me. 'It's full of thieves. People from the south who come looking for work and can't find any. Junkies too. They don't care what they do to pay for drugs. And for heaven's sake don't go on the Metro looking like a tourist. I did and had $200 stolen. They slit my money pouch with a knife.'

Jamil was not the first victim of Italian street crime I had encountered, and so, when I arrived at the station, I stashed my pack in left luggage and went out into the streets with my arms folded across my wallet-pocket and my blackthorn at the ready. Innocent Milanese, eyeing the stick, swerved to avoid me, but at least I was not robbed in Milan.

I saw whores but no potential muggers on my walk to the post office; only businessmen in tailored suits and businesswomen in tailored suits. All carried black umbrellas and sped along the streets as though hurrying to top-flight funerals.

Despite having been sent well in advance there was no mail awaiting me in the labyrinthine post office and so, disgruntled, I walked to the Piazza del Duomo to see the cathedral (my second since breakfast). But one cathedral a day is enough for anyone, and although Milan's is obviously grander and more intricate than Como's I was feeling – like Belloc before me – alienated from the milling masses. Like him I was impatient – and already nostalgic – for wild places where solitude is in keeping with solitary travel. Here, among millions, I was overcome by loneliness.

I did not want to see grand statues of Victor Emmanuel II or paintings by Tintoretto. I simply wanted to leave. But if you look at a map of Milan you will discover that it is exactly like a spider's web. And like an insect I felt trapped in its complexity.

It was too late to head out into the Lombardy Plain but as I walked out towards the dull suburb where the hostel is situated, the sky changed from slate to coal and sparks of lightning flickered in the north.

I passed a shop called Casa del Busto, which sells armour-plated brassieres and corsets for those with fuller figures, and took shelter from the storm in a bar run by two queer men in spotless white matadors' costumes.

They suggested a dry amber wine – which I would recommend had I not lost my note of its name – and I showed my approval by drinking several glasses while thunder echoed along streets turned to canals by the flood.

While I sat waiting for the storm to pass a dapper little man entered, shook his brolly, and fussed around a display of biscuit tins. After much soul-searching he chose one whose lid displayed a colour photograph of the Yorkshire countryside. Across gritstone outcrops and green dales were printed the words MRS KIPPAX COUNTRY RECIPE BISCUITS. Kippax? Who could have dreamed up such an unlikely English name? But I was thinking through ignorance for on my return I discovered that there is a town called Kippax, just outside Leeds.

I spent the evening in a pizzeria with Lars, a teenage Swede who, flushed with wine, insisted on telling me about his recent sexual conquests in Greece.

'Seventeen in two months. Not bad, huh?'

'Why so many?'

'Because when I get back to Sweden I will be doing national service far in the north where there are no women. So, like a camel, I drink all I can before going into the desert.'

'What will you be doing there?'

'Chopping down trees.'

'What for?'

'For paper.'

'No, I meant why does the army do that?'

'Oh I will not be in the army. I am a conscientious objector. I will be doing alternative service as a lumberjack.'

His arms were as thin as axe shafts. 'Do you think it's a wise decision?'

'It is better than fighting.'

'Do Swedish soldiers fight?'

'People fight them. Whenever there is any trouble in the world and the United Nations need a peace-keeping force they say, "Send in the Swedes. They are neutral. People will respect them." But they still get blown up by landmines or shot by terrorists. Besides, chopping down trees will make me strong, and women like that.'

'You're not doing too badly the way you are.'

'I have made a decision. From now on I want quality rather than quantity.'

I did not like Lars very much but it was a case of any port in a storm.

I was curious to learn if the international league table of promiscuity had changed since the sixties. 'Who are the easiest lays nowadays?' Did people still talk about lays? Obviously he understood for he answered without hesitation.

'English girls. They are too stupid to say no.'

Back at the hostel a distraught black American was being comforted by compatriots. Although built like a wrestler she had been robbed on a bus by a gang of children. It was a pity that she had not met Jamil and taken his advice for her T-shirt, stretched tight across grapefruit-sized breasts, was emblazoned with a big green apple and the words NEW YORK CITY. Even an illiterate Sicilian ten-year-old could not have mistaken her for a Milanese.

'Fucking Europe!' she kept saying. 'Fucking piss-pot! I wish I'd never fucking come. I wanna go home. Right now!' Without money or passport such spontaneity was impracticable. But no doubt the American consulate would sort it all out and in a couple of days she would be back in the safety of the New York streets and subway.

Milan to Lodi

I walked into the city through almost deserted Saturday morning streets.

My map of Milan, soaked the previous day, hung in damp tatters, and instead of taking the road to Lodi I unknowingly headed for Pavia.

After an hour I realised my error and cut across, alongside railway tracks, to join the right road.

At least it was warm. A sultry breeze blew litter along the gutters, and pigeons feasted on the festering remnants of discarded fast food.

Trudging through Milan was sheer folly, but having failed to walk in I felt duty-bound to walk out.

Southern Milan is hideous. Post-war development has turned it into an urban wasteland, and the only sign of community life I saw was a market where poverty-stricken migrants from Calabria and Campania were tending stalls piled high with fruit, vegetables and flowers.

A hook-nosed man with a drooping black moustache and matching eyebrows was polishing apples on the sleeve of a threadbare jacket. Two women, like ancient twins dressed all in black by their children, were arguing in high-pitched shrieks about the weight of a melon, their skeletal jaws moving vertically as though operated by puppeteers. A girl of four or five, barefoot, sat under a stall playing with an evil-looking cat displaying a suppurating socket where its left eye had been.

I bought half a kilo of green grapes and chewed them as I walked. Their skins were sticky – with the residue of pesticides probably – although their flesh was firm and juicy.

Milan goes on forever when one is on foot. Towns marked on my map as separate entities turned out to be suburbs linked by a dangerous road along which I slunk, there being no alternative.

Urban chaos was evident everywhere; dilapidated garages and factories, waste tips, scrap metal yards, jerry-built highrise apartment blocks, a caravan site beside a stinking drain.

Finally, after four hours on the road, I came to countryside – of a sort.

For a man who loves hills Lombardy is desolation, and I concur entirely with Belloc's appraisal of its purgatorial mudscape.

Far, far away, somewhere beyond the interminable flat black fields, the mountains rose heavenward; but here there was only hope to persuade one foot to follow the other. I was reminded of the Belfort Gap, although that was a mere square on a chessboard compared with the sixty-four of the Lombardy Plain separating me from Fornovo in the foothills of the Apennines.

At Melegnano I sat in the town square, swigging lemonade, watched by giggling teenagers who were waiting for buses to take them home to the sticks from Saturday morning school.

I wandered around the town like a journalist looking for a story, but all I witnessed was a police car whizzing around the streets, its tyres screeching, its siren sobbing. Round and round it went like a fairground attraction, its macho driver determined to track down the flasher or shoplifter who obviously merited such dramatic strategy.

Italy is Western Europe's biggest manufacturer of policemen. Somewhere there must be a factory where the workers slave night and day to provide the wax necessary to fill the myriad identical moulds from which the finished products emerge. Seamstresses must sew silly uniforms – designed to emphasise shoulders and crotches – around them. Armourers must arm them.

In Italy I must have seen a thousand policemen; local and paramilitary, and although many Italians are blond I did not see one fair hair protruding from beneath the rims of their ridiculous bonnets. And all are sallow with blue five o'clock shadow carelessly painted on their chins by overworked make-up artists. And their eyes are all the same shade of brown – although there are many blue-eyed Italians – and are made of glass.

A river, the Lambro, flows through Melegnano along whose bank Belloc had hoped to walk until its confluence with the Po. But the Italians do not go in for Rights of Way along their rivers, and the road is the only route for those riding Shanks's pony.

I stood on the bridge, looking down at the charmless Lambro, glad that there was no access to its banks, for a fetid gas rose from its slop-brown water. It was in spate and a flotilla of rubbish floated under the arch; the perfect target for a fusillade of stones flung by a ragamuffin with cropped hair and an old man's face. Mussolini as a child.

Fourteen kilometres still separated me from Lodi, and I walked it quickly, fuelled by adrenaline pumped into my system by a fear of destruction at the hands of demented drivers.

A thin yellow line painted a metre from the tarmac's edge indicates a safety-lane for cyclists, and along this I strode. But I saw no cyclists, and the drivers disregarded it. For them it was a line along which they could aim the centre of their bumpers.

If this was a sign of things to come, then I was in serious trouble.

Drainage ditches run parallel to the road, and I frequently heard the plop of vermin as they dived into black sumps leading to their horrid caves.

Fields of mud alternated with fields of rotting stubble. Trees were as rare as wells in a desert. Every so often I saw farms as impressive as English manors but lacking their picturesque surroundings. Walled gardens, rising out of the mud, adjoined huge dilapidated farmhouses. Deep-throated dogs, thankfully far away along puddled tracks, barked as I passed, and flocks of hooded crows rose squawking into the heavy air.

Many people must go mad in Lombardy.

One field I remember particularly. Its crippled crops were stained bright orange and I wondered what lethal overdose of chemicals had been sprayed there.

I ignored a signpost pointing to Lodi Vecchio – Old Lodi – which Belloc had found to be an unkempt and miserable village, and continued instead along the road to Lodi.

It was a providential decision, for at the bridge over the River Adda where Napoleon put the Austrians to rout in 1796 I witnessed a battle for survival waged against the river by the crew of a motorised barge.

The barge, eighty feet long, must have come adrift from its moorings and been swept downstream by the ferocious current.

Luckily it had become wedged under the central span of the bridge; luckily because 300 metres downstream there was an unprotected weir which the swollen Adda had turned into a thundering death trap.

I joined an enthusiastic audience lining the bridge and banks and watched as a man with miraculous cutting equipment began shearing the wheelhouse from the hull while the captain looked on despairingly. Instead of tethering the barge and waiting for the water level to fall they were trying to release the vessel, and the superstructure was simply too tall to clear the span.

It was a long wait, and as evening fell the metal-cutter sent showers of sparks cascading over the black water whose velocity was emphasised by occasional blocks of polystyrene flotsam dashing by like ice floes.

The emergency services had great fun rushing about, flashing their lights and blaring their sirens. Someone must have been in overall control of the fire engines, police, ambulances and inflatable rescue launch, but chaos seemed to reign. A ladder had been lowered from the bridge parapet to the stricken vessel and various people risked death to climb aboard and back again for no apparent purpose.

Eventually the bridge was cleared of spectators, and a gigantic mobile crane lifted the cabin whole, and dumped it into the barge's hold.

The crew who, to a man, had stayed on board were issued with luminescent lifejackets. Only the captain declined to put one on.

The boat's engine started, and the stern swung round. Under the arch it pivoted, then jammed again.

Jacks, wedged between deck and arch, were used to release it, and finally it broke free.

Spotlights illuminated the vessel as the captain fought to beach it before it was swept over the weir. With the motor at full throttle he turned the bow upstream and steered for the bank. If the engine failed there would be little chance of survival.

Not a sound emanated from the spectators.

A hundred metres short of the awful rim of white water a line was thrown ashore, was caught, and swiftly tied to a tree.

Anchors, chucked from the bow, helped to arc the barge into comparatively slack water and more lines were attached to more trees.

With a clunk the hull struck the bank. A disaster had been averted.

The onlookers broke into spontaneous applause, and as the crew jumped ashore they were handed bottles of wine. But the brave captain remained on board staring at the jagged square of metal which, like the remains of walls found at an archaeological dig, showed where his wheelhouse had once stood.

Spotlights were switched off. The show was over and I joined the crowd heading back through the delightful old town towards the cobbled central piazza where, being Saturday, much wine was destined to be drunk.

Planning to be off early in the morning I took this opportunity to pop into the cathedral where I was confronted by a sinister and shadowy statue of Christ, lit by candles from below, his wounds depicted in colourful and dreadful detail. He would not have looked out of place in the Chamber of Horrors.

Frescos displayed angels thrusting naked sinners into Hell where they were being attacked by serpents, while against one wall a line of contemporary miscreants sat on a bench on a dais, queuing to avoid a similar fate.

I sneaked a look into one of the confessionals. Here there was no anonymity. Priest and penitent sat eye to eye.

'Hello, Mario. How're things?'

'Fine thanks, Father. And yourself?'

'How'd anyone feel after eating Mrs Borelli's *frittatas*? But let's be getting on with it.'

'Let me think. Well on Thursday I had sex with my sister in-law.'

'That'll be Claudia?'

'What a memory you have, Father.'

'All part of the job. Besides she was in on Friday.'

'That's about it.'

'You disappoint me, Mario. I've ticked you off about all this adultery before, haven't I?'

'You have, Father.'

'Well it's got to stop! For your penance say five decades of the rosary.'

'Five?'

'Five! Now be off with you. And if you can't be good, be careful.'

As I drifted into sleep I was aware of something inching up the wall beside my pillow.

I switched on the light and saw a large centipede with spindly legs – like a boat race crew filmed from a helicopter – rowing up the choppy blue wallpaper.

Without waiting to discover if it was a leaping venomous variety I grabbed the nearest book – which happened to be *The Path to Rome* – and made an instant fossil of the creature by imprinting it into the wall. Cruel, I know, but you cannot be too careful with animals exhibiting excessive legs. Once, while I slept under an olive tree, a giant millepede crawled into my sleeping bag and bit my backside. Then it was not the pain that bothered me but the knowledge that it, like all foreign creepy-crawlies, only slip out of their loathsome crannies at night, silently.

Assuming the centipede had friends lurking behind the skirting board I slept with the light on, trusting in photophobia to keep the beasts at bay.

Lodi to Fidenza

Fog choked the cobbled alleys between Lodi's tall red-headed houses, although a woman, the shape and pattern of a Russian doll, was pegging sheets in a courtyard below my room.

It was only 6 a.m. but this insomniac must have heard an encouraging forecast.

I opened a window and the fog was sucked into my room like tobacco smoke into lungs.

Lombardy in daylight is dull. In fog it is invisible, and not wishing to be run down by maniacal deliverers of milk and Sunday papers I left the main road and took minor lanes, which, on this stretch of the plain, run more or less parallel to the Piacenzan Way.

The landscape was exactly the same as it had been the previous day except that I could see less of it, visibility being restricted to fifty metres.

I use the word 'lane' to describe my route although it is an inaccurate description. 'Lane' conjures up by-ways flanked by flowery banks and hedges where wrens and robins chirrup. There were no flowers here, and no hedges, although there were birds; not many, for the Italians delight in slaughtering everything that flies – apart from hooded crows, which thrive. Perhaps they are not as palatable as skylarks?

Soon, I promised myself, the sun would melt through and I would see the foothills of the Apennines rising like a wave on the horizon. But the fog persisted.

Occasionally I glimpsed stubbly men in stubbly fields doing nothing in particular, although some carried guns. Perhaps they were waiting for the fog to lift in order to shoot a few warblers flying down from English country gardens for a winter break in the sun?

Signposts pointed to villages always a kilometre or two off my road and I seldom saw more than a few houses grouped together. Only a dozen or so cars passed me all morning although a horse and cart, which I heard five minutes before I saw it, creaked and clopped out of the murk. Its driver, a septuagenarian with a face as wizened as the Tollund bogman's, was half asleep, a polished boot dangling only inches from the road. The bandy mare did not look much younger, and as she passed she hoisted her matted tail and left a trail of steam for me to follow.

I reached the outskirts of Codogno shortly before noon, just as the white ceiling of moisture was turning blue.

After trudging beside endless chilly fields the old streets of Codogno were a deliverance. Promenading families paraded in their best Sunday suits and dresses. The children, rewarded for sitting through sermons, sucked ice cream or sank their teeth into squelchy cakes.

I was the object of polite derision, for although the sun now shone brightly the transition had been subtle and I was still wearing an anorak, balaclava and gloves, while my rucksack, more suited to the Bernese Oberland than this quiet agricultural town, must have seemed absurdly incongruous. But I was glad to be amongst these smiling people and I did not mind their laughter at my expense. After all I was a strange stranger, and not many walkers dressed like alpinists could have interrupted Codogno's Sunday morning routine.

Outside the main church, stalls specialising in rosaries, plastic Virgins, missals and flowers for graves were manned by women raising money for charity.

Business was far from brisk but a late sung mass was in progress and most of the customers were still inside.

I entered the church, which was full to bursting, and stood at the back while a handsome young priest, shouting like a disc jockey into a microphone, exhorted the congregation to sing louder, *louder*!

Behind him a second congregation, composed entirely of priests and acolytes, performed ritual accompaniment with bells and thuribles.

The hymn was more tuneful than its singers, and after a dozen verses I left but not before having a collection plate thrust under my nose. I contributed more than I intended and suspect I might be responsible for an entire tile on the new church roof.

Behind the church, in the town square, I sat on a bench under chestnut trees and watched a wasp laying eggs in the gravel path while a sunken-cheeked old man – a widower I assume – talked to himself or his wife.

A leaf fell into my lap and I slipped it inside my map for a souvenir.

I had walked far too fast from Lodi, and my legs and back ached from the effort.

With my pack for a pillow I lay at full stretch on the bench and let the dappled light tickle my face. The heavy load of perpetual cold which I had carried more or less all the way from Toul fell from my shoulders, and like a man who has finally repaid the last penny of his debts I felt wonderfully insouciant. This was Italy as I had imagined it, and free from worry I slid into a deep sleep.

The muttering man had gone when I awoke, and the trees' shadows had shifted a few degrees to the east. It was not yet two o'clock and Piacenza, where I planned to spend the night, was only a dozen kilometres away.

Sleep had not dissipated my ebullience and so I chose a bar across the square and ordered a glass of spumante.

Men in a back room were playing a variation of bar billiards; their aim to pot balls without disturbing a cruciform arrangement of studs in the centre of the table. The champ, all greased hair and expensive jewellery, played shots worthy of a world-class snooker star, and each time he won he paid the penalty by buying a round of drinks for his opponents. In England the loser pays, in sport and just about everything else.

The bubbles rose straight to my head for I had eaten nothing since the previous evening, and I sat outside in the sun drinking a second and third glass while a Friesian cat with amber eyes slept on my knees, its claws hooked into my trousers.

A fourth glass served to weaken my resolve.

The Devil, perching languorously on my left shoulder, was perfectly reasonable. It was hot for me – although cool for him. And what *was* the point of staggering the short distance to Piacenza along shadeless roads? The angel on my right shoulder was having a siesta, and despite strenuous efforts I failed to wake her. Consequently, no tortuous ethical debate ensued. The die was cast.

The barman pointed me in the direction of the station where, for thirty pence, I bought a ticket to Piacenza.

The train was a double-decker bus on rails.

Upstairs the windows, all firmly fastened, were producing a greenhouse effect but I dared not break the age-old Italian tradition of keeping fresh air where it properly belongs: outside.

Perhaps they use double-deckers in an effort to make the monotonous countryside appear more appealing to the passengers? There is more land and less sky when you are four metres tall, but although heat-haze had replaced fog the empty fields remained empty fields. And in less time than it takes to expire from asphyxiation we were crossing the River Po whose pewter surface half submerged an island at its centre from which only the autumnal crowns of bowed trees protruded.

Invariably I find rivers without a backdrop of hills unappealing for they are usually straight and reflect nothing but the sky, which can be as dull as ditchwater. The Po is just such a river and not even clouds could enliven its swirls and surges.

Piacenza is built on its southern bank.

I did not have a map of the city but walked instinctively towards the centre, passing through a grubby park whose paths were separated by threadbare carpets of parched grass.

The park was empty apart from a gang of sullen youths and silent apart from the rattle of a can kicked by the only young woman I saw in the whole of Italy who had made a deliberate effort to look unfeminine. Greasy hair, unwashed for weeks, hung from a Guevara-style beret, and her matching suit of camouflage jacket and trousers did nothing to enhance a face whose muscles were rigid with anger.

As we passed I smiled but she replied with a scowl of contempt, revealing dirty teeth.

I turned to watch as she continued kicking the can with her black military-style boots.

When she reached the gang they began taunting her but she was unafraid. On the contrary, she picked up the can and threw it at them. She missed but hit them, I suspect, with some well-aimed words, for their good-humoured jibes turned to invective. But it was they who walked away, leaving her victorious and full of hate.

Via Rome led me towards Piazza Cavalli which was occupied only by equestrian statues. Colonnades, casting Stygian shadows, imbued the empty square with a nightmarish atmosphere and I was reminded of certain sombre paintings by Giorgio de Chirico, who, though born in Greece, was an Italian painter.

A dusty canyon of a street headed off Piazza Cavalli towards infinity, and having no desire to walk its entire length without purpose I chose a side street that brought me, by chance, to the cathedral, whose doors were locked.

Only one person shared the cathedral square with me, and she was a heart-rending sight.

She sat, hunched, on a step, draped in a tattered shawl despite the heat. She had hoisted her filthy skirt up to her thighs, and through the holes in her stained stockings I saw that her knees were raw and scabby. She must have been almost seventy but had dyed her hair black in a pathetic effort to disguise her decrepitude. Such women – bag ladies as they have come to be called – can be found in every civilised city but what made her particularly pitiful was the red plastic rose in her hair. I imagined her as she might be in a year or two when, if she survived, the same immutable flower would still be blooming.

As I watched her a yellow rivulet trickled from beneath her skirt and formed a fall on the steps.

I should have done something for her but I played the priest and passed by on the other side of the street.

Piacenza had oppressed me greatly. I felt stifled and had only one thought: to abandon it as soon as possible.

Back in the park I looked at my map and was faced with a problem I had anticipated but whose solution I had postponed.

From Piacenza the Emilian Way – Route 9 – follows an unswerving line the forty kilometres to Fidenza where my path would lead me south-east, away from flatness and into the foothills of the Apennines. But all the lanes leaving this busy road do so at right angles, like the teeth of a comb, and there is no parallel alternative for a walker.

Belloc, who trudged this way, wrote: 'And all these miles of road fade into the confused memory of that intolerable plain.'

And so, without regret, then or since, I avoided a night in Piacenza and a day of traffic-dodging by taking a train to Fidenza.

From an inter-city express laden with tourists I saw irrigation drains, crows and fields. Had I walked this stretch I would have described irrigation drains, crows and fields.

I expected to see the Apennines rising like giants in the south, but even their toes were hidden behind a blue haze.

I felt totally alienated from my fellow passengers and was glad to see the back of them when, after twenty minutes, I stepped on to the platform at Fidenza.

There are towns and there are my kind of towns.

Fidenza was my kind of town, and I am not sure why, unless it is because I have an affinity with places that can be traversed on foot in twenty minutes and have nothing to attract the international army of culture-snappers.

The evening promenade was just beginning and I joined families sauntering arm in arm along the main street.

A well-attended meeting of the Communist Party appeared to be in progress. Red flags hung from the balconies of houses grouped around a square. A crowd jostled. Policemen strutted. An ambulance was parked in readiness. However, the singing I heard was not the *Internationale* but a hymn to an older god.

The cathedral was overflowing and I only caught a glimpse of the stage. The bishop (hence the red flags) was performing an operatic mass aided by a milling chorus of lesser clergy whose sheer number made the Codogno mass seem like amateur dramatics. A grand production of Verdi's *Aïda* or the finale of a major fashion show would not have provided more resplendent and varied costumes. No wonder Catholicism still does such good business in Italy despite heavy leanings to the Left amongst a large proportion of the electorate.

In most Italian towns there are things you will not find in Iowa or Cornwall; brass plates engraved with hammers and sickles proclaiming the local headquarters of the Communist Party.

Later, in Siena, I met an American in a bar who could not understand why Communism not only flourishes in Italy, but is allowed to do so.

I tried to explain that there are differences between the Italians and the Chinese.

'Reds are Reds,' he said, 'no matter what colour they are. Besides, they don't need it here. They're doing all right.'

'Haven't you seen any signs of poverty?' I asked.

'I didn't come 5,000 miles to look for poverty. I'm here for the art.'

Leave the guided tours and you will find poverty in Italy. Villages perched on hilltops may appear picturesque from an air-conditioned coach, but if you walk the back alleys and smell the stink and peer into the sparsely furnished rooms of crumbling overcrowded houses you will find poverty.

As night descended on Fidenza I sat outside a jolly restaurant, eating pizzas, and watched a thermometer's digital display flickering between 23 and 24°C. Teenage boys in Levi's and T-shirts revved their motorbikes like cock birds performing mating rituals. Some struck lucky. Girls in pleated miniskirts would detach themselves from flocks of female friends to be swept away into the night, not sitting side-saddle as they would have done twenty years ago, but riding provocatively astride the pillions.

It was a night designed for the young. Stars speckled the sky, and the air was warm enough for moon-bathing.

In the fields around Fidenza sins of passion, destined for the following Saturday's confessions, were doubtless being enjoyed.

By nine o'clock I was in bed with a limp thriller and woke, as usual, with a naggingly clear conscience.

Fidenza to Calestano

The cloudless night had caused another autumn fog to form but I was impatient to be away and into the hills.

At half past six I thought I would have the streets to myself, but people were already hurrying to catch commuter trains to Parma or Piacenza.

The plain was in the past, or so I thought as I walked south briefly, then more or less east along little roads whose verges were laced with dewy webs. Only a couple of cars and a tractor passed me, which was just as well for once again I found myself the centre of a moving circle with a restricted radius of visibility.

But despite the fog I perceived subtle changes in the landscape. I actually found myself walking up and down hills, or rather inclines. Streams flowed faster and I saw livestock in fields far greener then before. Mares bolted round and round one paddock, appearing and disappearing in the fog as regularly as painted horses on a carousel.

I passed through hamlets that seemed devoid of life apart from roaming dogs, and hurried on in the hope that once I reached the valley of the River Taro the air would clear and I would see the Apennines rising all around me.

By ten o'clock I had reached the Taro Valley south of Nocelo, although the river was still some way to the east, separated from me by the trans-Apennine *autostrada* leading to La Spézia on the Ligurian coast.

At long last the fog was evaporating, and although I saw no startling individual peaks I perceived a line of hills rising to the south-west. I could not gauge their height for all detail was lost in a violet wash below a strangely crinkled sky the colour of parchment.

Ahead of me were the valleys and small towns that Belloc had described so vividly. It was the section I had been looking forward to most; and if section appears a prosaic word, more in keeping with a soldier on manoeuvres than a traveller, then I must reiterate that Belloc's route has no continuity apart from its line. It is a series of random sectors, defined by geographical boundaries, and this is both its charm and its weakness.

Somewhere in England an enemy – a creditor probably – was sticking needles in the kneecap of a voodoo doll created in my image, and so I rested on the roadside just north of Medesano.

I was lost in thought when a heap of a lorry, overloaded with stones, pulled up beside me. The haggard driver leaned out and said, 'Fornovo?'

'*Sì,*' I replied in my best Italian, pointing down the road. 'Fornovo.'

His head disappeared from the window, but the engine continued to tick over in neutral.

Half a minute later his head reappeared, tortoise-like, from the window. 'Fornovo?'

'*Sì!*' I pointed ahead and he pointed at me.

He had mistaken me for a hitchhiker and was offering me a lift.

And for his sake only – it would have been churlish to reject his kind offer – I clambered into the oily cab and we set off to the accompaniment of grinding gears and pebbles avalanching on to the tarmac. Windscreens would be lost on Route 357 that day.

A cigarette, pinched flat halfway along and held in place by a gap between his lower teeth, jerked up and down as he talked via a voice-box choked with ash.

The obvious handicap of mutual incomprehension did not deter him and while he chattered I tried not to look at him. But like an onlooker at a messy road accident my eyes kept straying back to a face stippled with blackheads more numerous than buttercups in an English meadow. Every greasy crease had been colonised, and I was reminded of nineteenth-century prints of tattooed Maoris.

Only when he pointed and said, '*Fornovo!*' did my horrid fascination end.

Belloc was carried across the Taro by a peasant.

I crossed by road-bridge although the Taro was not there. Instead of the raging mountain torrent I had anticipated there was a token stream which any toddler could have forded without assistance.

The rest of the wide and stony riverbed consisted of stagnant pools and drooping sun-blanched weeds. Rain and snow in the Alps might be filling the Adda, Lambro and Po, but here in the Apennines there was drought.

My lift of eight or nine kilometres with the kind-hearted lorry driver had saved me considerable time and I found myself at my day's destination by early afternoon. And so I mooched around the town, searching unsuccessfully for its soul.

Fornovo is not a Gateway To The Mountains sort of place: In truth it is a bit of a dump, ineffectively combining old stucco-fronted houses, modern flats and some kind of chemical works. An emerald river might have made it tolerable, but scummy puddles, above which squadrons of midges performed aerobatics prior to a night attack on the town, were an inadequate substitute.

In a smoky bar beneath a hotel I drank wine and asked if there were rooms.

They were all taken, the owner assured me, and I did not blame him for turning me down. I had failed to find a launderette in Fidenza and, frankly, my clothes were smelling none too fresh. Were there other hotels? No, apart from a motel sixteen kilometres down the *autostrada*.

I did not like Fornovo and was glad to have had my mind made up for me. I would press on to Calestano, only thirteen kilometres away which, with luck, I would reach by dusk.

I walked south for a little way, then turned up a minor road curling up into the foothills.

The Swiss Alps are masculine, strutting across the skyline like a victorious football team. Above Fornovo the landscape is feminine, its rounded features and folds gentle and demure. There are no great crags or jagged crests but pastures and brown corduroy fields, many ploughed on impossible slopes, like the domed fields in children's paintings. Every available square metre is cultivated although further away, and much higher, I could see scrub and the margins of forests made black by shadows.

In Belloc's day these roads were rough tracks, but having traced his route on my map I had discovered that even the goat paths he had described, linking the higher villages, are now metalled.

The sun beat down from a yellow-blue sky but the way was not too steep and I had enough liquid with me to prevent dehydration. Scientists tell us that we are 70 per cent water. The Queen? 70 per cent water? It's absurd.

I had not gone far when a bus full of laughter approached. I stood back to let it pass but it stopped. The driver obviously thought that no one is his right mind would voluntarily walk uphill, carrying a pack, in the afternoon heat.

'Calestano?' he asked, and this time I knew that he knew the way.

Guiltily I got on. I suppose that if, like Belloc, I had accepted lifts in rustic carts I would have seemed less irresolute. But I was pleased to be amongst these vivacious youngsters who were being scattered back to the countryside after a day's schooling in Fornovo. Besides, faces are always more fascinating than fields; and that is why, even now that the weather was warmer, I had no desire to pitch a sepulchral tent by the roadside and remain alone all night, like a corpse, awaiting resurrection at dawn.

The bus stopped at lonely farms and hamlets where impatient mothers waited to welcome their children with hugs and kisses. One of the boys fleetingly reminded me of one of my sons and I ached to be home with my family. I no longer glanced at their photograph in my wallet. Their faces were too definite, superimposing themselves on my almost abstract images of them. And I could not return their smiles.

From the broad saddle separating the Taro and Baganza valleys distant white villages were visible on the slopes of higher ridges, their outlines smudged by haze.

Then, as we rounded a corner, I saw Calestano in a coombe far below. My first mountain town.

There is only one inn in Calestano and I was welcomed with open arms by the owner, a strikingly handsome and confident man in his fifties with silver hair and a black moustache like a baby bat roosting under his nose.

In the restaurant adjoining the bar a tenor, accompanied by a chorus of cronies, was singing a ballad. His voice was rich and the harmony expertly and subtly improvised despite a score of empty wine bottles on the table. Perhaps because of them.

I have listened to the Welsh singing on countless occasions, but never with such bravura and instinctive melodiousness. There is never any hint of sex in a Welsh male voice choir. If you have ever heard the Glasinfryn Glee Club singing a Beatles number, then you will know exactly what I mean. One could be in a chapel on a wet Sunday.

Belloc's reception in Calestano was less effusive than mine. He had been told that no bed was available, and had been arrested – briefly – on a charge of being a suspicious character. Later, exonerated, he had enjoyed the contrite inhabitants' hospitality.

The people of Calestano are still hospitable.

Before I had time to set down my pack a glass of sparkling wine was pressed into my hands.

Two customers, Mario and Alberto, spoke excellent English and acted as interpreters.

Was there a room available?

Certainly.

A single?

But of course.

How much?

The inn-keeper consulted his wife. Much mumbling. Would 12,000 lira (£8) be acceptable?

I accepted, and with the deal clinched I bought wine for everyone, who, in turn, were duty-bound to return my gift. Let me recommend an empty stomach as an economic route to inebriation, but only if the company is entertaining and the sun is shining and you have a place to lay your head.

Very old men, wearing wide-brimmed hats indoors, sat at a table, playing cards, and I wondered if the oldest might have been a babe in arms when Belloc had stayed here. I asked if anyone had heard of him but heads were shaken. Obviously Calestano had excited Belloc more than Belloc had excited Calestano.

I bought green apples and red wine in the village shop and sat on my little balcony watching sparrows taking dustbaths. A distinctive hill – which I think is the one Belloc mentions – is now about 100 metres higher, its summit a steel television mast. But apart from this modern intrusion the surrounding ranges could not have altered much in ninety years. Bare slopes and fans of sand and scree divided spurs of deciduous trees whose leaves had yet to turn, and as the last flame of the sun was quenched the valley was flooded with purple shadows.

Something had to be done about my clothes.

I asked if there was a launderette in the village and was surprised to be told that there was one. But the launderette turned out to be a dry-cleaners.

The manageress, whose gossip with a friend I had interrupted, said that she could let me have my things back in two days.

'But I need them by tomorrow morning.'

'Sorry, but it is not possible.'

I turned to leave.

'Wait!' she called. 'Show me what you want done.'

I handed her the black dustbin-liner in which I kept my compost heap of festering clothes.

Like a child enjoying a lucky dip she delved and brought out each item, one by one, holding it aloft for her and her friend to scrutinise. Odd socks were neatly arranged in pairs on the counter. Pants likewise. And although she was as clinical as a nurse I could have died of shame.

When all had been assessed she looked at me long and hard, then said, 'Tomorrow. Eight o'clock.'

'In the morning?'

She nodded, and I fled.

At the inn a little girl, dressed all in white like a first communicant, brought me *vino frizzante*, and I ate a four course meal for which I was charged next to nothing.

I left my windows open and a warm breeze carried the sounds of cicadas into my room. Sunshine can simulate the south, even in Aberdeen, but not until you hear cicadas can you be sure of being there.

Content, I fell asleep beneath a ceramic Virgin with a broken nose.

Calestano to Reggio

The sun rose like a pearl into a pale blue sky, and infused with optimism I leapt out of bed and stood naked by the window until spotted by an early-bird woman shuffling along the street.

At eight on the dot I collected my weighty pile of damp clothes from the cleaners. Without batting an eyelid the manageress charged me £25; but cellophane wrapping for my three shirts was included in the price and so I did not quibble.

I packed, breakfasted, then made a fatal error.

With my rucksack on my back I left my room. I closed the door, then remembered that I had forgotten to look under the bed, a habit I had adopted since losing a book in France.

Without thinking to remove my pack I bent down and felt something snap in my back. I straightened up and everything seemed fine apart from a twinge where my vertebrae turned to hips.

I said goodbye to my kind hosts – who insisted I drink a parting glass of wine – then walked the short distance to the T-junction where the lane to Pastorello branches off along a hillside. And here the rest of my journey was put in jeopardy.

Walking uphill activated different muscles and a sudden excruciating pain in my back caused me, instinctively, to throw off my pack. But I had forgotten my waist-strap and the weight pulled me down towards the verge where I fell in a heap.

I struggled to rise, and when I finally got to my feet I could already feel my lumbar muscles seizing up.

The thing I had feared most had finally happened, and I stood opposite a cemetery, swearing at the top of my voice.

If past experience was anything to go by then it seemed likely that I would be totally incapacitated for several days, but before rigor mortis set in I had to return to the inn. Should I leave my rucksack by the road? No, I decided. Its loss would complicate matters considerably and so I lifted it, gingerly, on to my shoulders. Suddenly it was twice as heavy.

Normal strides were impossible and, using my blackthorn as a walking stick, I minced back to the inn whose steps I could not climb. I let my pack fall and, leaving it outside, eased my way into the bar.

The innkeeper and his wife, brimming with solicitude, gave me wine while I sat on a hard-backed chair wondering what the hell to do.

A boy fetched my rucksack and I swallowed an overdose of painkillers and muscle-relaxants. *Avoid alcohol* the bottles warned. I drank more wine. I was desperately disappointed and my disappointment turned to anger.

I was determined not to be beaten. Sitting still with an L-shaped back was not sensible, and so I spent half an hour hobbling around the bar.

The alcohol and chemicals seemed to be working. I could actually move, although a hike over the hills was out of the question. In retrospect I realise that I should have remained in Calestano, but I was behaving irrationally, and as the day wore on my decisions were to become less and less sensible.

I decided to take a bus to Langhirano, a small town in the next valley from which, should my condition worsen, I would go north to Parma. But when I enquired I learned that there were no bus routes across the hills. Plan two. I would hitchhike. It was only sixteen kilometres, and the following day, if it was feasible, I would walk to Castelnovo ne'Monte.

The innkeeper lifted the rucksack on to my shoulders and I took over twenty minutes to cover the 500 metres separating me from the road junction.

I stood under a tree for six hot hours, during which time only six cars passed. Three stopped but the drivers were only going a kilometre and, not wishing to be stranded in the middle of nowhere, I turned them down.

I dared not sit on my pack and every so often I popped pills down my throat. They certainly worked. Now it only hurt when I moved.

My sole entertainment, apart from lizards crawling over my boots, was a roadblock where two policemen with automatic weapons were stopping and searching vehicles on the Calestano to Parma road.

Eventually, and inevitably, they came across and demanded my documents. One of them spoke excellent English. His trained eyes had spotted my limp and we chatted about backs.

'You must lie on a board,' he advised. 'It is the only way. And no making love, eh!'

Just the thought made me wince.

At 3.30, despairing of ever leaving, I adopted plan three. I hoisted my rucksack and started to walk my original route. It was an insane decision and I can only think that the powerful drugs that I had been eating like sweets had deprived me of reason. But for the pain I might have shuffled into the sunset, but after several hundred metres ropes were pulled in my central nervous system and alarm bells tolled in my head.

I turned back, and twenty-four hours after first entering the inn in Calestano I entered the inn in Calestano.

I drank wine.

Across the street a bus, proclaiming its destination as Parma, waited patiently while I formulated plan four. Bus to Parma. From there another bus to Langhirano. Sixty-four kilometres to achieve sixteen. Perfectly logical.

And so I headed away from Rome, back on to the awful plain.

I remember little about Parma apart from the traffic, the crowds, and a wide dry trench crossed by splendid bridges. The trench was the Parma River, and I was reminded of the special effects used in the film *The Day The Earth Caught Fire* when, with the world spinning off its axis, climatic changes caused the Thames to evaporate. Imagine London without its river and you will have some idea of how Parma appeared to me.

'There are no buses to Langhirano until five o'clock tomorrow evening,' the tourist office man informed me. 'But if you go to Reggio nell'Emilia you could go to Castelnovo in the morning.'

Where was Reggio? I spread my map on his desk. Nearly twenty miles to the east. Plan five. Bus to Reggio. Sleep. Bus to Castelnovo. Then – and now I was really going crazy – I would walk *back* to Calestano.

'I think you are most wise,' said the man when I acquiesced to his suggestion.

'Where do I get the bus to Reggio?'

'No bus. You must take the train.'

My dream was turning into a nightmare.

It took me an hour to reach the station, but the train was two hours late, and when it finally arrived I had to stand in a crammed corridor with my pack on, inhaling breath smelling of dead rats exhaled by a neighbour with stumps in lieu of teeth. And, like a fool, I had swallowed more pills to ease the pain which was now creeping down my legs via the sciatic nerves.

Darkness had fallen by the time I reached Reggio.

Not far from the station I found a seedy hotel in whose entrance three ladies of the night – a Chinese, a mulatto and a mock Swede whose ash-blonde hair did not match her sable eyebrows – were touting for clients. And with their cheap scent in my nostrils, and the policeman's advice ringing in my ears, I booked in; paying in advance for a double room.

I drank too much vermouth, and after trying to get through for an hour managed to reach my wife in England.

Apparently I sounded demented and she thought that I was cracking up.

'Calm down!' she kept telling me, but by now I was paranoiac. After all, hadn't the hotel management conspired to prevent my voice escaping their switchboard?

Upstairs on the landing there was much giggling from strangely attired women.

I found my room, bolted the door, and lay down on the floor between twin beds.

And as I tried to sleep I was disturbed in a number of ways. Through curtain-thin walls I heard the antics of men and women whose backs were obviously in fine fettle.

Reggio to Ligonchio

Rubbish trucks woke me before dawn.

I lay perfectly still, not daring to move for fear of discovering that I could not move. What if I could not? The door was bolted. Axes would have to be used and strangers would have to carry away my urine in vermouth bottles.

With a hand on each bed I pulled myself into a sitting position. So far so good. Carefully I stood. There should have been a drum roll to accompany this stupendous achievement but I had to make do with the cymbalic clash of dustbins in the street outside my window.

I could walk, but my knee was painful again. And then, to cap it all, I discovered I had piles.

I only publish this intimate and unappealing revelation for two reasons; first, because it has some bearing on what happened later; and second, to warn other travellers against a surfeit of Italian pizzas, which are the world's worst. Exercise can do nothing to prevent this unsexiest of afflictions. After all, I had walked a considerable distance and if one reads accounts of Himalayan expeditions the pages invariably itch with the symptoms.

My bus left at seven and it took me over an hour to stagger, bow-legged, to the bus station. Thank God I was not on my way to a life insurance medical.

The deserted pre-dawn city seemed sinister.

I walked along arcades whose arches formed a crypted foreground to pale and ghostly houses whose shuttered windows were dimly lit by street lamps whose feeble bulbs bled their light into the foggy air. De Chirico by night.

The bus station, a converted cavalry stable by the look of it, was empty apart from a clerk under glass in the corner of a vast subfusc waiting room that coincided with childhood images of purgatory. A reconstructed *Tyrannosaurus Rex* could have been displayed in there with a metre to spare between ceiling and snout.

I walked through ethereal fog towards the ticket office (yes, there was fog *inside*), but the ancient clerk pretended not to see me.

Was this purgatory? Had I died from a drug overdose in the night? And was this clerk going to ignore me for 10,000 years before issuing a ticket to heaven?

The only other occupant was a sad young nun knitting bootees. Had she been sidetracked from paradise for wanting babies?

'*Scusi?*' I kept repeating like a full-bladdered child trying to attract a teacher's attention, but only persistent tapping on the glass with a coin stirred the clerk into a semblance of action. Like a mechanical doll with run-down batteries his arms and legs made minimal movements, and when he finally opened his mouth he did not say *Mama* but something which sounded onomatopoeically below the belt.

Grateful for my ticket to Castelnovo I approached a vending machine that offered a selection of appetising beverages to accompany my breakfast of assorted pills. Eagerly I fed it with lire although the drink I received – warm water, no sugar, no milk – was not one of those advertised.

The bus sped through ugly Slough-coloured suburbs.

The fog persisted as we left the interminable straight runway of a road and took off, circling, into the hills.

Rain did not fall. It was flung down on to the roof like shingle thrown at a tin bucket by a petulant child. Flashes, which at first I took to be the refraction of approaching headlamps, turned out to be lightning, and by the time we reached Castelnovo ne'Monte a storm of cataclysmic intensity was raging.

I sought shelter in a bar and drank coffee with pills while bulbs flickered and white cylinders of water exploded in the square outside.

A chain-smoking woman in her fifties at a nearby table was shaking visibly. Each thunderclap jolted her like someone receiving electroconvulsive therapy, and I wondered if her terror might be rooted in wartime experiences. I tried to make eye contact but she was in her own private hell and oblivious to everything around her.

For almost two hours the storm raged.

The brown filter-tips in the woman's ashtray grew to resemble a miniature log pile while my stomach began to echo the thunder. I had been so obsessed with my back that I had forgotten to eat for twenty-four hours, and this bar provided no food.

The storm stopped with tropical abruptness.

The woman surfaced from her trance-like state, picked up her bag, and left looking like anyone whose shopping expedition had been interrupted by a shower.

Moving like a hermit-crab across the pools formed in the square I found a restaurant.

Although only ten o'clock the bar was crammed with card-playing men drinking wine, and when the barmaid put a glass in front of me and lifted a bottle interrogatively I gave her the nod.

The restaurant was in darkness but I had to eat.

'Can you cook me something?'

'What would you like?'

'Eggs. Fried eggs.'

'How many?'

'Two. No, three.'

'Of course.'

She led me into the restaurant, switched on lights, drew curtains, and set me a table on which she put a clean cloth, a vase of fresh flowers, half a loaf and a carafe of red wine.

The eggs were special. Their creamy yolks were great pinkish domes, like children's sherbet flying saucers, and the fluffy white bread I dunked into them had arrived fresh from the bakery.

Of course it was the worst meal I could have chosen, medically speaking, but the wine gave me the courage to visit a pharmacy.

My pocket dictionary failed me. There was nothing under *piles* or *haemorrhoids* and I thought I would have to suffer the indignity of miming my affliction.

Like a teenager attempting to buy contraceptives for the first time, I prayed that a man would serve me.

The lovely blonde woman smiled and said, '*Prego?*'

'*Buon giorno. Parla inglese?*'

'Better than you speak Italian.'

'Thank goodness. I have a slightly embarrassing problem.'

She grinned and said, 'Then perhaps you had better speak to my husband.'

The pharmacist, in his thirties, took me aside and said. 'How can I help you?'

'I don't know the Italian for it, but I have haemorrhoids.'

'The Italian for haemorrhoids is haemorrhoids.'

We both laughed.

'You have been eating too much pasta and not enough fruit, yes?'

'Yes.'

'I have just the thing for you.'

He returned with medication for which I was charged very little.

I said, 'If I got that on a National Health prescription in England it would have cost me twice or three times as much.'

'I am not surprised. I have read a lot about your country in the newspapers and I do not understand what is happening to it. It used to be the model for other countries. Now it is falling further and further behind.'

And so, for a long time, we chatted about Britain; about the Thatcher years, and our iniquitous electoral system.

He said, 'But a country run by a minority is no longer a democracy.'

I could not disagree, for I have outdated ideas about the meaning of the word 'democracy'. For me it still means government of all the people, by all the people, for all the people and I tried to explain how, for a significant proportion of the population, it had come to mean nothing but the prospect of advantageous tax relief and increased personal spending power. Social conscience had become unfashionable. Cabinet ministers with even a spark of conscience had been ousted, and the hard men – the mediocre men – had survived. Something, I suggested, was wrong when the House of Lords was more radical than the Commons.

The pharmacist's wife had joined us.

'Have you children?' she asked.

'Two.'

'Then you must worry for their future?'

'I do. I do.'

Being a Briton abroad these days is comparable with being a Haitian or a South African. Everyone wants to know the reason for our moral decline. And wearying of apologising for my country I changed the subject by complimenting them on their English.

'We studied at a language school in Exeter,' he explained.

'I live near there.'

'Devon is beautiful,' she said. 'The moors and the sea. You must miss it a lot.'

'Yes.'

'Why are you here without your family?'

I told them, and although they had not heard of Belloc the husband noted his name on a pad.

'My wife and I read a lot of books in English. We like Anthony Burgess very much.'

'Me too. I admire people who go out on a limb. In writing and everything else. I can't stand people who hold everything back.'

'Have you read James Joyce?'

'Of course. *A Portrait of the Artist* was my bible when I was young. I think a copy should be presented to every Catholic at puberty.'

'We had a bit of trouble with *Ulysses*, and as for *Finnegans Wake*, well . . .'

'Don't worry. It defeated me too.'

And so we chatted about this and that until a backlog of prescriptions called the husband to his scales, and his wife to the counter.

I said goodbye and left with a tube of Preparazione H concealed in a pocket.

It was time to make a decision. I was now thirty kilometres east of Calestano as the crow flies, but my back was still painful and my feet still tingled from pinched nerves.

I had missed the villages of Tizzano and Lagrimone but was determined to cross the high Passo di Pradarena, which would take me from the district of Emilia-Romagna into Tuscany.

The hamlet of Ligonchio is about 2,000 feet below the summit of the pass.

I decided to go there and rest. Then if I felt capable, I would walk over into the Sérchio valley the following day. A local bus, alive with singing children – who by one o'clock had already finished their day's schooling – took me out of the town which is dominated by a spectacular tabletop mountain, the Pietra di Bismäntova, whose grey walls rose sheer from a moat of smoky mist.

Like a medieval castle it dominates the landscape for many miles, and each time I thought it had finally been lost from view behind a spur it would reappear, its outline, seen from a fresh angle, altered but still impressive.

The sun broke through as we crawled along barren and brushy valleys, which had the appearance of not having been blessed with a single drop of rain for many months. The storm-water had already percolated into the porous soil and everything was dry and dusty.

The River Sécchio, no more than a stream, flowed green amongst white stones whose source was a great cliff of faulted rock.

A broad-winged bird of prey, an eagle or buzzard, soared vertically, like a bubble through water, its silhouette black against the crag's splendid natural mosaic of sedimentary rocks.

Every so often a child would alight at a farm far less prosperous than those I had seen above Fornovo; for here the earth was too harsh for cultivation and the farmers had to rely on sheep or goats to provide a meagre living.

Most of the children lived in the hilltop village of Sologno, which is approached by a steep and exposed road rising above a gully which, in winter, must flow with a tributary of the Sécchio.

Sologno, seen from afar, is photogenic. Its fortress of a site is spectacular, and from its approaches one can see across wooded hills to the northern plain which stretches unbroken towards the Dolomites.

Sologno at close quarters is not so beguiling. Tiled roofs are not so quaint when they are seen to be in dire need of repair. Walls, a water colourist's dream of coalescing tones, are less appealing when one realises that the subtle shades of greys and browns are caused by damp.

Not every hilltop town in Italy has the advantage of having an international airport nearby to supply it with coach-loads of prodigal tourists weighed down by credit cards and Nikons.

The tamed hills of southern Tuscany are fashionable with foreigners. Those in Emilia-Romagna are not. It is as simple as that.

From Sologno we followed a twisting lane through hillsides of oak and chestnuts where solitary shepherds and goatherds tended their flocks.

How pastoral it all looked. Put Beethoven on the soundtrack, film the sheep backlit so that their fleeces are burnished with gold, intercut a close-up of a doughty peasant (having told him to gaze wistfully into the middle distance) and there you have it. An award-winning documentary for city dwellers who can say, 'How peaceful. How simple. If only I . . .'

I looked closely at these lonely men as we passed. I had seen that expression before: on the faces of checkout girls in supermarkets. They were dying of boredom.

As we approached Ligonchio the sun was obscured by a black cloud billowing like smoke from a forest fire; a forest of rubber trees. And the Passo di Pradarena, whose difficulty I had hoped to evaluate, was lost from view.

Ligonchio is the end of the line for buses, and along with the few remaining children I stepped out into a drizzly little square.

Luckily – in some senses – one of the inns had forgotten to close.

The Ritz it was not. I was escorted upstairs and given a cell which the Howard League For Penal Reform might have condemned as unfit for human incarceration. The dun-walled room reeked of damp, and after I had pressed my hand into the mattress to test its firmness I found moisture on my fingertips. Dead woodlice lay in the basin and when I tried the taps I found them both *freddo*. I snatched back the sheets and although nothing scurried away I decided against actually sleeping in the bed.

My back was aching terribly and so I spread my sleeping bag on the floor, lay on it, and soon fell asleep.

The town clock, right outside my room, woke me at four. It was time for tea, or rather its Italian equivalent.

The bar downstairs was sombre but I bought the landlord wine and he returned my gift with grappa.

Groups of engrossed men sat playing deafening card games; each hand offered being flung down, like gauntlets, with a slap of fingers across table tops. Anger seemed to be in the air but it was only histrionics; old men playing eighteen. And at the end of each game laughter and rounds of strong drinks were exchanged.

I sat by a grimy window whose sill displayed a vast and diverse collection of dead flies. Live specimens butted the panes in an effort to escape but they were banging their heads against a glass wall. At a guess the window had not been opened since 1945.

Pulling focus from the flies to the surrounding hills I saw that the slopes had been carelessly painted by one of Mother Nature's less talented children. A contour line artificially separated summer from autumn. Below this horizontal band the leaves were green. Above they were as brown as winter bracken. No intermediate yellows or reds divided them, and I thought perhaps that a variation in species might account for this strange phenomenon; but no, both levels comprised the same mixture.

Directly below the window there was a grey reservoir and the bunker of a hydroelectric power station, its concrete stained by rain.

Flies began to settle on my hands and eyelids, and so I absconded into the dusk.

Even at a speed of only one kilometre per hour it took a mere twenty minutes to explore the village. I saw no people, only hens, cats and mongrels who looked too fed up to bite.

Not wishing to return to the flies or my slummy room I entered a bar.

A gargantuan bald man in his sixties greeted me. His shirt showed through the elbows of his sweater; a sign, in Italy, that he was either a bachelor or a widower.

I asked him for wine but he laughed, displaying teeth the colour of cork. He was a customer and he called to a blithe flamingo-thin girl who served me.

I bought the man wine and he clunked his glass against mine.

A young couple, whose smart clothes announced that they were from elsewhere, were sitting in a corner. I sat at the only other table.

When I had finished my wine the bald man said something I did not understand.

'He wants to buy you wine,' explained the young man in perfect English.

'Thank him for me but tell him there's no need.'

'That is not the point. You bought him a drink. Now he must repay you. It is the custom here.'

'In that case I'll accept. Ask him to join me.'

And so the four of us spent an hour together.

Marco and Rosa, both medical students in Genoa, were visiting Rosa's mother who lived in a nearby village. The bald man was Enrico.

After we had introduced ourselves Marco said 'We know that you are not an American, but we have made a bet that you are not English.'

'What then?'

'Irish?' suggested Rosa.

'Because of my Irish nose?'

'Because you seem more relaxed than most English people we have met.'

'Have you met many?'

'Oh yes,' said Marco. 'We have been to England several times, but we have not found the people sympathetic. Well? Are you Irish?'

'My passport's British, but three of my grandparents were from Ireland originally.'

'I love Ireland,' said Marco. 'And Irish music. So happy one moment and suddenly so sad, so melancholy. Like Italians.'

'Genoa is called the most English of Italian cities,' Rosa said.

'Why?'

'Because the people are so restrained.'

We talked of this and that until Enrico, who had been left on the sidelines, spoke. Marco, looking embarrassed, translated.

'He wanted to know if you are English or American, and when I said English he said he prefers Germans.'

'Ask him why.'

Enrico answered at length, but Marco summarised the monologue. 'He says it's because the Germans have more money and are better businessmen. He got to like them during the war. According to him they were good soldiers. He says that in 1943 he captured three English parachutists and found them very – proper. Very rigid.'

'They were probably scared stiff. Ask him what happened to them.'

'He says he does not want to talk about it.'

'What happened here during the war? When Italy joined the Allies?'

'It was terrible,' said Marco. 'Some still supported Mussolini but many joined the partisans. It is always terrible when there is civil war. Brothers fighting brothers, sons against fathers. But in this region there was much resistance and there were dreadful atrocities committed by the Nazis in Bologna.'

Enrico's ears pricked up when he heard Bologna mentioned, and a heated argument ensued between him and Marco.

Rosa finally managed to calm things down. I asked what had caused the row.

'This man is still a fascist at heart,' explained Marco whose face was flushed with anger. 'He started talking about the bombing at Bologna station in 1980. He said it was because of the Communists. He is mad. It was terrorists of the Right who did that wicked thing. He wants Italy to be the way it was fifty years ago. I do not. And so we argued.'

'Is he from this village?'

'No. He is from Reggio. He has only come here for the *funghi*.'

'It is the season for them here,' Rosa explained, 'and many people come into the mountains from the cities to collect them.'

Enrico stood up to go and held out a calloused hand. I hesitated but shook it perfunctorily, and for a moment our eyes met. He grinned, said something to Rosa and Marco, then left. I asked for a translation.

'He said you are all right for an Englishman but you hold hands like a woman.'

With Enrico gone we talked more freely, and for the second time that day I was asked for my opinions about the direction in which Britain was heading. And fuelled by Lambrusco my language was distinctly non-ambassadorial.

Meanwhile food was being prepared for me at the inn, and on my return I was led down into a basement dining room, which I shared with an asthmatic-sounding man and an extraordinary stuffed animal with a corgi's body and wolverine's head that bore no resemblance to anything Noah had taken into the ark. If such creatures existed in the forest then I would have to watch my step. And why was a string of garlic hanging from a peg?

A woman with astigmatism plonked a huge bottle of red Barbera in front of me.

I was not offered a menu. I would eat what I was given. A steaming volcano of cannelloni arrived, but the woman did not leave. She kept repeating '*Coniglio?*' and I explained that I did not understand.

It was time for a charade. She placed both hands above her forehead, fingers extended, and began to waggle them. I was confused, and seeing this, she tucked up her top lip and began to twitch her nose, squeaking as she did so.

'Ah,' I said. 'Rabbit!'

I looked up 'rabbit' in my dictionary just to make certain that she had not been miming corgi or wolverine.

'*Coniglio. Sì. Grazie.*'

I had not eaten rabbit since the fifties, when it was frequently served up in greasy stews at school. But I was ravenous (I had not yet eaten the cannelloni) and any qualms about eating flopsy bunnies were effaced by hunger.

As I began my cannelloni the wheezing man opposite began tapping his fork on his plate to attract my attention. He said something in a strangled high-pitched voice, and smiled. I smiled back and muttered a greeting.

But as he tackled his pasta the most terrible gurgling noises filled the room. I thought he was suffocating, and was about to rush to his assistance when I noticed a bandage, like a choker, around his throat, a safety pin perilously close to his Adam's apple. Obviously he had recently undergone a tracheotomy, and the gurgling was air escaping from the hole in his windpipe.

He continued to eat pasta, and I ate mine, although my enthusiasm was somewhat impaired by the constant guttural bubbling.

Replete, I pushed away my plate which was immediately replaced by a rabbit, complete with rib cage, lying like a wrecked vessel on a yellow beach of mushy polenta.

The woman smiled sweetly and I dared not refuse.

'OK?' she asked bashfully, inviting my appraisal of her cookery.

And while the gurgling man gurgled I detached bruise-coloured flesh from bone and began to chew. It must have been a very old rabbit, a suicide probably, but the woman was so sweet that I smiled and said, '*Mi piace moltissimo.*'

She bowed modestly and hurried back to her kitchen.

I ate it all although a significant percentage remained wedged between my teeth. I must have resembled a fox after a kill.

Fruit fit for a Caesar followed, and I realised how snotty I had been about her efforts. It had been a feast.

In the bar flickering footballers were fouling on a TV screen, while outside thunder and lightning were providing *son et lumière* around the power station.

Aching, and with a strenuous day ahead, I went up to my floor.

Something small and black fled behind the wardrobe when I switched on the light, and so, as in Lodi, I left it on. But my dreams were like the undersides of bricks in gardens, and when I woke at six I saw an enormous spider spread-eagled on the wall above my head.

But as my eyes focused I saw that it only had four legs. It was a crucifix.

Ligonchio to Castelnuovo di Garfagnana

By 6.45 a.m. the bar was already full of hawking village elders drinking coffee laced with grappa, and as in Calestano I was sent on my way with sparkling wine fizzing like Alka-Seltzer in my stomach.

Towards the pass the clouds were dark and ominous, and when rain began to fall I sheltered in the lee of a roadside shrine to the Virgin in order to put on waterproofs.

The lane, bordered by scrub, wound around gullies frothy with cappuccino-coloured streams.

Below the hamlet of Ospilatello the lane rises steeply, and with my back protesting I climbed at a snail's pace.

Ugly new apartments for skiers squatted cheek by jowl with traditional houses, and I was not tempted to stop.

I had already passed into autumn and the only sounds were raindrops dripping from black branches on to the forest floor where various fungi, like coral, floated on the leaf mould. No birds sang, and to break the awful silence I recited Gerard Manley Hopkins' poem 'Spring and Fall' aloud. It begins:

'Margarét are you gríeving
Over Goldengrove unleaving?'

and ends,

'It ís the blight man was born for,
It is Margaret you mourn for.'

Far from cheering me up this poem threw me into a melancholy frame of mind and so I sang instead, choosing 'Molly Malone', who, I had forgotten, died of a fever.

I lapsed into silence.

There was mist but no mellow fruitfulness, although my spirit soared temporarily when, though a break in the clouds, I briefly glimpsed the Pietra di Bismántova glowing like a spectral citadel in a stray shaft of sunlight.

The Passo di Pradarena approaches 5,000 feet and with altitude came winter. Icy fog, rising from the west, blew between trees stripped of their leaves and any hope of seeing the Tyrrhenian and Adriatic Seas from the summit were lost.

I was not having much luck with my mountain passes and I was reminded of similar conditions on the Ballon d'Alsace.

There is no rocky crest to this final ridge of the Apennines and I only realised I had reached the top when I saw a gloomy building, devoid of light, and noticed that I was beginning to walk downhill.

I was in Tuscany.

The loneliness was intense and I longed – as on the Ballon d'Alsace – to experience human contact; but not a single car passed, for there are easier routes to north and south.

I descended delicately through opacity, praying that my throbbing back would not let me down.

The fog's base was lower on the western slope and for several kilometres I neither heard nor saw anything other than tiny tributaries trickling towards the Sérchio Valley somewhere far below. And gunfire. Intermittent rifle shots informed me that deep in the woods hunters were slaughtering deer or wild boar.

The seasons reversed. Winter became autumn and autumn almost summer again when, just above the village of Capanne di Sillano, the fog lifted and I saw stands of chestnut trees so heavy with clusters of green fruit that, from a distance, they resembled apple orchards.

I picked plump chestnuts from the roadside, ate their sweet flesh and, filling my pockets with them, walked into Capanne di Sillano where the first building I saw was a restaurant.

Beneath a scythe-tusked boar's head I drank beer, while in a back room a party of leather-booted hunters, their chests bandoliered with bullets, were enjoying a rumbustious meal.

After the cemeterial silence of the pass I was glad to be amongst men again, although their laughter and snatches of songs only served to highlight the isolation which every lone traveller, flitting from place to place, must experience.

The lovely lane to Sillano twists and turns through forests, and while I sauntered along it the mist evaporated from the Sérchio, revealing a white hamlet on the steep wooded slopes opposite. Windows winked as a beam of sunlight crossed the river, scaled the hillside, and briefly encircled the houses. And for the first time that day I heard birdsong.

I did not stop in Sillano, where Belloc slept, but rested a little below the houses.

From above and from within Sillano is just another village, but seen from below its setting on a spur transforms it into a sight worthy of an Alitalia poster.

Soon I would be leaving the mountains for good. Beyond Lucca there would only be hills beside the road to Rome and I felt that fate had dealt me a succession of niggardly hands.

At every mountain pass Belloc had held five aces. Fine vistas, awaiting his arrival, had invariably materialised as soon as he poked his head over a ridge; whereas I, since crossing the Jura, had experienced rain, sleet, snow and fog. I was like a gambler with only one chip left, and that was on my shoulder.

Below Sillano my luck changed.

A high cloud to the west, brighter than the rest, was refusing to conform to the laws of nature. Instead of blowing along with the rest it stood firm. And as the sky cleared I saw that it was a mountain covered, so I thought, with snow. But it was not snow. It was pure white marble. And as I watched the skyline a succession of serrated rocky peaks emerged to form a truly alpine range rising from the green forests of the Garfagnana – as the Sérchio valley is called.

So myopic had I become, constantly referring to The Route, that I had failed to realise how close I had come to Carrara, which lay beyond these splendid peaks of the Apuan Alps, whose summits – unlike those of the Apennines – are inaccessible to all but mountaineers.

And, with Michelangelo in mind, I perceived them not as mere lumps of rock but as natural sculptures; and for the second time that day I found myself reciting Hopkins' poetry aloud, this time from 'No worst, there is none':

'O the mind, mind had mountains; cliffs of fall
Frightful, sheer, no-man-fathomed. Hold them cheap
May who ne'er hung there.'

In case you are thinking that I can quote from all the great poets then I must disabuse you. Once it was my good fortune to direct a biographical film about Hopkins that concentrated my mind wonderfully on his words, which, once learned, are unforgettable.

Thus I had my one vision in the hills, and feeling that the gods – possibly nudged by Belloc – had finally done me a good turn, I carried on down the steep road, vaguely aware that something was amiss.

After a kilometre or so I realised what was wrong. I had been so enraptured by the mountains that I had left my blackthorn beside the road. Never mind, I thought. I will buy another. And for a while I continued until I knew that I would have to return for it as I would do for a lost friend. And if this sounds absurdly anthropomorphic then all I can say in mitigation is that it had been my sole companion since Toul, fending off dogs and providing a calming mantra-like tap-tap-tap on a hundred lonely roads.

The sky had expelled all its clouds and in the stifling afternoon heat I retraced my steps and found my blackthorn resembling an alien sapling sprouting beside a rowan.

Down again I went, the river audible on my right as it rippled over boulders and snaked between gravel banks, until I reached the little town of Piazza al Sérchio, where the southern road to Castelnuovo di Garfagnana disappears into a limestone gorge.

I could hardly move and so, bent like a hunchback in an effort to alleviate the pain, I entered a bar, drank a litre of mineral water, and ate many pills.

I had hoped to continue to Castelnuovo on foot but I was all in. My crossing of the Passo di Pradarena had been foolhardy, but I was glad to have salvaged something of the Apennines.

Now I desperately needed to rest and so I took a little train the last thirteen kilometres to Castelnuovo along a delightful valley where I noticed the first of the famous Tuscan cypresses which were to accompany me all the way to Rome.

Belloc describes Castelnuovo as a 'horrible little place' but I liked its narrow alleys, which I followed, crossing the bridge Belloc sketched, to an inn whose plain wooden door belied the cool Moorish palace within.

Like a sultan I lay on a bed wide enough to accommodate my entire family, and slept.

I awoke a little later to cicadas chirping in a lemon tree outside my window.

The town square was restless with people milling around a cinema displaying an obscene poster for a sado-masochistic film.

Little children promenaded with their parents under a naked woman being lashed with whips, and I felt the deep-seated reactionary within me rising to the surface. It seemed so incongruous amongst these medieval streets, and although I realise that one cannot expect people to live in a museum of the mind I was angered by this tacky exploitative image of the present.

I dined, from the contents of a supermarket bag, on a terrace above the Sérchio.

The river, still glowing pink under an effulgent sky, was the trysting place for young lovers who stood, whispering and embracing, on its pebbly banks.

There was not a whip amongst them.

Brimming with a middle-aged man's memories of past amours I returned to my room where I lay wondering what might have happened to all those plain and pretty girls who had filled my youth with joy and torment. Where were they all? Was I still dimly remembered when certain pop songs were played on the radio? And I recalled how, a year previously, when returning from seeing a solicitor about my late mother's will, I had bought a ticket at a Surrey station close to where my childhood had unfolded into manhood.

As I turned away from the ticket office I had seen the woman who, as a teenager, had encouraged my first sexual relationship.

For a quarter of a century I had remembered her as she had been then: bright, funny, lithe and seductive. Now she was careworn and grossly overweight, a dress like a tepee unsuccessfully disguising her matronly bust and hips.

Our eyes had met but we had both feigned blindness and had gone our separate ways, forever probably, without saying a word.

And as I slid between the cool sheets in Castelnuovo I recalled lines from T. S. Eliot's 'Rhapsody on a Windy Night' which, at first reading, had so excited me with their acrid understated power:

'Smells of chestnuts in the streets,
And female smells in shuttered rooms.'

I remembered how smug I had felt when the priest teaching me English had glossed over these lines, blushing embarrassment. In my mind I had chanted, 'I know something you don't know. I know something you don't know.' Of course he had known a great deal about rhyme and metre and such things, but from that day on I have felt a healthy disrespect for literary types who delight in dissecting the human heart whose passionate beat they have never known.

> 'Bald heads forgetful of their sins,
> Old learned, respectable bald heads
> Edit and annotate the lines
> That young men, tossing on their beds,
> Rhymed out in love's despair
> To flatter beauty's ignorant ear.'

So begins Yeats' 'The Scholars', with which I caused a minor stir in the English Department at university when, instead of handing in a critical essay on Yeats' love poetry, requested by a withered fig of a lecturer, I offered her this poem.

Hopkins, Eliot, Yeats. Enough poets for one day.

Meanwhile, back in Castelnuovo, I lay in my shuttered room, malcontent with only the smell of fresh linen to excite my senses.

Castelnuovo di Garfagnana to Lucca

Sunshine grinned through the slats of my shutters, and on the rim of a terracotta jardinière in the garden a tartan lizard lay soaking in the heat.

I had slept for twelve hours and the firm mattress had done wonders for my back.

I popped into a little riverside church and sat for a while beneath a statue of the Virgin whose head was encircled by an electric halo, then wandered into the town centre, where, below the Rocca – the governor's crumbling palace – stalls laden with fruit and knick-knacks were already attracting vociferous customers under the shady arcades.

I asked a woman in the tourist office (yes, even in this little-visited place there was one) about the parallel roads to Lucca, and she told me that I would surely be knocked down, for each has the river gorge on one side and sheer cliffs rising on the other with no provision for pedestrians, particularly in the tunnels.

And so, in Castelnuovo di Garfagnana I made an important decision, for me if not for you.

Belloc's narrative dealing with the stretch from Castelnuovo to Rome is short and thin, for not only was he in a desperate hurry to finish his journey but was also taking a route that bypassed many of the places that give Tuscany its unique character. His path, now a straight, dull and dangerous main highway, circumvents the hills on which many of the Tuscan towns and cities are built, and never having visited this part of Italy I was determined to avoid a slavish adherence to his ruler of a route.

Coupled with this was the gnawing fear that my injury would prevent me completing the journey, and so I decided to walk only when circumstances merited the risk. Instead I would take local buses and trains, never travelling more than the equivalent of a day's walk within a twenty-four hour period.

Even Belloc, who had tackled this section mainly at night, had been tempted, and had succumbed to a rail journey from just south of Lucca to Siena.

Had I trudged along the valley I would not have visited Barga, an ancient hill-town a little to the south of Castelnuovo.

There, under a pergola threaded with vines, I sat in an eyrie with the green flames of cypresses below leading my eyes upward to the spiny peak of Pánia di Croce rising above ravines into a vibrant and violet sky.

I drank fruity white wine as cold as spring water and rejoiced at having finally caught summer's tail as it crept south along the peninsula towards Africa. Languorous cats sprawled on red-tiled roofs while the sound of someone practising the flute drifted up through the midday heat.

Empty alleys took me steeply up to the Romanesque cathedral where I did the things all tourists do. I admired the sculpted pulpit and the vaulting, then strolled back to the town, seeing no one.

All was peace and harmony until a sandy bitch like a lioness leapt at me from a bead-curtained doorway. This was no feint. She came straight at me and I hit her hard across her muzzle with my blackthorn. I shouted, filling the old town with my panic.

A liquorice-moustached woman emerged through the beads, waving her arms about and screaming abuse at me for attacking her pet monster. And walking backwards I retreated while the bitch growled and the woman snarled until I reached a corner. Then I ran.

I slept on the bus to Lucca, waking only once at Borgo a Mozzano, where I saw an extraordinary fourteenth-century footbridge, the Ponte della Maddalena, which crosses the Sérchio in one elegant span. And I took comfort from the fact that the tourist-office woman in Castelnuovo had been right. The roads were a death trap for pedestrians. Aftercomers beware.

Lucca is full of architecture. It is also full of the most beautiful women I have ever seen: tall, chic, with renaissance faces framed by curly honey-blonde hair, and an air of confidence – almost arrogance – about them. If you know the paintings of Botticelli, then you will be able to picture the women of Lucca better than I can describe them.

No hotel would accept me and so I wandered out through one of the four gates, Porta Elisa, which breach the red stone ramparts surrounding this perfectly preserved city.

I found a bed in a modern apartment block; in a flat owned by a widow who rented her daughter's room to tourists.

She still wore black but was bubbly and funny and brought me tea and biscuits as I sat by my window on the sixth floor gazing out across the northern plain towards distant hills from which a tidal wave of storm clouds thundered towards the city.

Forked lightning struck the fields and rain battered the window, but the squall was brief and left the gift of a double rainbow in its wake.

As the sun set over Lucca's rooftops I walked on its wide walls, which, having been planted with trees, now form a raised boulevard from which I hoped to understand the complicated layout of the streets better. But Lucca is flat and the walls not high and so I descended and wandered at will among its warren of alleys, popping into every church I passed, drinking in the atmosphere of each like a man on a pub crawl.

Belloc had treated himself to a lavish meal in Lucca and it was time, I reasoned, that I did the same.

Finding myself in a bustling piazza not far from the cathedral I chose a restaurant with tables geometrically arranged under an awning and, adopting a bourgeois manner, I ordered food from a food-waiter and wine from a wine-waiter.

It was a fine restaurant, but I had not counted on a cabaret.

A screeching of brakes and a crunch of metal heralded the entertainers.

Cars had been racing around the piazza like dodgems, and a male tailgater had smashed into the rear of a Fiat driven by a Medusa-haired woman who jumped out and began haranguing the offender, her arms flailing like Kali's, her voice rising above the cacophony of horns rebounding from the walls of historic buildings.

The police, who had been hanging around in gangs, preening, were immediately on the scene, but instead of clearing the two cars, thereby allowing traffic to flow, they began taking statements.

And so I ate my hors d'oeuvre to the accompaniment of discordant electronic music not unlike certain compositions by Lukas Foss.

A German-speaking family of four, all in shorts, sat at an adjoining table and began arguing about a watch the father had just bought his son.

Father perused the instructions like a lawyer going over the small print of a dubious will while the beneficiaries looked on. He turned to me and said, 'All this modern technology. The translation is terrible, but I think I understand it now. It works from water.'

Modern technology? I expressed scepticism.

'Really,' he said. 'When the digits start fading you must hold it under a tap.'

I had heard of water-clocks – but water-watches? Obviously the simpleton had been conned. But he handed over multilingual instructions which convinced me that he spoke the truth.

'Where are you from?' I asked.

'Switzerland,' he said, 'but we prefer Italy.'

'Why?'

'Switzerland is so dull. Nothing ever happens there. In Italy everything is unpredictable.'

'What do you do for a living?'

'I'm in motor insurance.'

His wife joined in. 'And the weather in Switzerland is so cold and damp. Here it is wonderful!'

There were goose pimples on her arms and legs, and our breath was condensing in the chill evening air. But this was Italy and so we all pretended for everyone's sake.

While I was eating my main course, Quasimodo sat at the table opposite and ordered a Carlsberg lager which he drank from the can. Soup followed, and being toothless he dunked his bread and sucked it noisily, dribbling diced vegetables down his filthy jacket and collarless shirt.

In England he would have been asked to leave, but when the restaurateur made his round of the tables he treated the poor man with the same courteousness he extended to the rest of his clientele.

The city was deserted as I walked through alleys and past houses that could hardly have changed in 600 years, but once beyond the walls I was back in the twentieth century and its bunker culture.

An unlit street passed the football stadium, and from the shadows beneath its overhanging concrete buttresses five youths emerged and crossed the road behind me, walking unsteadily.

Ready to break into a run I listened to their footsteps gaining on me, but at a junction they went their own way. Not a gang of muggers after all; probably just a few kids experimenting with solvents underneath the arches.

The widow was waiting up for me and pressed a finger to her lips as she led me on tiptoe past her daughter sleeping in a foetal position on a cramped sofa.

And, cosy in the daughter's comfortable bed, I slept like a log.

Lucca to San Gimignano

I took pot luck the next morning and, ignorant of the country, stuck a pin in a place called Empoli, which is about forty kilometres south-east of Lucca across a featureless plain.

I was so close to Pisa that I decided to take a C-shaped route to Empoli via this famous city. And so, after a morning of sightseeing in Lucca, I took a bus into the little range of barren hills separating the two cities.

From the crest I could see an architect's model of Pisa. There was the Tower, the Cathedral and the Baptistery, all white and gleaming in the sun. There were the red walls and the slug-slime River Arno mooching to the sea which I may have seen, for the horizon was all blue and I could not distinguish between air and water.

The bus took me to the north of the city where I confirmed that the Leaning Tower was still leaning. But among all these fine wedding-cake buildings there were thousands and thousands of tourists. By moonlight it must be magical, but I was still not attuned to the hordes and could not face the suited Japanese and baseball-hatted Americans with *Dot* and *Skip* pinned to their lapels.

I decided to move on, for Pisa is a place in which to stay, not do in a day.

Along the banks of the Arno there are elegant nineteenth-century houses where Byron and Shelley chose to live for a time – on opposite sides of the river – while to the south there is a concrete bus station where I boarded a sardine tin on wheels.

Away from all this beauty I sped along the Arno Valley. How wonderful it sounds. The Arno Valley in Tuscany. How awful it looked.

Ribbon development stretched for mile after mile; and all was ugliness: factories, apartment blocks, advertisement hoardings, filling stations and the visible smog from exhaust fumes forming a toxic stratum in the streets.

No one got off the bus but people kept getting on, and with my rucksack still strapped to my back I was crushed into a corner, my nose only centimetres from a dank and hairy female armpit. I could smell ravioli in the air.

On and on we went past flat dusty fields and into nondescript dusty towns. I had no idea where I was but was past caring. All I wanted was oxygen.

At Pontedera there was a general exodus and I grabbed a plastic seat designed for people with one buttock. To the south low hills disappeared into haze although I saw the odd tower rising from villages half hidden amongst vineyards and olive groves.

Empoli is a dump. There may be gems of Romanesque architecture hidden in backstreets but I did not find them. All I found was concrete and bricks.

The day had turned sultry and the ambience of the town reminded me of Fargo, North Dakota. I had taken a Greyhound straight out of Fargo and I took a train straight out of Empoli, to Certaldo, the first town of any size in the Elsa Valley, which leads south to Siena.

I was back on Belloc's rails, for he, despite his younger and perfectly functioning vertebrae, had given up hereabouts and taken a train to Siena.

At last I was amongst the hill country of central Tuscany; the hills so beloved by calendar-makers and wealthy sexagenarian English hippies.

The novelty of the landscape attracted me at first: the domed hills resembling old-fashioned beehives with their concentric furrows rising to crumbling ochreish farms perched on their tops; the windbreaks of cypresses; the chapels miles from anywhere.

Perhaps, in early summer, when these hills are golden with crops and aflame with poppies they are a wonder to behold but this autumn desert of perpetual brown clods soon palled and I sat back, playing Polonius, straining my ears to overhear a conversation between two young American girls hidden from view by the back of my seat.

'You didn't let him?'

'Sure. Why not?'

'You're crazy. You're not going to tell Steve, are you?'

'I haven't decided. We're usually totally honest with each other about the sexual side of our relationship.'

'Aren't you afraid of catching something?'

'Oh I made him wear two rubbers just to make sure.'

'Ssssh! Someone might hear.'

'Don't be stupid. We're not in Baltimore.'

As we pulled into Certaldo I made for the door, and passing the Americans I advised, 'Don't tell Steve.'

Boccaccio spent the last thirteen years of his life in Certaldo, and in 1793, 418 years after his death, the good citizens of the town, moved by righteous indignation at his lascivious and blasphemous stories, tore down a monument erected to his memory.

No one has erected a monument to the iconoclasts.

High above Certaldo there is a castle. Down below I traipsed through Certaldo's baking streets before returning to the station where I sat in the sun outside a bar with my trousers rolled up to my knees like a character from a Beryl Cook painting.

Two women in their early twenties sat nearby. Like the two in the train they also spoke English, but with plummy Roedean aplomb. I shut my eyes and listened. I could have been in an Islington wine bar.

I gathered that they were well-heeled art students, and although I never learned their names I will call them Tracy and Bev.

Tracy, the dominant one, was informing Bev that Michelangelo was really rather kitsch.

Bev attempted to contradict Tracy but Tracy knew more and longer words than Bev, and Bev, concealing her obvious resentment, said, 'I suppose I can see your point.'

I saw Bev's point. When sharing a room with a bossy travelling companion it doesn't do to disagree.

'Excuse me,' I interjected, 'but I haven't spoken to any English people for a while and I couldn't help noticing that you were – well – English.'

Tracy gave me the once-over and I found myself encountering the class barrier for the first time since leaving home.

She was confused. My accent, standard English, was acceptable, but I was unshaven and I was exposing my knees.

'Oh,' she said, her lofty thoughts sidetracked into a cul-de-sac.

'Why have you come to Certaldo?' I enquired, adding, 'if you don't mind my asking?'

As though quoting from some textbook Tracy said, 'There's a very fine example of a Mackintosh-designed building here so we popped over from Firenze to take a look.'

'The same Mackintosh who designed the Glasgow School of Art?'

'Yes, actually.' She frowned the frown of someone who is afraid of being shown up in front of an underling.

I know next to nothing about nineteenth and twentieth-century architecture and had only heard of Mackintosh in connection with the Glasgow building, which is revered by those who know about such things. But Tracy could not be sure that I was not an eccentric Professor of Art Nouveau on a sabbatical.

'You prefer recent architecture, do you?' I asked.

'Yes, actually. I mean all this old stuff's nice enough in its way, but, I mean, if I was living in the fourteenth century I wouldn't go on and on about the ninth and tenth centuries all the time so why should I become obsessed with the Renaissance? I live in the now and so I'm naturally more interested in now things.'

'Then you should go to Empoli,' I suggested. 'You'd love it.'

'Oh?'

'We could stop off there,' said Bev. 'It's on the way back to Florence – I mean Firenze.'

'What's there to see there?' demanded Tracy.

'Steel. Concrete. And there's a wonderful multi-storey car park.'

'Ha, ha, highly amusing,' said Tracy, looking far from amused. 'Now if you don't mind I don't think we wish to continue this rather silly conversation, actually.'

'Actually,' I said, 'neither do we.'

It was time for a map.

Up in the hills a few kilometres south-east of Certaldo I saw a name that appealed: San Gimignano. I would go there for the night even if it turned out to be the headquarters of a multinational petrochemical corporation.

Italophiles will wince at my Philistinism, and I have no excuse but my ignorance whose roots have grown from seeds sown long ago. I have never bought guidebooks, in the belief that personal discovery is preferable to being told what to expect. It is a policy doomed to produce great gaps in my knowledge but one to which I still adhere when travelling; for without a constant element of surprise the whole purpose of itinerancy is nullified.

San Gimignano surprised me.

Its slender towers soar from a hilltop like a medieval Manhattan. And these towers were built for the same purpose: to impress; not rival companies, but rival families.

As I approached it through olive groves I knew that I had discovered a gem, but why did no one else know of its existence?

They did.

Outside the main gate, tour buses encircled a park like wagons preparing for a Sioux attack – with hardly the space for a Winchester 73 between front and rear bumpers.

Via San Giovanni was chock-a-block with day trippers, but even they and the trinket shops could not detract from my realisation that I had stumbled upon a place that was not merely special but unique.

I learned that a convent had rooms to rent and so I crossed the town, found the airy and almost deserted Piazza Sant'Agostino, and rang the bell.

I waited for a long time while a small white-furred sleeping dog rose and fell on the chest of an old white-haired sleeping man taking a late siesta in the shadow of the church which is contiguous to the convent.

The huge wooden door finally creaked open and I was ushered in by a woman without a wimple who demanded money, but not a lot, and nicely.

Thus I entered the Convent of the Millepedes.

The pale walls of the cloister were like quarried limestone ornamented with living fossils, some curled in spirals like ammonites, others as linear as trilobites.

In the centre of the cloister there is a well and cypress trees, and a mood combining relief and peacefulness enveloped me as I followed the woman up a staircase smelling of polish and carbolic.

An aunt of mine was the Reverend Mother of an Ursuline convent school in London, and whenever I was taken into the strange, slippery and plaster-sainted nuns' quarters I smelt that same obsessive odour of sanctity.

An extraordinarily narrow corridor – against both sides of which the woman's wide hips brushed – overlooks the cloister. Along one wall there are a series of identical doors, one of which the woman opened with a key selected from a jangling bunch.

I was about to write that my room was like a cell. Of course it was exactly that, comprising a simple metal bedstead, a table, a chair, and the recent addition of a washbasin. Two millepedes formed a stencilled *D* on the wall, while human bloodstains, squeezed from the flattened corpses of mosquitoes, smeared the whitewash.

The woman gave me a set of keys and left me alone to reflect upon the lives that had been lived in this 8 x 6 foot box. All those solitary and celibate nights of voluntary incarceration stretching back for centuries. The interminable incantation of prayers. The examinations of conscience. The acts of contrition. The terror of hell and the hope of heaven. The sublimation of intellect and desires. The despair of those who found themselves confined at the behest of others.

I had had the foresight to buy a bottle of local wine while wandering through the town and I sat by the window watching the sun slide behind hills, which, now I was among them, were asserting a subtle and unexpected charm.

Cypresses and olives cast long shadows over dusty earth which was not, as I had first thought, a uniform brown but a combination of intermingled colours ranging from cinnamon to beech-grey.

Far to the north the ridges of the Apennines seemed no higher than a hedge, while the Elsa Valley below San Gimignano had been transformed into a white lake of mist.

The courtyard beneath my window had been allowed to run wild. Rusting netball hoops hung askew over a garden of weeds where giggling novices must have sported under an oblong of sky. An ancient tree, whose drooping boughs knelt amongst the yellow grass, was covered in orange leaves. In my notebook I wrote 'orange leaves', but then I saw that they were not; for among the leaves hung oranges and they were not remotely the same colour.

Hollows in the hills filled with shadows which overflowed into night.

I lay on the bed with a cup of wine and listened to a cicada clicking as regularly as a metronome. And through my open window I heard another guest, an Irishman, singing *She Moved Through the Fair*.

This plaintive song had been one of my mother's favourites, and as the singer sung in a lilting tenor voice I was overwhelmed with melancholy; for to travel alone means confronting all those thoughts which the routine distractions of ordinary life can suppress for months or years on end. But alone in a cell in the Convent of Sant'Agostino, with my mother's photograph in my hands, my grief welled to the surface, and I wept.

An almost full moon had turned the travertine streets to ice and the towers gleamed blue and silver.

I saw no one as I walked up to the Rocca and climbed steps leading to the wall which entirely surrounds the town. Olive trees stood in puddles of moon shadow, and when I gazed back towards the towers I saw nothing to remind me that I was in the twentieth century. No vehicles. No electronic sounds from TVs or stereos.

Only the moon and the stone.

San Gimignano

A blackbird singing in the orange tree whistled me awake. Overnight the mist had risen and the hills had become islands in a calm pink sea, and each farm a fortress.

I liked my cell and decided to stay another night.

No gibbering nuns had returned from the inferno to haunt my dreams. Here, perhaps, they had led scandalous and jolly lives behind their high walls. After all, Boccaccio's stories are tumescent with naughty nuns and abbesses; and Certaldo is just down the road.

The tap water smelt odd and so I cleaned my teeth in wine and walked out into the town where I saw no one apart from an old man in the Piazza del Duomo taking his Siamese cat for a walk amongst the pigeons.

Coffee was unavailable so early and I strolled out through Porta San Giovanni into the countryside where I found an olive grove into which I wandered.

Propped against a gnarled trunk I sat and watched the day arriving, the shadows cast from the towers creeping crookedly over the rooftops like the shadows from gigantic sundials.

A warbler fluttered silently from tree to tree, and weary of sitting I joined it in its search for insects on the bark and amongst the leaves, hoping to find a praying mantis. But I saw nothing except a speckled spider moving like a crab. I levered stones with a stick but no snakes or scorpions emerged and I returned to the town a failed naturalist.

How pleasant it was to walk without the encumbrance of a rucksack dragging me down like a bad conscience.

Going uphill still hurt a little, but on the flat and downhill I was almost back to normal.

In the Piazza della Cisterna – named after the well at its centre – I was the first customer to order breakfast, which I ate alone on the perimeter of a square which, on my arrival the previous evening, had been full of the nouveaux riches with their sophisticated video cameras taking shaky hand-held shots of the towers. In thousands of homes bored relatives and neighbours, inveigled into watching abysmal home videos, would rise in excitement and exclaim, 'Why didn't you tell us you were there during an earthquake?'

At least in the old days, when 8mm film was the stock-in-trade, the movies were mercifully short. Now they can go on forever or even longer.

An elderly couple staying at the hotel sat nearby and I immediately knew that they were English, not only from their dry hair, irregular teeth, and clothes (she in a sensible tweedy two-piece suit and clasping brooch, he in twills and golf-club tie), but from the way they did not talk to each other.

Even at 7 a.m. her blotchy face was protected by a straw hat. ('We always come to Tuscany in the autumn. The sun doesn't agree with Thelma.')

I had bought my first newspaper since leaving England, an international edition of the *Guardian*, and the first headline I read was *Moore chill on child benefit*. Mr John Moore, the Social Security Secretary, had decided to freeze payments because '. . . *resources had to be directed in such a way as to help and encourage people to improve their lives and aim for independence. This meant social security should not be seen as a safety net.*'

If not a safety net, then what? *What was the matter with Britain*? And so furious was I with this hired mouthpiece of Our Leader that I wrote him a letter there and then explaining how, throughout my journey, I had regularly been asked to explain Britain's odious decline back into the nineteenth century. But of course my letter was a waste of time. One cannot point out wickedness to its practitioners: men and women who are too morally bankrupt to know what the word – which I have chosen most carefully – means.

Meanwhile the Englishman had actually spoken to his wife. Politely, as though addressing a total stranger, he had said, 'Would you be so kind as to pass me the sugar?'

'You know too much sugar isn't good for you.'

'Only one spoonful.'

'Very well – provided it *is* only one.'

I entered the Romanesque cathedral long before the coach parties arrived, and almost had this extraordinary building to myself.

Even before my eyes had grown accustomed to the dark interior I was enchanted by the frescoed walls. Lunettes like comic strips entirely cover the space between floor and ceiling; those on the left depicting scenes from the Old Testament, while those on the right portray the life of Christ.

There are far too many to describe, but the Creation of Eve struck me as the finest. While Adam sleeps in a Garden of Eden bright with fruit and flowers, God, acting as midwife assists in a bizarre Caesarean section with Adam as mother. With God's help it appears there is *nothing* a woman can achieve that a man cannot equal.

Near the entrance Saint Sebastian, bristling with arrows, resembles an ecstatic porcupine, while above him are three frescos showing Heaven, Hell and the Last Judgement. Naturally, as an ex-Catholic, I was attracted to Hell with its bloated sinners being systematically and horribly tortured by gleeful devils.

The images corresponded to those that had terrorised my childhood; their source the priests who had, in my prepubescent years, kindly consented to oversee our religious retreats. 'Love God and He will love you. Turn your back on Him and He will revenge Himself on you for all eternity.'

It was an offer I could refuse.

I did not see the amputated finger belonging to Saint Geminianus, after whom the city is named, nor the bones of a child, Saint Fina, who, in an interesting reversal of The Fall myth, was given a foul disease by God for accepting an apple from a boy.

Boccaccio wrote a satirical tale, set in Certaldo, which tells of a friar who travelled the countryside raising funds for his brethren. To encourage foolish people to part with their crops he promised to show them a feather from the Angel Gabriel's wings, which he had brought back from the Holy Land.

This is not the place to recount the entire story, and I only mention it because I find it impossible to understand how, 600 years later, such nonsense is still encouraged by the Vatican.

And for those who think I exaggerate, let me point to the fact that there is now an international airport at Knock, in Eire, specifically built to ferry pilgrims, including the Pope, to a place where a statue of the Virgin moves in mysterious ways.

By ten o'clock flash-cubes were creating local electric storms inside the cathedral, and so I fled into the piazza where those too scantily clad to enter through the church's portals sat tanning on its steps.

Up at the Rocca an ancient ruin had been converted into an art gallery where there was an exhibition of contemporary West German art.

My heart sank as soon as I entered and saw an enormous spoon carelessly constructed from papier mâché. The maker was, I think, trying to concentrate my thoughts on the throwaway society. But worse was to come. Upstairs there was a series, numbered one to a million, of tin cans painted (by which I mean paint was the chemical used) on paper. Some tin cans had green acrylic labels, others blue, others red. You see? Even by describing them I have begun to give them credence. Readers of art reviews will know exactly what I mean. Time and time again the reviewers are too pusillanimous to call junk junk. And so they describe, sitting on fences which have their mortgage statements plastered all over them.

My favourite story is *The Emperor's New Clothes*, a lousy choice if you want to win friends and influence people. But who wants those sort of friends?

And so I quit this naked insult to intelligence and returned my attention to a load of medieval stuff, which, despite a tendency towards representation, had sufficed in its day.

Sated by art I spent the afternoon in the suburbs beyond the Wall of Culture. The housing estates and supermarkets could have been in Nottingham or Portsmouth although the bars here supplied wine far superior to the plonk served up in any number of Robin Hood Inns or Lord Nelsons.

In one crowded bar a man came over and asked what I was doing there.

'Just having a drink.'

'Tourists don't come here.'

'Why not?'

He shrugged. 'Because they cannot look at other tourists.'

'I've seen enough tourists.'

He laughed. 'Then you cannot be a tourist.'

And slapping me violently on the back he bought me a drink. Reciprocation led to a boozy afternoon that was marred only by the man's insistence on talking about football, about which I know even less than I do about the architect Mackintosh.

That evening I was given a table in the display window of an empty restaurant in order to encourage more customers, and there I sat eating cold fungi resembling, and probably tasting of, pickled slugs. But more appetising food followed, and assisted by a bottle containing several hairs of the dog I was beginning to enjoy myself when two Scottish maiden ladies entered, sat at the next table, and began discussing cancer of the bowel.

'It's her own fault. She never took roughage. Always sticky cakes and boiled sweets. I said, "At your age it's important to have regular motions," but would she listen?'

'Is she still living at home?'

'Oh no. They took her to the infirmary a fortnight last Thursday.'

'Have you sent her a postcard?'

'You know what the Italian post is like. It probably wouldn't arrive in time.'

For my own sake I intervened. 'Good evening, ladies.'

It did the trick. They nodded a greeting but were not pleased, and began conversing about the shortcomings of the cattery to which Blackie had been condemned during First Woman's absence.

'Let's hope it's an improvement on the last place. Don't you remember when we got back from Spain and discovered she'd caught worms?'

Later I got lost in a backstreet and ended up outside a building I assumed was a monastery; for screwed to an impressive gate set in high walls was a sign: *Casa del Recliso*. An enclosed order, I thought. But when I glanced up I saw bullet-proof machicolations complete with gun-ports like the arrow-slits in a medieval castle. It was a prison, and I thought how dreadful it would be to be locked up behind walls within walls within walls, with the open Tuscan landscape stretching to infinity.

Iron grilles concealed the windows, and I was reminded of the time when, while filming near Cardiff Gaol on a hot summer day, I had seen a prisoner sunbathing with his back against the bars. He had shifted and I had seen that his back was red where the heat had burnt him, with white vertical stripes where the bars had protected his skin.

All these walls and towers. I had had my fill of San Gimignano.

On the ceiling of my cell, directly above my head, a large spider was daintily stalking mosquitoes too high for me to flatten. And with this ally waving its palps I fell into a deep sleep enclosed by unclimbable walls.

San Gimignano to Siena

It was still dark when I closed the convent doors behind me and walked through San Gimignano's empty streets, passing its lean towers for the last time.

Beyond the walls the stars in the west still glimmered, while those in the east had already been extinguished by the white glow of dawn.

Once again the surrounding hills were cut off by a high tide of mist, down towards which I walked, for pain had been replaced by discomfort, and I was anxious to move under my own steam again.

Tuscany, I realised, is composed of straight lines and right angles: the rows of vines; the rectilinear houses; the furrows; the cypresses; the roads and tracks bisecting the fields; the towers.

Poggibonsi is only a few kilometres from San Gimignano and the first part of the walk was pleasant enough, although I soon sank under the mist into a sub-aqua world of cold currents where nothing stirred amongst a bed of ploughed sand.

On the foggy outskirts of Poggibonsi people were arriving for work at depots and factories, and after San Gimignano's medieval churches and palaces these post-war buildings struck me as particularly execrable. But the valleys of Tuscany are littered with industry and one cannot complain. It provides employment, and not everyone can toil picturesquely in the vineyards for the delectation of passing travellers.

Lira-less, I sat in the main square waiting for the banks to open; and there I decided that my walking days were certainly over as far as this journey was concerned.

Willpower was not enough, and some devil, having escaped from the hellish fresco in San Gimignano's cathedral, was busy hammering a wedge between two of my vertebrae.

Belloc popped into Siena to collect money and stayed only an hour.

I was also there to collect money which had not yet arrived despite having been sent from London by Telex ten days previously. Pony express would have been quicker. And so I remained in Siena for three nights.

Each morning the smiling bank official would shrug and say, 'Maybe tomorrow?', and I soon realised that all my efforts to discover the reason for this foul-up were a total waste of time. It would arrive when it arrived.

When I remember Siena I immediately think of a man standing in a hole in the middle of a street along which hundreds of tourists jostled one another, each with *I'm only here for the art and I still haven't seen The Campo* expressions seriously engraved on their faces.

The bearded man had a Christ-like visage with compassionate eyes half hidden beneath long blond hair, and I soon discovered that there was no hole. His legs had been severed or amputated below the pelvis, and he balanced precariously on the stones, begging. Each morning someone must carry him there, deposit him, and return for him later. A cardboard notice around his neck proclaimed *No means of support* and he fended off collisions with preoccupied tourists' legs by holding aloft arms as muscle-bound as a weight lifter's.

Few people contributed to his plate despite the fact that thousands and thousands of dollars and

Deutschmarks were passing him by every minute. Perhaps they thought he should get a proper job?

Siena was hosting an international conference, and all the hotel rooms had been snapped up by professors of Etruscan archaeology. Consequently I was forced to stay in a hostel in the suburbs, where I shared a room with a damp English student of Italian who had come for a year to 'brush up' the language he had been studying at university for two years.

'Why Siena?' I asked.

'Because they speak the purest Italian here. It's the sort of Surrey of Italy.'

That evening, while a woman removed her bra as an integral part of some TV game show, I sat in the hostel bar, drinking. The student joined me and I offered to share my wine. He called for a glass, in Italian, and the barman arrived with another bottle of wine.

'No, a glass,' the student of Italian repeated in Italian.

'But this is a glass,' replied the barman, using a similar language.

I pointed to my glass.

'Oh,' said the barman in perfect English; addressing the student. 'You want another glass. You were asking for a bottle.'

Earlier two elderly and indomitable Australian women had arrived looking distraught. They needed to talk, and as I was nearest they had picked on me.

'We've spent two bloody hours looking for a hotel, and the only one we could find wanted to charge us 180,000 lire a night!'

I explained about the conference.

'In the end we had to hire a taxi. I said *pension* to the driver, and he took us to the bloody post office!'

I could not help laughing.

'What's so bloody funny?'

'I'm sorry. You left the *e* off. It's not *pension*. It's *pensione*.'

'How long've you been here then?'

'Only a few hours.'

'Anything to see?'

'It depends what you're looking for.'

'We're just travelling.'

'Well there're a lot of churches and museums and galleries.'

'We've already seen them.'

'I thought you'd only just arrived?'

'In Florence. That's where we've just been.'

'And where're you going next?'

'We haven't decided exactly, but we're heading back to Austria and Germany in a few days. We prefer them.'

'Why?'

'They're so much cleaner and the food's more to our taste.'

'Have you been to Venice?'

'No. Where's that?'

'In the north-east. Not too far. And it's more or less on the way back to Austria.'

'What's there then?'

I thought I would give churches and galleries a miss. 'Canals.'

'Canals? You mean water canals?'

Were there any other kind? And briefly I thought they were taking the mickey. They were not.

'Instead of streets.'

'How the hell do they get about then?'

'They use boats. It's very beautiful.'

'OK. Then we'll go there.'

It was as simple as that. I had irrevocably altered the pattern of their lives, and I imagined them walking the shadowy alleys of Venice like the two weird sisters in *Don't Look Now*. If a dwarf in a red mac got them, then I would be responsible.

The view of Siena from Via di Camporegio, just below the Basilica di San Domenico, is unforgettable. Red-tiled houses with pinkish-brown walls descend into a valley then rise up the opposite slope to the white marble cathedral with its great dome and striped raccoon tail of a campanile.

I sat on a bench beside an American girl (she had Pan Am labels on her knapsack) and watched her failing to capture the scene on her sketch-pad.

She caught me sneaking a look and – assuming I spoke English – said, 'It's no damned good. I'll never be able to get it right.'

'It's not so bad.'

'You're kidding? It's crap! Mind you, it took them 150 years to build it so I don't suppose ten minutes is enough to do it justice. God, you English are so lucky. You can just hop on a plane and spend the weekend here.'

'If you can afford to.'

'Hell, it's only a $300 round trip from London.'

The interior of San Domenico, built in the thirteenth century, is stark.

Saint Catherine, who was born in the valley below this red brick Gothic church, was received into the Dominican Order in the Cappella delle Volte where there is a portrait of her, probably painted from life by her disciple Andrea Vanni. It is very simple with a serene

Catherine delicately holding a white lily. Her face, painted 600 years ago, is still fresh and full of vitality. And this pictorial representation is all the more poignant because, only a few steps away, in the chapel named after her, her mummified head is displayed in a reliquary.

If you put a coin in a slot you get a minute's worth of light in which to view it surrounded by frescos depicting scenes from her life. And this juxtaposition of portrait and shrivelled flesh is the most forceful personification of *ars longa, vita brevis* I have yet experienced.

Seeing human heads is not an everyday occurrence, and so I went for a stiff drink in a nearby bar, where, among the collection of bottles, I saw an enormous black scorpion suspended in a bottle of clear liquid. Thinking it was the Italian equivalent of Mexican mescal, which has a cactus bug in the bottom of every bottle, I asked the barman what the drink was called.

'Formaldehyde,' he explained, laughing.

'Did you find the scorpion near here?'

'Oh no. In Italy they are very small. Like this.' He showed me his little finger. 'That one is from North Africa. A souvenir of the war.'

And relieved that I would not be duty-bound to sample scorpion juice I settled for a vermouth.

Having had a surfeit of human and animal remains, I strolled to the southern quarter of the city, where I found myself outside the church of Santa Maria dei Servi where a flamboyant old queen, assisted by his pretty young boyfriend, was taking photographs of the austere red façade and campanile.

Not many tourists bother to walk so far from the Piazza del Campo (the main square where the Palio, frenetic horse races, are fought twice a year), and so, for a while, I had the church to myself. But had I left death behind? No. The place was rife with it.

There is a painting *and* a fresco of *The Slaughter of the Innocents*, each depicting in graphic detail babies being hacked to death. There is also a *Herod's Banquet* complete with severed head, and to the right of the main altar a contemporary sculpture of a dragon being impaled on a stake. A statue of a Madonna with eight gold daggers in her heart leads to a corpse in a glass coffin.

Photographs of children had been slotted into the ornate frame, and a printed card read:

B. Giovacchino Piccolomini
Protettore dei Bambini edegli Epilettic.

As I stood there a man, the father of an epileptic child I assume, arrived and lit a candle.

I left him alone and he stayed for a long while, his lips moving in silent desperation.

His prayers completed he put banknotes into a collection box on which was written *OFFERTA PER LA CANONIZAZIONE DEL B. GIOVACCHINO PICCOLOMINI.*

If only it made sense.

The white cathedral is undoubtedly splendid, although I am not sure if I like it. Certainly I have no overwhelming desire to revisit its striated pillars and pavement of clever graffiti, the former so numerous as to resemble a herd of zebras' legs viewed through a telephoto lens. But I have never enjoyed elaborately ornate buildings and much prefer the solidity and simplicity of certain English cathedrals.

The Piccolomini Library, left of the nave, is conspicuously ornate, with its illuminated manuscripts and frescos. And there are secular touches here, including a Roman copy of Greek statues depicting the Three Graces, all naked and one without her head – as one might expect in Siena.

A man wedged in a corner was using binoculars to study the ceiling. I looked up and there, above a portrait of Pius III, satyrs with enviable hard-ons were cavorting in wild abandon amongst voluptuous nymphs.

I was surprised by this apposition of the sacred and profane, but having seen so much holy anatomy and horror I was relieved to find something celebrating life.

However, my mood darkened again when, while eating an apple on the cathedral steps, a car screeched to a halt and a man in a terrible state of shock pulled a child from the rear seat. Surrounded by nurses he rushed in through a hospital entrance. The child's face was as white as marble and her arms hung down as stiff as bones. I doubt if she was alive.

In the fan-shaped Piazza del Campo local youths, hunting in packs, prowled among young female tourists sunbathing near the Fonte Gaia. If the boys did not get them then the pigeons surely would, for they flew in formation around the piazza saturation-bombing the red brick pavement with an unlimited supply of biological weapons.

I saw many other things in Siena but will mention only one more: the Pinacoteca Nazionale, a picture gallery displaying hundreds of works by Sienese artists.

I had never enjoyed Byzantine painting, for having seen various examples in isolation I had found them too stylised for my taste. One, I thought, was much like another, but this gallery swept away my ignorance and prejudice.

Here there are rooms full of Madonna's and bambinos, all entirely different and breathtakingly beautiful.

Later, when I went out into the streets, having spent three hours in the gallery, I saw those same faces all around me.

There are many later Sienese paintings on show, and it would be futile for me to emulate a guidebook; although if I could choose only two works they would be Duccio di Buoninsegna's *Madonna col Bambino* and Sodoma's *Christ Being Removed From The Cross*. Words must fail. You must go and see for yourself.

On my third morning in Siena money arrived at the bank.

The teller counted out a sheaf of Monopoly money, and I asked if I could convert them into travellers' cheques.

'Impossible.'

'Why?'

'Because it is not possible.'

'You mean I have to carry all this cash around with me?'

'Of course.'

And so, with my living expenses and airfare home stuffed in my wallet, I went out into the streets where, all of a sudden, every third person had become a footpad.

Siena to Montalcino

Twenty miles south of Siena, above Buonconvento in the dusty Ombrone Valley, is the hill-town of Montalcino; a San Gimignano without towers.

There are several churches, a castle, a museum, and fine views towards forested hills from its ramparts. And it was wonderfully empty, probably because all the historic buildings were locked.

Owing to a dearth of tourists accommodation was scarce, and I was forced to choose a hotel where I was ripped off for the first and only time during my journey. Still, I had a TV in my room, and while I showered I watched Roger Moore as James Bond speaking perfect Italian. Even 007 had acquired a depth of character I had hitherto thought superficial.

I suspect that half the so-called art films I used to watch so avidly in the Academy Cinemas in Oxford Street would have lost much of their mystique had the actors spoken Liverpudlian. Had I really enjoyed all those Jean-Luc Godard and Antonioni films or had I been a victim of self-deception? Were all those nihilistic studies of bourgeois ennui (with the *auteurs'* homespun philosophies about life and death clogging up the soundtracks) really as boring as I dared not believe? Probably.

Montalcino, surrounded by vineyards, is famous for its wine, and feeling flush I ordered a bottle of Brunello in a delightful family-run restaurant on the main street.

Hunger had driven me in before anyone else, but I was soon joined by a family and a couple; stereotypes both.

The German family were very loud and extremely rude to the sweet girl who took their order. Had I been her I would have kept a secret supply of joke shop fart-powder to sprinkle on such louts' coffee (it would have to be the coffee, for earlier spiking would result in an own goal).

The couple – dry hair, crooked teeth – were upper-crust English, and whispered. Celia Johnson and Trevor Howard. I suspected that they were having an affair, for amongst their sibilance I kept hearing references to she (from him) and he (from her). But perhaps it was wishful thinking on my part? Maybe they were a perfectly respectable married couple from Cirencester who were merely discussing their servants?

After a sumptuous dinner, for which I was charged next to nothing, I walked behind a rat hopping along an alley, saw the castle by moonlight, and returned to my room, where I discovered that even Benny Hill could speak Italian.

But in his case it added nothing to the mystery.

Montalcino to Bolsena

At dawn I heard shooting in my room.

At the end of my bed Randolph Scott was plugging me with a six-shooter.

The ramparts were quieter. Delicate strands of white mist, like spiders' webs, overlaid the vineyards but dissipated as soon as the sun balanced on a hilltop.

I had decided to go no farther than Acquapendente that day, but when I reached the valley I found that there were no buses going south and so I took a complicated route by train and bus via Orvieto. Had I been fit enough to walk it would have taken half the time.

On the train to Orvieto I sat opposite two meaty US servicemen on leave.

Both wore T-shirts printed with Ivy League logos, and each had cropped hair no longer than a newborn baby's. Their features, protruding from roast pork skin, were adequately formed – by which I mean they possessed recognisable noses, ears, lips, etc. – but something vital was missing. Of course they could have been Stepford husbands or clones or identical twins from an emotionally deprived background, but I suspect that they were just plain jocks.

Both were reading comic books, but at one point one of them glanced out of the window and said, 'Grapes.'

'Where?'

'There.'

'Where?'

'Those plants. They're vines.'

'What?'

'Vines.'

'Is that where grapes come from?'

'Yeah.'

'Oh.'

Jumpy introduced himself on the bus from Orvieto to Acquapendente.

The bus was packed with exuberant students heading back to their homes in the hills, and when I heard, 'Hello. Are you English?' I thought it was simply someone showing off in front of his peers. But the accent was odd. It sounded South African; which it was, almost.

Jumpy had been raised in Rhodesia, but the family had split after the country became Zimbabwe, his mother moving to South Africa, his father back to his native Italy where his son now studied fashion design in the Orvieto Art School.

Jumpy was charming and sophisticated and glad of the chance to speak English.

'Are you fluent in Italian?' I asked.

'Oh yes. I've been here a while now.'

'Do you think in Italian?'

'Some of the time.'

'And dream?'

'No. I still dream in English.'

We talked of this and that, and then I asked, 'What are you planning to do when you leave art school?'

'Work in the fashion business in Rome for a while, and then come back to help run my father's factory.'

I was nonplussed. This was agricultural country, and I could not fathom how a knowledge of fashion would help in the production of farm machinery or fertilisers or whatever else his father manufactured.

Jumpy laughed when I voiced my perplexity.

'He makes clothes. Good quality clothes. And I'll help design even better ones.'

Obviously his future was all sewn up.

The bus twisted and turned through the Umbrian hills until we reached the high plateau of the Monti Volsini, where teams of pure white oxen were ploughing the black soil.

Jumpy pointed to a field and said, 'During the war there was a military airfield there. And you see that building?' An old farmhouse stood amongst trees just beyond the perimeter. 'That's where my father lived as a boy.'

We stopped at the next village and Jumpy shook my hand. 'This is where I must say goodbye. My friend Alfredo will show you where you can stay in Acquapendente.'

'Good luck.'

'And to you.'

He got off, waved, and walked into his father's childhood memories.

Soon we reached a hole in the world.

Far below, surrounded by the green caldera of an extinct volcano, I saw the circular Lago di Bolsena, its surface so calm and white with reflections of sky that it resembled space rather than water.

Lanes led down past poor farms to the airy little town of San Lorenzo Nuovo, which occupies a lip of the hills overlooking the lake.

I was now in Lazio, the last region I would cross.

My route to Rome lay south, but I was determined to see Acquapendente several kilometres to the north. Why? I am not sure, for Belloc described it as a dreary place where he ate in a restaurant full of flies.

The road lies along a dismal marsh whose flatness is alleviated only by factories. Monte Amiata should have been visible to the north-west but it remained muffled in clouds.

Jumpy's friend Alfredo led me down alleys to the heart of Acquapendente, a square which was being torn apart by wobbly men with road drills.

Apart from the din, the town seemed pleasant enough although it is built in a hollow that trapped the muggy air like mud in a pool.

Alfredo pointed to a seedy hotel and said goodbye.

I drank wine in a gloomy bar and made up my mind to spend the night beside the lake at Bolsena, where the air would surely be fresher and the outlook less claustrophobic. And so I retraced my route to San Lorenzo, on the outskirts of which a massive roadblock had been set up. A dozen *carabinieri*, armed to the teeth with automatic weapons, were stopping all traffic. I was the only passenger on the bus, but obviously my Irish features did not coincide with the description of the terrorist or bank robber they were after, and the bus was waved on.

Down the hill we sped towards the lake, along the same road where Belloc had hitched a ride on a cart.

My map lied, for the road does not follow the lakeside but takes a parallel route a kilometre to the east, and between road and water rutted tracks lead to campsites, none of which were open. Secretly I was glad, for the sites looked uniformly depressing with their brick launderettes, lavatory blocks and mini-supermarkets.

But Bolsena more than made up for this dross.

With its castle and old town perched on a crag, Harlech-like, Bolsena immediately appealed, not only because of its picturesque silhouette, but because it is a mock seaside resort.

An avenue of sycamores led me to a beach of grey granular sand and a harbour in which the boats seemed ice-bound; for only in a glass have I seen calmer water.

I walked to the end of the jetty where a man was fishing. On cue his float dipped and he struck. His rod formed an omega, and I thought the wood would surely split; but the fat fish was whipped up on to the stones, where, with one quick flick of his wrist, the angler succeeded in stabbing a hand with the hook. But this was Italy where men are men and no one cries over spilt blood, and affecting not to notice he dripped a crimson trail to his moped, where he put the twitching fish into a plastic bag along with several more of the same species.

Lovers strolled hand in hand beneath the pines fringing the shore while a papery sun set behind the castle. Far out in the lake haloes of mist formed above distant islands, and all was peace, until the police arrived.

One cannot get away from them in Italy; anywhere.

A launch like a motor-torpedo-boat vandalised the silence with its high-powered engines as it entered the harbour at full throttle, causing the fisherman to abandon his nook on the jetty.

Perhaps they had just performed some vital function like rescuing shipwrecked mariners from the millpond, but they infuriated me. They could not simply arrive. They had to do it in style with the crew, all in black like Action Man toys, lining the gunnels.

In the sycamore avenue I found a shrine; a little statue of Our Lady of Lourdes set in a hole in the bole of a tree. A bulb was affixed above her head and an electric cable led along a bough and across a garden into a house.

I was reminded of my father and how, for many years before his marriage, he had acted as a *brancadier*, helping the sick on pilgrimages to Lourdes; and of my brother, who, while paying a nostalgic visit there, had been hospitalised with mumps; and of the story of the man who was so desperately ill that he had been immersed in the holy baths while strapped to a wheelchair. As he was pulled out, dripping from head to foot, there was a cry of wonderment from the onlookers. Sure enough there had been a miracle: four new tyres on the wheelchair.

Bolsena is a miraculous place. In 1263 blood dripped from a host on to an altar cloth and Pope Urban IV ordered the building of Orvieto Cathedral on the strength of this story. Seven hundred years later, in the chapel of Saint George's College, Weybridge, I was told a similar tale by a clever Jesuit conducting a retreat. A wicked boy had stolen a consecrated host and had thrown darts at it. Sure enough – yes, you have guessed it – the host began to bleed and the boy, conscience-smitten, had ended up a priest or a saint or some such. And although I may no longer be an adherent of Catholicism at least I can still admire the continuity of its mythology.

In Bolsena Belloc had eaten fresh fish from the lake and I went in search of a restaurant that would cook me some, but everywhere, apart from a pizzeria, was closed for the winter. But at least I ate fish: microwaved anchovies like astronauts' footprints on a moonscape of cheese.

A smoky bar in a cellar was crowded with men sitting at long wooden tables. Carafes of urine-coloured wine were being consumed at a prodigious rate, but when I asked for a glass the barman, suspecting I was not local, tried to palm me off with some superior stuff in a bottle. No, I said. I wanted the same as everyone else.

I half expected it to taste like retsina, but it was sweet and thick. And having no pressing engagements I remained for some time watching and listening to men laughing, arguing and singing while, no doubt, up in the quiet houses wives lay abed under portraits of Pope John Paul awaiting the clomp of unsteady footfalls on the stairs.

Passing the sycamore grotto, where Our Lady's radiance was attracting moths, I returned to the beach, where I watched a red moon floating like an autumn leaf in the lake.

It was cold and cicadas thrummed half-heartedly in the pines.

Something heavy, a carp perhaps, splashed just offshore, and the moon's reflection became splinters of stained glass.

Bolsena to Ronciglione

I sat under the corbelled towers and walls of the castle and watched the sun building a golden causeway across the lake. In the umbrella pines greenfinches chirped, their feathers gilded by the dawn light. A black cat trotted by with half a lizard in its mouth.

Down in the main square women were buying fish and still-alive eels from stall holders, while the village elders had already taken up position under the trees where they would spend the day watching the world pass them by.

The road to Montefiascone is flat at first, following the lake and passing a British military cemetery where those killed in the 1944 offensive are buried.

At war with Italy? Were we? Really?

But it was German troops who laid these men to rest in some corner of a foreign field.

Despite the proximity of unlimited water, the farms here seemed poor with ramshackle houses set among narrow strips of olive trees, vines and flowers.

All along the verges women in peasant garb were swaying towards Bolsena with baskets of produce balanced on their heads. I would have expected to see such sights in Calabria, but not here, so close to Rome. But I had divided Italy artificially, bisecting it along the latitude on which Rome stands. South of Rome is The South geographically, but poverty does not conform to such preconceived concepts.

The road soon left the lake and climbed through parched country towards Montefiascone with its impressive outline of castle and cathedral. Belloc, frantic to reach Rome, had passed by and continued on to Viterbo whereas I, travelling as lazily as any tourist, decided to stop there for a while.

In the square outside the Roman gate leading to the old town there was a dreadful noise. A taped tenor, amplified and distorted through rudimentary loudspeakers, was filling all available ears with sobbing love songs. Every minute or so the tape would stop abruptly and arbitrarily, to be replaced by a live woman's voice. 'Ladies and gentlemen! We are proud to present an exhibition of the world's most terrible creatures. See the venomous snakes – the cobras and vipers. Thrill to the scorpions, tarantulas and crocodile! Here for three days only.' Crackle. More tenor.

I thought it might be amusing to visit this old-fashioned travelling show, and was about to mount the steps leading into the trailer when I saw a pathetic old lady peering through the dusty pane of the only window. The expression in her eyes was intensely lugubrious, and she had dyed her hair ginger in a doomed attempt to appear younger, echoing the sad bag-lady of Piacenza.

Only when she stuck out her tongue at me did I realise that I was face to face with an orang-utan.

English conditioning asserted itself, and I turned away determined that my money would not contribute to the incarceration of this most unterrible of creatures.

There is a story, possibly apocryphal, that a bishop once sent a servant to sample all the wines of this region. When the servant found an inn serving good wine he marked the place with an *est*. In Montefiascone the wine was so fine that he marked all the inns with *est, est, est*. The prelate's palate coincided with his servant's, and so enamoured was he with this local wine that he promptly moved to Montefiascone and drank himself to death. And whatever the truth of this tale it is certain that Montefiascone's wine is called *Est, est, est* to this day.

It is also certain, subjectively, that the wine has done nothing to sweeten the nature of Montefiascone's citizens.

Invariably, in Italy, when asking for information about this and that I had found people courteous and only too willing to help. Not so in Montefiascone. And the entire city reeked of decay and poverty.

Gangs of unemployed youths hung around street corners while others, wearing jeans and simulated-leather jackets, roared around the piazzas performing highly dangerous stunts on motorbikes. Their code forbade helmets, and if what I saw was typical of their behaviour then entire hospital wards must be given over to the victims of such bravura.

A slummy alley led up to the cathedral whose great dome I had seen on my approach to the city.

The door clanged shut behind me, and standing alone under the cupola I listened while weird and unmusical chords emanated from the organ. No lights were on in the church, not even candles, and the baroque interior was veiled by shadows.

Perhaps it was simply the horrid lid-like dome intimidating me, but I experienced a powerful intuition that something was not quite right about the place.

I was reminded of Bellinzona and its darkened church, but here the feelings of unease were far more intense and I knew that sanctuary lay *outside*. And so I fled.

How glad I was that I did not have to walk the hideous road from Montefiascone to Viterbo.

Cables slung between pylons formed a gigantic wire fence flanking the highway while hoardings advertising booze and cigarettes filled the gaps between factories and vast cones of wrecked cars. And when I saw the suburbs my heart sank.

Viterbo is the Aldershot of Italy. Conscripts are sent there to be turned into soldiers; and barracks, surrounded by high-security fences, form a linear penal colony stretching all the way to the city walls.

Viterbo has a reputation for violence, and I can understand why, for the streets were full of strutting off-duty servicemen swigging from cans of beer. No doubt when night fell they would do what all soldiers do best: fight.

The old city, encircled by a stone curtain, is pleasant enough with its market, cathedral and medieval houses. For 300 years, during the Middle Ages, it was a rival of Rome. But there is a run-down air about it. Belloc had heard fountains splashing here, and although I saw fountains the only water I saw in them was stagnant and full of rubbish.

I bought grapes in the market and sat on a bench, watching a crippled dog dragging itself across the road on its two front legs.

A suited man with a glittering tiepin came up to me and said, 'Hey, man, you wanta room?'

'No, thank you,' I replied even though I had intended to stay here.

'Very nice room.'

'No.'

'You gotta girl?'

'Yes. In England.'

'You not in England now. I know very nice girl. Very friendly. Very clean.' He winked.

'No thank you.'

He moved closer. 'Maybe you like boy?'

'Go away.'

His smile evaporated and his tone turned nasty.

'You all the same you English. No money, no prick.'

The pimp spat and glided away into the crowd in search, no doubt, of indigenous clients amongst the conscripts. I decided to move on.

Ronciglione is only thirteen kilometres to the south and I boarded a bus in Viterbo's chaotic bus station.

On the city's outskirts the conductor, a Marcello Mastroianni look-alike, apologised operatically when he saw my ticket. The journey, he explained, would take two hours.

'It's a school bus, you see? We stop at every village. You should have taken the express.'

'Don't worry. I'm in no hurry.'

'Then I hope you will enjoy the ride.'

I did. I sat at the back and was surrounded by girls returning home from high school. Apart from one, a raven-haired beauty of seventeen with silver earrings, they seemed shy, but the beauty wanted to practise her English.

'What is your name?'

'Peter.'

'Peter,' she repeated. 'Pe-ter.'

Her voice had a throaty Claudia Cardinale quality, and my name had never sounded so exotic.

'I am Maria and this is Giannina and this is Elena . . .' And so it went on, each girl shaking my hand as we were introduced.

'May I sit with you?' asked Maria.

'Of course.' Of course.

She fanned herself with a hand, causing her earrings to jangle; and if I am guilty of having a fetish then it must be dangling earrings.

'It is too hot,' she said, removing a loose-fitting jacket and revealing wonderful breasts constricted in a white cotton top.

Oh God! Even Odysseus lashed to his mast had not suffered more than I did with this siren beside me, her perfume all honeysuckle and roses.

I acted casual, asking her what she planned to do when she finished school.

'I think I will become a nurse and marry a rich doctor.' She laughed, showing teeth as white as snow.

We travelled up through chestnut groves and followed a ridge above Lago di Vico, the second in a line of volcanic lakes leading to Rome; but my mind was not on the landscape.

Too soon – after only an hour – we reached an extraordinary village called Caprarola, built on a spine of rock protruding from the forest.

Maria smiled and said, 'Goodbye.'

I shook her hand, but was tempted to kiss it for I had fallen a little in love, as middle-aged men are wont to do, and I was sad that I would not see her lemon-shaped eyes again.

She skipped down the steps, her miniskirt flouncing around her brown thighs, and ran up a narrow lane until she reached a corner where she turned and waved. And was gone. Forever.

Lago di Vico is unspoilt, its round reedy shore rising into dry forests.

Ronciglione, originally an Etruscan settlement, lies just above the lake but hidden from it by a low ridge, and there I found a room overlooking a sandstone gorge where, in the fig tree below my balcony, warblers warbled.

Turner visited the town and sketched the springs here, but perhaps he came earlier in the year for, try as I might, I could only find dusty stream beds.

Strolling through the old quarter I came across an exquisite eleventh-century chapel where an old woman in black was reciting the rosary; and not wishing to interfere I left and climbed towards the castle through cobbled streets too narrow for cars.

Here too I felt like an intruder, for these poor houses were not exhibits in a tourist village but people's homes. Families sat outside open front doors, enjoying the balmy evening air; the grandmothers knitting, the children playing, the parents chatting while they waited for supper to cook. Food smells filled the alleys. In pots in dark kitchens all manner of feasts were being prepared, and I became acutely conscious of how little a traveller can understand without remaining in one place for a considerable time.

In Ronciglione there were perhaps 3,000 people, none of whom I would perceive other than as figures differentiated by facial features, age, sex and clothes. And beyond this town? Millions. No, billions.

Journeying like this, constantly on the move, can never assuage loneliness; merely compound it.

Having eaten alone in an otherwise empty restaurant I returned to my single room, where, with a bottle of wine for company, I sat on the balcony watching bats flapping among the moonlit crags.

Ronciglione to Rome

I was now only 40 kilometres north of Rome but decided to spend one more night outside the city.

I chose Bracciano on the west shore of the third and final lake, Lago di Bracciano – although I knew nothing whatever about the town. Another Bolsena, I hoped.

My map showed a railway winding out of Ronciglione, and so I bought a ticket and sat on the empty platform. For some reason no one used this line and I soon found out why.

The hands of the station clock reached the appointed hour and continued to turn.

Thirty minutes later the Thin Controller, wringing his hands, told me that the train was kaput but that a replacement would arrive any time.

The station cat, accustomed to such exaggeration, wandered on to the track and lay on a sleeper, its tail looped over a rail. And so I sat on the baking tarmac for three hours, reading, while the Thin Controller supervised the ticket collector (who had no tickets to collect) while he weeded the station garden (where not a weed was visible).

I had given up all hope of leaving Ronciglione when a rattling and scraping heralded the train's approach. Technically, I suppose it was a train, although it resembled two nineteenth-century trams welded together by rust with its wheels miraculously staying on rails that were far from parallel.

There were no other passengers on board, and I could choose any wooden bench I liked. I could even open a window without fear of retribution.

The country through which we – the driver and I – passed was unremarkable and the only excitement occurred when, at an unguarded crossing, a car sped across only metres in front of the train, which was hurtling along at 20 kilometres per hour, rolling from side to side like a boat in a heavy swell.

I had missed my connection at Capránica by three hours, and as we pulled into the station I saw another train pulling out, my alternative connection.

Thus I spent two hours in the station bar, drinking wine, for the platform was shimmering like a salt lake in the intense heat.

A sweaty puffing man wheeled a racing-bike into the bar and propped it against a wall.

He was wearing all the right gear: skintight Bermuda shorts, T-shirt, cycling cap and special cycling shoes although his fifty-year-old body was fifty per cent overweight. A paunch overhung his crotch and his buttocks appeared far too plump to balance on the knife-edged saddle.

He smoked cigarettes smelling of pipe tobacco while he ate a pastry and drank copious amounts of beer.

He noticed my rucksack and asked what I was doing. I explained.

'That's the spirit!' he said. 'We mustn't let middle age get the better of us.'

'You cycle a lot?'

'I've only just begun. The doctor said it would be good for my heart.'

'How far have you come today?'

'From Capránica.'

Had I got off at the wrong station? 'But we're in Capránica.'

'The doctor says I should take things easy at first.'

A hunter cradling a shotgun entered and draped a dead rabbit on the bar. Blood oozed from an ear, but the barmaid cleaned the stain with a cloth and, grasping the rabbit by its scut, carried it into a back room and returned with a bottle. He had his wine and she her family's supper, and all without a lira changing hands.

I glimpsed the lake from the train, but as soon as we pulled into Bracciano I knew that it was not for me.

It is too close to Rome and has a Southend air about it. The roads were choked with traffic and the pavements almost impossible to walk along. And when I asked the price of a room in a shabby hotel I was quoted an outrageous sum.

Rome was only 16 kilometres away. I would sleep there. A black cloud overhung the city as I approached it through billboard country that soon gave way to suburbs on a par with Viterbo's.

I did not know Rome and naively expected to see the white dome of Saint Peter's rising above ancient ruins spilling down from the Palatine Hill. What I saw was post-war development. Block of flats. Thousands of them.

It was an inglorious entry, but as I walked towards the centre from the north-east corner of the city I knew that here was a place in which I could happily stay for many days. I saw no ancient monuments – they were to come later – but there was an indefinable ambience which I have rarely found in cities. No doubt my appreciation was heightened by the realisation that I had finally reached my destination, although my sense of partial achievement was tempered by sadness. Was it really over?

I remembered the Moselle, along whose valley I had walked all those weeks ago. Only weeks? It seemed many months. I pictured myself there, far beyond the Apennines, the Alps, Jura, Vosges, limping along rainy lanes with my blistered feet and the apprehension I could not share.

I hardly recognised that stranger. The man who had left Toul no longer existed.

And that, I suppose, is the only criterion by which one can judge a journey.

Rome

If you do not book in advance, a single room is impossible to find in Rome unless you arrive at a hotel at the crack of dawn.

Evening was falling upon the city, and I had no alternative but to stay in a hostel close to an Olympic Stadium, which is already going the way of most grandiose Roman architecture. It is falling apart.

Urchins skateboarded among rubbish littering the entrance to the stadium and I could see that the concrete façade of the indoor swimming pool was rent with fissures.

A fire smouldered beside the road, and as I approached it I saw a silhouette kicking the coals into flame.

It was a whore's beacon. She was haggard and dirty, and as I passed she lifted her skirt and adjusted the seams of stockings full of holes.

The wretched hostel, built to house Olympic athletes, is the twin of the police headquarters opposite, and although the hostel does not have electric fences, security cameras and guard towers it is just as spartan. Never have I stayed in such a dosshouse and I vowed to be up before the sun in order to find a hotel room.

I was too weary to explore the city and so I ate in Alcatraz.

Australian men and women were throwing food and beer at each other while, at an adjacent table, a blond South African was chatting up three very plain English girls. He was trying the intellectual approach.

'Of course,' he was saying, 'yoo hev a lot of bleks in Britain.'

'Of course. Oh yes we do.'

'Sem as us. Sem problem.

'Absolutely.'

'Not quite,' I interjected. 'There's a difference.'

'Oh yis? What's thet?'

'In Britain they have the vote.'

He smiled a pearly smile. 'Yoo bin to Seth Efrica?'

'No.'

'So how ken you understend?'

'I can't.'

'Then yoo should go there.'

'I meant I can't understand people like you.'

'My friend, yoo should mek an appointment with our femus Doctor Barnard. I'm told he ken perform miracles with a bleeding heart.'

The English girls were impressed by his wit and one of them, who was well-spoken, said. 'What are you anyway? Some sort of middle-aged hippy?'

'Just someone who's already returned to one of the things he was trying to get away from.'

'I suppose you're one of those liberals.'

'I don't object to being labelled a liberal.'

'Liberal. Dodo. It's all the same thing.'

'Spoken like a true Thatcherite.'

'And what's wrong with being a Thatcherite I'd like to know?'

'No you wouldn't.'

Besides I was too tired to argue and I sloped off to Cell Block 'B' where I slept on a metal bunk above a man who, from the smell of him, had not seen soap for a month.

★ ★ ★

Before dawn I went to the troughs to wash but, finding them piled high with puke, I left immediately in search of a hotel.

I found one in a little street off Piazza Farnese run by a fanatical John Lennon fan. Photos of Lennon filled the lobby, and when I booked in the beaming owner said, 'Ah! English! You like John Lennon?'

'Some of his songs.'

'Eez eencredible, John Lennon. Eencredible! You have seen the Beatles?'

'Yes.'

'You have seen John Lennon?'

'Yes.'

'Eez dead now.'

'Yes.'

'Eencredible, eencredible . . .' His voice trailed off into melancholic silence.

People not only shoot pop stars, they shoot popes; and I was not prepared for the security in and around the Vatican.

Policewomen with hair like shampoo advertisements carried machineguns at the entrance to the Piazza San Pietro, and as I glanced up at Bernini's splendid colonnades I saw men with guns peeking from between statues.

Mass was about to begin in the Basilica. Not any old mass but one starring Pope John Paul himself. The Choir and Orchestra of the Bavarian State Opera from Munich were to perform Beethoven's *Mass in C Major*, and seats in the back stalls were free.

Security was tight. An armed guard with a metal detector was frisking everyone, and when it came to my turn his device went 'ping'. The offending article, whatever it was, was in my jacket's inside pocket.

'What have you got there?' he demanded.

I opened my jacket, displayed the pocket, and said, 'Passport.'

'Ah,' he said. 'That's all right then. You may proceed.'

As I walked up the steps leading into the Basilica I suddenly realised how illogical our conversation had been. Why should my passport activate his detector? I delved in my pocket and felt metal. It was my knife.

And so, armed with an offensive weapon, I entered Saint Peter's for the first time.

Yes, the sheer magnitude impressed me, but I was unable to appreciate it on this visit owing to a congregation numbering several thousand, most of whom, for some reason, were German.

I managed to find a seat at the back and waited to hear Beethoven in the world's largest church. And waited. And waited. Where was the Supreme Pontiff?

Rumours started to spread, and religious groupies, some in their eighties, began to stand on their chairs.

Ushers ran among them, trying to calm them down, but hysteria was sweeping the auditorium.

I glimpsed the arrival of robed figures but pandemonium ensued. *Everyone* stood on their seats and I did likewise – for it is not every day that one gets the opportunity to see a pope. But I saw nothing despite being taller than most. He was there though, somewhere; for wild applause and cheering rang out all along the nave.

Even John Lennon could seldom have experienced a reception like this and it certainly refuted his claim that the Beatles were more popular than Jesus Christ; for was this not Christ's representative on earth?

Here was John Paul, without need of George and Ringo, slaying them in the aisles.

A dozen rows down towards the altar someone slipped off his chair and a domino effect caused several more to follow.

Officials moved in to restore order, and after five minutes – the time it takes to process from one end of the church to the other – the music began.

I heard it via a speaker attached to a nearby pillar and the sound quality was comparable to listening to the BBC World Service on a cheap South Korean transistor radio in Yakutsk during a solar storm.

But Beethoven is Beethoven and during the *Gloria* I did my best to let my spirit soar to the ceiling, although I have to admit that I only got halfway up a pillar, for all around me people were chatting like customers in a *bierkeller*.

A sermon followed, all in German, and after ten minutes I left, my seat being pounced upon by several members of the congregation who began whispering argumentatively.

Pope John Paul must have been thoroughly fed up with the sermon too, for soon after I re-entered the Piazza a gathering crowd began gazing expectantly at apartments where a papal flag hung from a balcony.

Then I saw the Pope. At least I think I did, for he was so far away – for security reasons – that it could have been a waxwork. He gave his blessing, but that could have been a recording. Perhaps he was still in the Basilica; yawning at the sermon? Perhaps I was witnessing a miracle?

All the people knelt to receive the blessing although I, along with a battalion of security men, remained standing. At least I had seen the Pope even if he had not seen me. No matter. Even Belloc had failed to secure a private audience. On an impulse I visited the Venerable English College and introduced myself. I was given an exceptionally warm welcome, and was taken under the wing of a young seminarist, John; who invited me for lunch.

And sitting in John's room, along with several of his friends, I drank gin and tonic and answered questions about my journey, glad to be in the company of people who had not only heard of Belloc but had read his books.

How good it was to speak my own language without having to worry that my words might contain too many syllables. How stimulating it was to exercise my brain again in debate with people whose lives were devoted to intellectual pursuits.

In the refectory I ate like a glutton and drank far too much wine.

Afterwards we adjourned to the common room where, for an hour or two, we chatted about Catholicism and the role of the clergy, as they saw it, in the modern world. I asked them how they thought they would cope when they left their cloistered life in the College, and they generally agreed that this was the one aspect of their training which gave them the greatest cause for concern.

'Don't any of you have any doubts?' I asked.

'Of course,' said John, 'after all you can't separate education from scepticism.'

'So all you have to do is convince yourselves of the existence of God, then convince others, then convince them that He's a benevolent deity and should be worshipped. Not only worshipped but according to your particular creed.'

In his autobiography, *A Path from Rome*, Anthony Kenny describes his life at the English College where he was a student from 1949 to 1955 before his return to the laity. He tells of how the students were subjected to a narrow and rigid regime. Beyond the confines of the College they were only allowed out in groups of four, while under their cassocks they had to wear canvas underpants specially designed by nuns.

Things have changed. I did not see one cassock in the College, and female guests roamed freely through the corridors. On a dais in the common room there was a drum kit and an electric guitar. And although I generally experience a phobic reaction while in the company of priests – even priests-to-be – I found these students' company delightful and was disappointed when they began drifting away to perform various religious and academic duties.

John took me up to the roof and pointed out the sights of Rome, whose seven hills I saw for the first time.

'If you could choose only one thing I should see while I'm here, what would it be?'

He did not hesitate. 'The Catacombs.'

In the College chapel he showed me the plaque commemorating alumni who had been martyred during the Counter Reformation; for during the reign of Elizabeth I a statute proclaimed that it was high treason for those ordained abroad to enter England. Many paid with their lives.

I said goodbye to John and left this somewhat enclosed and privileged place to pursue the life of a tourist for the next couple of days.

I did all the usual things: watched poseurs posing on the Spanish Steps; wandered around the clever but hideous Colosseum where the smell of barbarism still lingers; visited the Forums, which stimulated my imagination far less than the ruins in Athens; sauntered beside the Tiber whose water was not yellow but Palmolive green; entered the Pantheon and many churches; saw famous fountains; was dazzled by the white stones of the Vittorio Emanuele Monument that rears like a monstrous Mighty Wurlitzer amongst the ancient sites.

But mostly I walked; for Rome is not too large to explore comfortably on foot.

On my last evening I took John's advice and caught a bus along the narrow and cobbled Via Appia to the Catacomb of San Callisto.

The sun was setting and cypresses cast spindly shadows across the fields.

I arrived just in time for the last tour of the day conducted by an extraordinary old man who managed to make my first guided tour an intimate, indelible and personal experience. I was lucky. There were only two others in the party.

'How long have you been doing this job?' I asked.

'Seven years.'

'Don't you ever get bored with seeing and describing the same things day after day?'

He flung up his hands and said, 'Of course not. It is the best job in the world for I am a Christian. And each day, though I see the same things, each day I see the different effects it has on different people. People like you.'

We climbed down into the passages cut in the soft tufa, where the early Christians were laid to rest in excavated shelves; wide ones, like double beds, for married couples; cots – so many of them – for infants. And to see the sign of the fish painted and scratched on the walls of cavernous chapels was to experience, in tangible terms, the very foundations of the Christian religion. It was like delving deep into my subconscious, each successive gallery corresponding to memories of a Catholic upbringing.

It was dark when we emerged.

No one felt inclined to say a word, and our guide, accustomed to such a response, shook our hands silently and left us to reappraise our doubts.

★ ★ ★

On my last morning in Rome I returned to the Vatican to see the Sistine Chapel, but for some reason it was closed to the public. Instead I wandered back into the Basilica where I saw Michelangelo's *Pietà*, which, since the attack by a madman in 1972, now lies behind a protective glass screen which prevents one from viewing it properly. But the grief was still apparent: grief that I transposed; for I did not see the grief of a mother for her son but that of a son for his mother. And passing the Chapel of the Holy Sacrament I stopped, for a mass was in progress, and the small congregation was singing the Lourdes Hymn.

'Ave, ave, ave Maria . . .'

I had not heard it since my mother's funeral the previous year, and in the middle of Saint Peter's I broke down and wept, not only for her, I think, but for a lost childhood of certainty, which my faith, such as it was, had provided.

And with tears streaming down my cheeks I walked out into the sunlight.

★ ★ ★

Forty-five minutes from Rome and eight kilometres above the Alps I looked down at the Bernese Oberland. There was the Jungfrau, the Mönch, the Eiger and just beyond them two puddles; the Lakes of Thun and Brienz whose shores had taken up an entire day's march.

The steward handed me a meal on a tray, and when I next glanced out of the window we were already a week's walk farther to the north.

TOM CUNLIFFE

good
vibrations

COAST TO COAST BY HARLEY

'A PITHY THROBBER OF A BOOK' CHRIS STEWART

summersdale *travel*

two feet,
four paws

walking the dog 4,500 miles

Spud Talbot-Ponsonby

Foreword by Ffyona Campbell

summersdale *travel*

For a current publishing catalogue
and full listing of
Summersdale travel books,
visit our website:

www.summersdale.com